The
LONG
PURSUIT

Abraham Lincoln's Thrity-Year Struggle
with Stephen Douglas for the Heart and Soul of America

ROY MORRIS, JR.

University of Nebraska Press
Lincoln

Library of Congress Cataloging-in-Publication Data
Morris, Roy.
The long pursuit: Abraham Lincoln's thirty-year struggle with Stephen
Douglas for the heart and soul of America / Roy Morris, Jr.
p. cm.
Originally published: Washington, D.C.: Smithsonian Books; New York:
Collins, c2008.
Includes bibliographical references and index.
ISBN 978-0-8032-3928-9 (paper: alk. paper)
1. Lincoln, Abraham, 1809–1865. 2. Lincoln, Abraham,
1809–1865—Adversaries. 3. Douglas, Stephen A. (Stephen Arnold), 1813–
1861. 4. Legislators—United States—Biography. 5. Legislators—Illinois—
Biography. 6. United States. Congress. House—Biography. 7. United States.
Congress. Senate—Biography. 8. Lincoln-Douglas Debates, Ill., 1858.
9. Illinois—Politics and government—To 1865. 10. United States—Politics
and government—1815–1861. I. Title.
E457.35.M689 2010
973.6'8—dc22
2010019732

To Leslie, Lucy, and Phil—
Three facets, one diamond.

Contents

Introduction

One stands today as perhaps the most revered figure in American history. The other is remembered, if at all, for a hard-fought election victory that most people believe mistakenly was a defeat. The gap between the two could scarcely be wider. Yet for much, indeed most, of their careers, Abraham Lincoln and Stephen Douglas held vastly different positions in the eyes of their countrymen. For the better part of two decades, Douglas was the most famous and controversial politician in the United States, renowned for his defeats as well as his victories, a "steam engine in britches" who worked tirelessly and combatively for the Democratic Party and, not incidentally, for himself. Lincoln was merely Douglas's most persistent rival within their adopted home state of Illinois. A leader in both the House of Representatives and the Senate, Douglas was nearly nominated for president twice in the 1850s. Lincoln served a single undistinguished term in the House, one that he freely admitted was "a flat failure." It was not until Douglas passed, almost single-handedly, the Kansas-Nebraska Act of 1854, ushering in half a decade of unprecedented civil strife in Kansas, that Lincoln reentered politics and began his inexorable and seemingly inevitable rise to the White House. Had it not been for Douglas, Lincoln would have remained merely a good trial lawyer in Springfield, Illinois, known locally for his droll sense of humor, bad jokes, and slightly nutty wife. Nationally, he was barely known at all.

If, as Lincoln said, there was a "race of ambition" between the two men, until 1860 Douglas not only led the race, he virtually lapped Lincoln in the backstretch. While Douglas had little need for Lincoln, Lincoln badly needed Douglas, both personally and politically, as a goad, a pace horse, and a measuring stick. When Lincoln's law partner, William Herndon, remarked famously that Lincoln's ambition was "a little engine that knew no rest," he might well have added that it was the portly, combative figure of Stephen Douglas who stoked the engine. It is doubtful that Douglas, who had many rivals, ever fully realized how intensely Lincoln studied, plotted, and mulled over Douglas's every move. He had the time. While Douglas strolled the marble halls of Congress, trailing friends and foes behind him in a cloud of smoke from his ever-present Cuban cigar, Lincoln trudged the muddy streets of Springfield alone and climbed the back stairs to his paper-strewn law office on the second floor above a haberdashery. His one link to the outside world was the stack of out-of-town newspapers that he read each morning as avidly as a marooned sailor reads strange footprints on a beach. Whenever Douglas returned to Illinois—and it was more and more infrequently—Lincoln was usually on hand to hear what he had to say and to respond, invited or not, to his remarks. In his shambling, slightly hangdog way, Lincoln functioned as a one-man truth squad for Douglas's often flexible public pronouncements. Inherently honest himself (although not entirely immune from the professional politician's constant temptation to stretch the truth as far as it might credibly stretch), Lincoln watched Douglas perform his regular philosophical about-faces with a certain degree of amused wonder, if not necessarily admiration. Douglas, he said, did not "tell as many lies as some men I have known, but I think he cares as little for the truth . . . as any man I ever saw."[1]

Like all ambitious politicians growing up in America in the 1830s, Lincoln and Douglas entered public life in the overbranching shadow of Andrew Jackson, and each man defined his political philosophy by how strongly he supported or opposed Jacksonian democracy. From boyhood, Douglas imbibed the heady brew of street-level, common-man politics as embodied by the far from common figure of "Andy" Jackson— commanding general, plantation (and slave) owner, and natural-born elitist. It was a tenet of faith with Douglas that the voice of the people spoke most loudly and clearly when it bubbled up naturally from below.

"The voice of the many" was how he termed it. Lincoln, born somewhat lower on the social scale, had a less romantic view of stubble-bearded democrats with a small *d*. Along with his idol, Henry Clay, he believed that a wise and enlightened federal government was necessary to oversee the everyday workings of the American people, who were no better or worse than people anywhere, and generally could be counted upon to put their selfish interests ahead of their altruistic ones, although they could sometimes be induced to follow "the better angels of [their] nature." Douglas's view of politics was expressed most fully in his concept of "popular sovereignty," or the right of the majority to decide how they would live. Lincoln took the opposite tack, defending the primacy of the individual—black and white—against the intrusions of his often-domineering neighbors. "No man is good enough to govern another man, without that other's consent," he maintained. One way or another, it is a debate that still reverberates in American society.[2]

Race was the crucible in which the Lincoln-Douglas rivalry was fired. Ironically, it was the frontier-born Lincoln, a son of slave-state Kentucky, who better intuited the corrosive effect that slavery had—and was having—on the nation as a whole. Douglas, born and reared in free-state Vermont, exhibited a perplexing, lifelong obtuseness on the issue. For him, slavery was essentially a political question, of interest mainly to the high-strung southerners who profited from it. Taking his cue from the Missouri Compromise of 1820, which sought to manage the conflict by separating the slave and free regions of the country much as a boxing referee separates two clinching fighters, Douglas devoted his career to seeking workable solutions to the question. To him, slaves were merely a form of property, different in kind but not in law from land or horses or cattle, and owners had a God-given right to manage their property. Beyond that, and perhaps more to the point, slaves could not vote, and Douglas was nothing if not a politician, the most gifted perhaps of his generation. Lincoln, while no wild-eyed abolitionist, had a deeper well of sympathy, forged in part by his own dirt-poor childhood, which allowed him to see black men and women as recognizable human beings engaged in the age-old struggle for food and shelter—not entirely equal to white men, perhaps, but certainly deserving the right, as he often said, to eat the bread they earned with their own hands. While no less political than Douglas (and personally more aloof and inward-looking), Lincoln could see beyond the voting booth. Men, at any rate, could not eat ballots.

For nearly three decades, well before the issue of slavery tore the nation apart, Lincoln and Douglas battled each other for political supremacy on street corners, public squares, and village greens. In so doing, they helped define and determine the course of American politics during its most convulsive era. It was an accident of timing that plunked these two larger-than-life individuals down in the same thumbprint-sized corner of backwoods Illinois, yet it now seems almost mystically predetermined that they would take their great debate, so to speak, onto the national stage. How completely Lincoln won that debate—with the eventual help of 2 million blue-clad Union soldiers—explains in part why Douglas is so comparatively forgotten today. History, as they say, is written by the winners. Despite his many electoral, legislative, and personal victories, Stephen Douglas eventually lost the political war with Abraham Lincoln the same way that he lived his life—largely, loudly, and comprehensively. But while it lasted, it was quite a fight.

The

LONG
PURSUIT

1

The Paradise of the World

Some time during the winter of 1855–56, as he struggled with the galling disappointment of having lost a surefire seat in the United States Senate to his late-coming colleague Lyman Trumbull, Abraham Lincoln sat in his law office in Springfield, Illinois, and jotted down a few lines of rueful reminiscence. He was thinking not of Trumbull, as might be expected, but of an altogether longer-lived opponent, Democratic senator Stephen Douglas. Looking back on their often tumultuous rivalry, Lincoln tried his best to be objective. "Twenty-two years ago Judge Douglas and I first became acquainted," he recalled. "We were both young then; he a trifle younger than I. Even then we were both ambitious; I, perhaps, quite as much as he. With *me*, the race of ambition has been a failure—a flat failure; with *him* it has been one splendid success. His name fills the nation; and is not unknown, even, in foreign lands."[1]

About Stephen Douglas, Lincoln could speak with some authority. Indeed, few if any political opponents have ever known each other as well or as long as he and Douglas. Almost from the time they arrived, sixteen months apart, in their adopted home state of Illinois, they were fated to be rivals—first on the local, then the state, and finally the national scene. Lincoln, who was four years older, got there first, literally washing up on the shores of the tiny village of New Salem in the spring of 1831. Douglas, originally from Vermont, took a less direct route, going first to Cleveland, Ohio, then heading west to St. Louis, and finally settling down in the same west-central corner of Illinois that Lincoln had staked out a few years before him. The two men, so different from each other physically and temperamentally—Lincoln unusually tall, Douglas unusually short; Lincoln calm and rational, Douglas combative and excitable; Lincoln abstemious, Douglas a lover of whiskey, women, and fat cigars— would carry on a thirty-year struggle for political dominance. Between them they would debate and define the preeminent issues of their time. Unlike so many politicians, then and later, no one ever had to guess where they stood. They would say so, and by their actions they would give voice to millions of their fellow citizens who had not trained themselves, as Lincoln and Douglas had done, to mount the public stage and speak the truth, as they understood it, to both the powerful and the powerless.

In heading west to seek their fortunes, the two young men were following an already well-worn path. For decades, Americans by the thousands had been flocking westward, drawn by the lure of cheap land and wide-open opportunities. The chance to re-create or reinvent oneself in new surroundings—a peculiarly American concept—was particularly appealing to Lincoln and Douglas, each of whom was leaving behind a less-than-idyllic home life. Lincoln and his taciturn father, Thomas, had always had a distant relationship. The elder Lincoln could neither read nor write, and had little patience for his only son's inherent inwardness, which served perhaps as a painful reminder of Abraham's late mother, Nancy Hanks Lincoln, a tall, melancholy woman who died of "milk sickness" when her son was nine. Like countless other hardscrabble frontiersmen, Thomas Lincoln was a subsistence farmer and an inveterate wanderer. His own father, also named Abraham, had been shot down before his eyes by Shawnee Indians when he was eight, and that shocking death, his son later observed, placed Thomas in "very narrow circumstances" and set him on the path of "a wandering laboring boy." In the twenty-one years that Abraham Lincoln lived at home, his father uprooted the family four times—twice the national average, even for that itinerant era—moving successively from Kentucky to Indiana to Illinois in a more or less vain search for economic stability.[2]

Along the way, Lincoln acquired a lifelong aversion to physical labor that was ironically at odds with his later image as a hardy rail-splitter.

"Lincoln was lazy—a very lazy man," recalled his cousin Dennis Hanks, who lived with the family while they were growing up. "He was always reading—scribbling—writing—ciphering—writing poetry." Neighbors, too, remembered the young Lincoln as being "awful lazy . . . he was no hand to pitch in at work like killing snakes." It was not so much that Lincoln was lazy—few men ever worked harder at improving themselves—but that, gifted with a genius-level mind, he cared more about intellectual than physical pursuits. That dislike of the grindingly hard labor of the frontier did not stop Lincoln's father from placing an ax in his son's hands when he was seven, or from hiring him out to other farmers, for twenty-five cents a day, whenever he had a debt to pay. By the time he was seventeen, Lincoln had plowed, mowed, planted, and shucked hundreds of acres of his father's and other people's corn, cleared land, split fence rails, and hauled wool eighty miles back and forth to the nearest mill. That year, he began working on flatboats, an experience that opened up a "wider and fairer" world to the land-bound youth and eventually transported him far beyond his father's hemmed-in world.[3]

Lincoln's new life began one late-April morning in 1831, when the residents of New Salem, Illinois, awoke to a diverting spectacle. A makeshift flatboat bound for New Orleans and loaded down with wildly thrashing hogs and heavy barrels of bacon, wheat, and corn had become lodged athwart a dam on the Sangamon River. In the middle of the river, hatless and sweating, a tall, homely young man with a wild shank of black hair was striving mightily to dislodge the boat, which was taking on water at an alarming rate. It was Lincoln. With his tattered blue jeans rolled up to his knees and his blue-and-white striped shirt clinging wetly to his chest, Lincoln helped his three companions offload several barrels of cargo to shore. Then he borrowed an augur and drilled a hole in the foredeck of the boat. When enough barrels had been removed from the rear of the vessel, water drained out through the hole and the boat tipped easily over the dam and back into the river. It was a simple but ingenious solution to the problem, and the townspeople of New Salem were suitably impressed. One old settler, Caleb Carman, initially judged Lincoln to be "very odd" and "very curious," but admitted later that "after all this bad appearance I soon found [him] to be a very intelligent young man." So did the rest of the village. Two months later, on his return trip upriver, Lincoln settled in New Salem to manage a new dry goods store that his financial backer, a Micawberish businessman named

Denton Offutt, planned to open. He would live there for the next six years, and when he left he would leave behind a wealth of memories, anecdotes, and tall tales that, taken together, would constitute the bedrock of the much-loved Lincoln legend.[4]

Like its newest resident, New Salem in 1831 was rough-hewn and rustic. Founded two years earlier by mill owners James Rutledge and John Camron, the village was a thrown-together conglomeration of about a dozen cabins clustered around a handful of stores and taverns on the bluff overlooking its lifeline, the Sangamon River. Lincoln, an experienced river hand, fit right in. He took over the management of Offutt's store, whose owner, "a gassy, windy, brain-rattling man," spent most of his time talking and drinking. Lincoln, too, did his share of talking, if not drinking—he was a confirmed teetotaler. The one useful trait he had inherited from his father was a gift for storytelling, and he entertained his new friends with shaggy-dog stories and rambling jokes, including one slightly off-color jab at the English. In Lincoln's telling, Revolutionary War hero Ethan Allen makes a postwar visit to England, where he is annoyed by his hosts' derisive habit of placing a portrait of George Washington in their privies. This is entirely appropriate, retorts Allen, since "there is nothing that will make an Englishman shit so quick as the sight of General Washington." Another Lincoln story involved a Baptist preacher who confidently announces to his congregation that he is the physical representation of Jesus Christ. When a blue lizard runs up his pant leg, the startled preacher throws off his pants and shirt and cavorts across the stage in his underwear, at which point an old lady stands up and announces: "If you represent Christ then I'm done with the Bible."[5]

Along with his storytelling talents, Lincoln won over the locals with his strength and grit. In a frontier society that valued courage above all other qualities, Lincoln was inevitably challenged to show his moxie. The challenger, a burly tough named Jack Armstrong, was the leader of a gang of homespun layabouts known locally as the Clary's Grove Boys. Denton Offutt, as was his wont, had been bragging loudly that his new employee was the strongest man and the best rough-and-tumble wrestler in the area. Armstrong took exception. Despite his stated aversion to the "wooling and pulling" of a wrestling match, Lincoln had no choice but to accept the challenge—to have walked away would have branded him ineffaceably as a coward. He met Armstrong in the village square at the appointed time. Memories differed on the winner of the match, but everyone agreed that the funny-looking new shop clerk had shown the right stuff, and Armstrong and his gang eventually would become a combination private bodyguard and personal cheering section for Lincoln when he entered the hurly-burly of public life.[6]

More refined friends included millwright James Rutledge, New Salem's de facto mayor; transplanted Vermont physician John Allen; village schoolteacher Mentor Graham; and 300-pound justice of the peace Bowling Green, nicknamed "Pot" for his enormous overhanging stomach. Besides welcoming Lincoln into the local debating club, the quartet made a suggestion in the spring of 1832 that surprised and flattered their callow young friend—in fact, it changed his life. Harking back to his experience on the river, they encouraged him to enter politics by running for the Illinois legislature from Sangamon County. It was not as much of a stretch as it seemed. Most of the legislators who met once a year at the hardscrabble state capital in Vandalia were as unpolished as Lincoln—farmers, millers, and humble tradesmen who typically voted on nothing more elevated than whether or not to fence in their neighbors' cattle. Lincoln, if elected, would be expected to focus primarily on a subject of vital importance to all New Salem residents—improving the Sangamon River. Rumors of a new railroad linking Springfield and Jacksonville to the Illinois River and bypassing New Salem altogether had everyone in the village worried. Without navigational improvements to their sluggish, driftwood-choked lifeline, there would be no way for them to effectively transport goods to and from St. Louis. New Salem would die.[7]

With the help of Graham and fellow storekeeper John McNeil, Lincoln crafted an announcement notice for the *Sangamo Journal*. Acknowledging that he was "young and unknown to many of you," Lincoln conceded that he had been born and remained "in the most humble walks of life," with "no wealthy or popular relations to recommend me." Besides being true, the admission was also good politics. Most of "the independent voters of this county" upon whose judgment and mercy he was throwing himself were also poor and undistinguished, and Lincoln, at the very beginning of his career, was shrewd enough to make a virtue of his—and their—unfavored upbringing. An enterprising scholar later counted no fewer than thirty-five references by Lincoln to his "humble" background before he ran for president in 1860. The heart of his announcement stressed his experience on the river. "From my peculiar circumstances," Lincoln wrote, "it is probable that for the last twelve months I have given as particular attention to the stage of the water in this river, as any other person in the country." He underscored his experience a few days later by helping to guide the riverboat *Talisman* upriver from Beardstown to Springfield and down the Sangamon to New Salem, where Rutledge's dam had to be partially destroyed to allow the vessel to pass through it—further highlighting the need for improvements to the river.[8]

Lincoln's entry into politics was interrupted as soon as it began by worrisome news from the western frontier. Chief Black Hawk, the aging leader of the Sauk and Fox Indians, had crossed back into Illinois from Iowa, where he had grudgingly removed himself and his people after signing away 50 million acres of tribal land to Indiana territorial governor William Henry Harrison in 1804. Citing boilerplate language in the treaty that gave the Sauks continued use of the land until it was sold by the government, Black Hawk wanted to return and plant corn again on his ancestral stamping ground. White settlers now squatting on that ground naturally disagreed, and the call went out for 1,700 Illinois miltiamen to join 340 regular army troops in putting down the uprising. Among those answering the call was Lincoln, who was motivated less by military than financial reasons. By that time, Denton Offutt had run off, literally, to join the circus, taking a position as a horse trainer for a traveling show in Georgia, but not before getting his reluctant clerk to split enough rails to pen up 1,000 hogs behind the store. With his newfound livelihood threatened, Lincoln had pressing need of the $125 salary being offered by the state of Illinois for warm-blooded volunteers.[9]

To his immense surprise and gratification, Lincoln was elected captain of the New Salem militia company (Jack Armstrong was his sergeant). For the next two and a half months—he reenlisted twice—Lincoln and his charges trooped through an invariable sameness of swamps, gullies, and underbrush in pursuit of Indians they never found. The closest they came was discovering the remains of five settlers who, unfortunately for them, had been more successful in finding Indians and had their scalps lifted for their troubles. The sight made an understandable impression on Lincoln, who recalled many years later: "The red light of the morning sun came streaming upon them as they lay heads towards us on the ground, and every man had a round, red spot on top of his head, and the red sunlight seemed to paint everything all over." Lincoln's company was far away when the main force of white soldiers caught up with Black Hawk's band on the banks of the Mississippi in southwestern Wisconsin on August 2, 1832, and killed 300 of them at the Battle of Bad Axe. The "small and foolish war," as historian Alvin M. Josephy, Jr., termed it, ended soon afterward, with Black Hawk being escorted in leg irons to Jefferson Barracks at St. Louis by a young army lieutenant named Jefferson Davis.[10]

Returning to New Salem on foot after his horse was stolen, Lincoln got back too late to do much campaigning before the August 6 election. Deeply suntanned from his weeks in the field, the neophyte candidate told potential voters—no doubt needlessly—that he was "almost as red as those men I have been chasing through the prairies and forests on the rivers of Illinois." A local observer captured Lincoln during his first campaign: "He wore a mixed jeans coat, clawhammer style, short in the sleeves and bobtail—in fact it was so short in the tail he could not sit on it; flax and tow-linen pantaloons, and a straw hat." Despite his undeniably eye-catching appearance, Lincoln failed to capture many votes, finishing eighth out of thirteen candidates, although he did receive 277 of the 300 votes cast in his hometown precinct. It would prove to be, as he never failed to remind listeners afterward, the only time he was ever beaten "on a direct vote of the people."[11]

With the desertion of Offutt, Lincoln went back to looking for full-time work. Attempting to capitalize on his recent experience, he threw in with a former member of his militia company, William Berry, and opened a new grocery store. It proved to be no more successful than Offutt's had been, even after the partners acquired a license to sell liquor on the premises. Not even the addition of wine, rum, peach brandy, and whiskey served by the dipper enabled the store to turn a profit, and it gradually "winked out," in Lincoln's gentle phrase. Still, his popularity in the community was such that Lincoln's friends managed to convince government officials in Washington to appoint him village postmaster after the current officeholder, Samuel Hill, unexpectedly resigned. Lincoln made no secret of his Whig political leanings—he had voted for Henry Clay for president against Andrew Jackson in the last election—but the post was "too insignificant" in the larger scheme of things, he noted, for his own party affiliation to matter much to higher-ups. In May 1833, he began selling stamps and delivering letters, undemanding occupations that permitted him to stay in the public eye while performing useful little services for his would-be constituents. It also gave him access to all the newspapers passing through the post office, a particularly pleasant perk for a constant reader such as Lincoln. Less than a year after arriving in New Salem unceremoniously on the deck of a flatboat, the twenty-four-year-old stranger was now a valued member of the community.[12]

◆ ◆ ◆

Stephen Douglas's entry into Illinois was considerably less dramatic than Lincoln's. He rolled into Jacksonville, the seat of Morgan County, in the middle of the night, climbing down from his stagecoach near dawn on November 2, 1833. He had less than $5 in his pocket. Not yet twenty-one, Douglas had followed Lincoln's similarly wandering path to Illinois, but with a few important differences that reflected the not-insignificant gap in their social status. While Lincoln was the son of an illiterate back-woodsman, Douglas had been born into upper-middle-class privilege, the son of a Vermont physician with sturdy New England connections going back 200 years. His people had fought in King Philip's War and the Revolution, acquired large landholdings in Connecticut, New York, and Vermont, and showed a natural bent for politics and public service. Douglas's paternal grandfather, Benajah Douglass (Stephen dropped the second "s" some years later), served five terms in the Vermont General Assembly, and also held office as a selectman and justice of the peace in Brandon, Vermont, where Stephen was born on April 23, 1813. Besides the modest financial bequest that Douglas inherited from his grandfather when he died in 1829, he also inherited his stumpy legs, large head, stentorian speaking voice, and boundless self-confidence. He would, in time, put all these traits to good use.[13]

It was lucky for Douglas that his grandfather was so generous, genetically and financially, since his own father—through no fault of his own—was a complete void in his son's life. He died, in fact, when Douglas was two months old, dropping dead from an apparent heart attack at the age of thirty-two while dandling his infant son on his knee near an open fire. According to family legend, an alert neighbor named John Conant scooped the baby from the flames in the nick of time. Douglas's narrow escape coincided with an immediate drop in the family's fortunes. His still-young mother, Sarah Fisk Douglass, with a newborn son and a one-year-old daughter to provide for, moved in with her brother, Edward Fisk, who owned the farm adjoining the widow's land. Fisk was a bachelor—

"an industrious, economical, clever old bachelor," his nephew later wrote, with a subtle undertone of distaste—and he quickly combined the two properties into a single holding, his own. Besides acquiring his sister's land, he also acquired the services of her son as a common laborer, not unlike Abraham Lincoln's filial indenture to his father. Like Lincoln, Douglas came to resent both the work and the master. "I thought it a hardship that my uncle would have the use of my mother's farm and also the benefit of my labor without any other equivalent than my boarding and clothes," he recalled in an autobiographical sketch in 1838.[14]

Determined to get out from under his uncle's control, Douglas convinced his mother to permit him to see "what I could do for myself in the wide world among strangers." The wide world was fourteen miles away—one mile for each year of his life—and located at Middlebury, Vermont, where Douglas apprenticed himself to a local cabinetmaker with the sturdy New England name of Nahum Parker. Douglas already had learned the rudiments of woodworking from another maternal uncle, Jonathan Fisk, and he commenced helping Parker make tables, washstands, and beds. Eight months later he was back home in Brandon, having fallen out with his master over the nature of his duties (apparently, Parker wanted him to be a house servant as well as an apprentice) and his burgeoning interest in politics. The fall of 1828 was a polarizing time in American political life. Incumbent president John Quincy Adams was facing a monumental challenge from Tennessean Andrew Jackson, the same man he had narrowly defeated in 1824, when the undecided presidential election was thrown into the House of Representatives. Charges of a "corrupt bargain" between Adams and Kentucky congressman Henry Clay, who became Adams's secretary of state, had arisen immediately after the election and subsequently had been nursed, like a festering sore, for four long years by Jackson and his supporters. They fully intended to pay back "King John the Second" for what they saw as his underhanded subversion of the popular will.[15]

The ensuing campaign was one of the dirtiest in American history. Jackson's supporters railed against the "lordly purse-proud aristocracy" embodied by the patrician Adams, who lived in "kingly pomp and splendor" in his "presidential palace." Adams's supporters countered that Jackson, a self-made product of the southwestern frontier, was little more than a bumptious rube, "destitute of historical, political, or statistical knowledge . . . a man . . . wholly unqualified by education, habit and temper from the station of President." But Jackson was a legitimate war hero, the destroyer of a crack British army outside New Orleans and the scourge of Native Americans everywhere. A new political party, the Democrats, took shape around Jackson and began sketching the outlines for a more representative, populist-oriented philosophy of governance centered on the needs and wishes of the working class.[16]

One of Jackson's acolytes was the fifteen-year-old Stephen Douglas. As the campaign progressed, the apprentice cabinetmaker regularly stole away from work to follow the political debate on street corners and in taverns, often spending his evenings in lively discussions with other young men in the community. When ghoulishly illustrated "Coffin Handbills" began appearing on Brandon's fences and walls, charging Jackson with murder for having executed six deserters during the Creek Indian War in 1813, Douglas and his fellows angrily tore them down. The bare-knuckles politicking captivated Douglas, who later observed: "From this moment, my politics became fixed, and all subsequent reading, reflection and observation have but confirmed my early attachment to the cause of Democracy."[17]

Parting company with the Adams-favoring Parker, Douglas found a new position back in Brandon with a woodworking church deacon named Caleb Knowlton, but he soon discovered that he had lost all taste for furniture making. By this time, Douglas's Uncle Edward, hitherto a confirmed bachelor, had surprised everyone by getting married, and Douglas, with an eye toward supporting himself, enrolled in the Brandon Academy, a college preparatory school. There he studied English, mathematics, and classical languages and indulged his newfound interest in politics by joining the school debating society. He remained at the academy until November 1830, when his mother remarried a widower from upstate New York named Gehazi Granger, whose son had married her daughter, Sarah, earlier that year. Douglas and the rest of the family moved to the Granger homestead on the shores of Lake Canandaigua in Ontario County.[18]

Located in the Finger Lakes country of western New York, Canandaigua was a center of social and religious ferment. Not long before the Douglases immigrated there, another transplanted Vermonter, a young mechanic in Palmyra named Joseph Smith, made a startling claim. According to Smith, he had unearthed, with the help of the angel Moroni, a set of mysterious gold tablets on which were inscribed the tenets of a new religion. Smith's ethereally inspired 500-page *Book of Mormon* went on sale the same year that the family moved into the region. Meanwhile another self-anointed mystic, Charles Grandison Finney, was leading the Second Great Awakening in nearby Rochester, preaching an individualized approach to salvation that was remarkably similar to modern self-help books. A third rising national movement with roots in Ontario County was less religiously, if no less mystically, based. William Morgan, a disgruntled member of the intensely secretive Masons, had announced his intention to expose the secrets of freemasonry. Morgan subsequently was abducted from jail in Canandaigua, where he was serving time for unpaid debts, by unknown men believed to be Masons. When his badly decomposed body washed up on the shores of Lake Ontario a short time later, it ignited an Anti-Mason movement that swept the Northeast and threatened for a time to derail the presidential hopes of Stephen Douglas's champion, Andrew Jackson, himself a Mason. The controversy was still smoldering when Douglas arrived.[19]

With his stepfather's assistance, Douglas enrolled in Canandaigua Academy, where for the next two years he excelled more at student politics than formal studies. Continuing his interest in forensic debate, Douglas gave a number of spirited speeches in defense of Jackson, who nevertheless lost Canandaigua and Ontario County by a better than two-to-one margin to Anti-Masonic candidate William Wirt when he ran for reelection in 1832. Surprisingly, Douglas's Democratic advocacy did not harm him with the town's leading politicians, future congressman and postmaster general Gideon Granger (a cousin of his stepfather) and Congressman Mark Sibley, both of whom were staunch National Republicans and Anti-Masons. The two men befriended Douglas, as did the town's leading Democratic attorney, Levi Hubbell, who allowed the young man to study law with him for six months in the winter and spring of 1833. The state of New York required seven years of classical education and legal study before one could become a practicing attorney, and Douglas, with no long-range hope of financial support by his family, did not want to wait that long. In June 1833, armed with letters of introduction from Gideon Granger and Mark Sibley and a $300 parting bequest from his stepfather, Douglas set out for the West to seek his fortune. When his mother asked when she would see him again, he supposedly responded, "On my way to Congress."[20]

After brief stopovers in Cleveland, Cincinnati, Louisville, and St. Louis, Douglas arrived in Jacksonville, Illinois, in November 1833. Despite being named for his longtime hero, the town held few immediate opportunities for the boyish Douglas, who was twenty years old and looked even younger. Taking the advice of a well-meaning local attorney, Murray McConnel, who would become one of his lifelong friends, Douglas headed off for the Illinois River town of Pekin, where McConnel said there was more opportunity for a would-be attorney. Unlike New York, Illinois did not require a seven-year term of study for a law degree. Indeed, all it required was an examination by a member of the state supreme court and a certificate of good moral character. Douglas was confident that he could manage both, but first he had to wait until spring—there were no more riverboats going to Pekin until then. Marooned in the tiny village of Winchester, he somehow managed to scare up enough students to open a one-man school. He also worked part-time as an auction clerk and spent his spare hours discussing politics with the local denizens. By March 1834, he had put together enough of a nest egg to return to Jacksonville, where he soon received his law examination from Judge Samuel D. Lockwood and hung out his shingle at the county courthouse. He was on his way. Praising his adopted home as "the Paradise of the world," Douglas informed his family in enthusiastic capital letters: "Illinois possesses more natural advantages, and is destined to possess greater artificial and acquired advantages, than any other State in the Union or on the Globe." In a few short months, he told them, "I have become a *Western* man, have imbibed Western feelings principles and interests and have selected Illinois as the favorite place of my adoption."[21]

✦ ✦ ✦

Lincoln, born in the West, did not have to make a conscious transition to western values—he simply went on with his life. While continuing to serve as postmaster in New Salem, hand-delivering letters that he stuck for convenience into the headband of his hat, Lincoln also signed on as an assistant to county surveyor John Calhoun, a fellow Black Hawk War veteran and a distant relative of the fiery South Carolina politician of the same name. Scraping together enough money to buy a compass and chain and a couple reference books on trigonometry and surveying, Lincoln was soon thrashing through briar patches and river bottoms, measuring off farm lots and roadways, witnessing deeds, and mediating property disputes. The work was hard—Lincoln shrugged it off as "a

poor man's lot"—but it was necessary to "keep body and soul together."
The $2.50 he earned for each quarter section he surveyed was also nec-
essary to begin chipping away at the mountain of debt he had incurred
during his brief, inglorious business partnership with William Berry, who
soon would die of chronic alcoholism and leave Lincoln alone to face
their increasingly importunate creditors. Embarrassingly, the Sangamon
Circuit Court sent the county sheriff to attach Lincoln's horse, saddle,
bridle, and surveying equipment and sell them at auction. In another
example of his high standing in the community, Lincoln's horse was returned to him free of charge, and a helpful neighbor, James Short, bid
$120 for the surveying equipment and immediately handed it back to
him as well. Although legally responsible for only half the store's debts,
Lincoln vowed to pay them all, even though it would take him several
years to do so. He took to calling it, only half-jokingly, "the National
Debt."[22]

The wide-ranging work as a surveyor—he often had to travel as far
away as 100 miles at a time—coupled with his local duties as postmaster,
kept Lincoln in the public eye, and in the summer of 1834 he decided to
run again for the state legislature. Party lines were beginning to harden
in Illinois and across the nation, divided unevenly between those who
loved Andrew Jackson (the majority) and those who hated him (an increasingly vocal minority). Lincoln counted himself among the latter. He
had to walk a fine line politically—most of his neighbors in New Salem
were fellow Whigs, as Jackson's opponents were becoming known, but
the farmers in rural Sangamon County were Democrats. Even his old
friend and wrestling opponent Jack Armstrong was a Democrat, although it did not stop him from continuing to support Lincoln personally, or prevent his wife, Hannah, from sewing their friend a new pair of
buckskin-reinforced blue jeans to wear while he was tramping through
the underbrush on surveying jobs.[23]

As a way, perhaps, of walking the political tightrope, Lincoln in 1834
did not issue a public letter announcing his candidacy or expanding on
his previously held positions. "My politics are short and sweet, like the
old woman's dance," he told his listeners from the stump. "I am in favor
of a national bank. I am in favor of the internal improvement system and
a high protective tariff. These are my sentiments and political principles.
If elected, I shall be thankful; if not, it will be all the same." Meanwhile,
he continued delivering the mail and surveying the countryside, count-

ing on his personal contact with voters to carry him through. It was enough. On Election Day, he tallied 64 percent of the countywide vote, more than doubling his 1832 total, and finished second in a field of thirteen candidates. It was rumored later that Armstrong's Clary's Grove Boys had made a deal with fellow Democrats to trade votes for Lincoln in an attempt to defeat the better-known and better-connected John Todd Stuart, a Springfield lawyer who had been Lincoln's militia major in the Black Hawk War. If so, it didn't work. Stuart squeaked by as the fourth and final state representative from Sangamon County, all but one of them Whigs.[24]

No one could say why, exactly, Lincoln had done so well in the election. Fellow Whig William Butler made a stammering effort to explain his newfound appeal, and in so doing gave as fine a capsule description of Lincoln's ineffable political talents as anyone would ever produce. "Well, it is hard to say just why," Butler said. "It was because of the standing he had got in the county, and especially the prominence given him by his captaincy in the Black Hawk War—because he was good fellow—because he told good stories, and remembered good jokes—because he was genial, kind, sympathetic, open-hearted—because when he was asked a question and gave an answer it was always characteristic, brief, pointed, *a propos*, out of the common way and manner, and yet exactly suited to the time, place and thing—because of a thousand things which cannot now be remembered or told."[25]

Delighted by his victory, not least because it would mean another $250 of income, Lincoln approached a wealthy neighbor, Coleman Smoot, and asked to borrow $200 to pay down some of his debts and buy a new dress suit—his first—"to make a decent appearance in the legislature." Smoot agreed, and Lincoln set off for the state capital in Vandalia, seventy-five miles away, on November 28, 1834. He arrived the next afternoon, after a thirty-four-hour journey by stagecoach, to find himself in the distinct minority. There were sixty Democrats and only twenty-one Whigs in the legislature. One of those Democrats (although not yet an elected official) making the rounds of the two-story brick statehouse was Stephen Douglas. Exactly when and how Lincoln and Douglas first met is unknown. Lincoln put it down vaguely in his 1856 note as having taken place "twenty-two years ago," making it 1834. Douglas never mentioned a first meeting. They were both so young— Lincoln was twenty-five, Douglas was twenty-one—and traveled in such different social and political circles, that it is not surprising they did not initially take much notice of one another. That would soon change.[26]

While Lincoln was a duly elected legislator, Douglas was a one-man lobbying effort—mainly for himself. He had come to Vandalia at the behest of Jacksonville legislator John Wyatt, a fellow "whole hog" Democrat (as opposed to the more watered-down "milk and cider" Democrats who waffled in their support of Jackson and his policies). Wyatt had a personal and political score to settle with State's Attorney John J. Hardin, a former Democrat who had turned Whig after getting appointed to the four-year post in 1832. Hardin had helped defeat a number of the same Democrats who had backed him for the position, and Wyatt was determined to get revenge for Hardin's "ingratitude." With Douglas's help, he prepared a bill stripping the governor of the power to appoint state attorneys. Under the new bill, the two houses of the legislature would elect the attorneys. After a lengthy wrangle, the bill was approved over the objections of newly elected governor Joseph Duncan, another Democrat-turned-Whig. In the subsequent legislative election, Douglas defeated Hardin by four votes and was appointed state's attorney from the First Judicial District. Lincoln voted against both the bill and Douglas, who disgruntled lawmakers called, somewhat inelegantly, "Jack Wyatt's tomtit."[27]

In winning the appointment, Douglas fell afoul of Illinois Supreme Court justice Samuel Lockwood, the judge who had examined him for his law license eleven months earlier. "What business has such a stripling with such an office?" Lockwood complained. "He is no lawyer and has no law books." Douglas was unabashed by such criticism. "I occupy precisely the position I have long wished for *Politically* and *Professionally*," he told his family. "I am doing as well in my '*profession*' as could be expected of a Boy of twenty one." He attributed his success to "the Lord, the Legislature, and General Jackson," presumably in that order. His new duties encompassed eight western Illinois counties, including Lincoln's bailiwick of Sangamon. It was the fastest-growing part of the state, and Douglas took the opportunity to foster valuable political connections with many leading lawyers and jurists. Again he bragged to his family. "I find myself on a new theatre of action," he wrote, "and I may say a very important and critical one, when conducting an important trial alone, with three or four of the best lawyers in the state on the opposite side ready to take advantage of every circumstance, never asking favors nor granting them."[28]

One of those lawyers on the opposite side was Lincoln's old friend and fellow war veteran, John Stuart. As a newly elected Whig legislator and longtime supporter of the now-deposed Hardin, Stuart hoped to embarrass Douglas personally and the Democrats generally. When the young attorney made his first visit to McLean County, Stuart moved to dismiss all of Douglas's indictments on the grounds that he had misspelled the very name of the county in which he was lawyering—he had written "McClean." Conceding nothing, Douglas demanded that Stuart prove he was wrong. After a two-day delay while a copy of the appropriate statutes were retrieved from nearby Peoria, both men were surprised to find that the original spelling of the county name indeed was McClean. Henceforth, Douglas vowed, he would "admit nothing and require my adversary to prove everything." It was a good lesson to learn, but it made Stuart a lifelong enemy. No doubt the story quickly got back to Lincoln.[29]

Douglas soon became disillusioned with the law as a profession, or at least as a moneymaking venture. "Out of the long list of Lawyers that come to this country and settle," he told his brother-in-law, Julius Granger, in May 1835, "there is not one out of an hundred who does one half the business enough to pay his expenses the first year . . . practicing Law in the Sucker State will not make a man rich the first year or two." Increasingly, his legal duties took a back seat to his political activities. The rapid influx of settlers into Illinois—the population almost tripled between 1830 and 1840—created both challenge and opportunity for would-be politicians of all stripes. The political makeup of the state was changing overnight. Its traditional ties to the South, solidified by decades of immigration into the southern part of the state, were being challenged by an increase in new arrivals like Douglas from the East and New England. The easterners, by and large, brought with them a more sophisticated approach to politics, including the convention system of nominating candidates and the need to enforce party loyalty.[30]

Quick to recognize the changing environment, Douglas took the lead in organizing the state's first-ever political convention, timed to coincide with the opening of a special session of the legislature in December 1835. The subsequent convention of Illinois Democrats, although small in numbers, provoked a firestorm of protest from Whig legislators like Lincoln, who were more or less captive onlookers to the proceedings. The Whigs denounced the gathering as "anti-republican" and "dangerous to the liberties of the people." But Douglas, recalling his early political experience in New York, defended the system as "the only way to manage elections with success." The *Chicago Democrat* concurred, advising delegates that the only proper response to Whig criticism was "pooh—pish—pashaw." The convention voted to support the presidential bid of Jackson's vice president, Martin Van Buren, in the upcoming election "as the man best qualified to carry on the principles which have marked, distinguished and elevated the political course of Andrew Jackson." It also supported, somewhat contradictorily, "the rights of states, and the supremacy of the general government"—but that was a debate for another time.[31]

The state convention increased Douglas's visibility, and he decided to run for the legislature in 1836. His principal opponent was a familiar enemy—John J. Hardin, the man he had deposed as state's attorney one year earlier. The Whig-leaning *Sangamo Journal*, which had taken to calling Douglas "Squire Douglas" in its columns, observed of his nomination that "the Van Buren men of Morgan must not possess a very fastidious taste, if they can swallow such a dose as this." Douglas relished the fight—"the warmer the better for I like excitement." He had exchanged his tailored clothes for a more homespun suit of blue-denim "Kentucky jeans" and readily adopted the twangy pose of true man of the frontier. "I find no difficulty in adopting the Western mode of Electioneering by addressing the people from the Stump," he informed his family, adding that "I live with my constituents, eat with my constituents, drink with them, lodge with them, pray with them, laugh, hunt, dance and work with them; I eat their corn dodgers and fried bacon and sleep two in a bed with them." However suspect the authenticity of Douglas's new image, it worked politically, and he tallied the largest number of votes in his district. In neighboring Sangamon County, Lincoln was reelected to a second term in the legislature, joining eight other members of the local delegation, each of whom was over six feet tall, as part of the so-called "Long Nine."[32]

Putting the best face on things, the *Sangamo Journal* hailed the Tenth General Assembly for having "more talent than any legislative body ever before assembled in Illinois." It was no exaggeration. Counting Lincoln and Douglas, the 1836–37 legislature included one future president of the United States, five future senators, seven future congressmen, a governor, and three generals. Although on opposite sides of the aisle politically, Lincoln and Douglas sometimes found themselves voting together on local issues, including the selection of a new speaker of the house, a mammoth internal improvements project, and the relocation of the state capital from Vandalia to Springfield. The latter project was one of particular interest to Lincoln, who was preparing to make a similar relocation personally. He had been spending more and more time recently in Springfield at the law office of his friend Stuart, and Stuart eventually convinced him to become a lawyer himself.[33]

It did not take much convincing. Lincoln had always been interested in the law, regularly attending informally conducted sessions of Pot Green's court in New Salem, and Green sometimes allowed him to argue cases before him. Thus encouraged, Lincoln purchased a book of legal forms that enabled him to draft simple documents such as wills, deeds, and bills of sale. With books borrowed from Stuart's law library, Lincoln managed to educate himself, reading so much and so long that concerned neighbors worried about his health. Five weeks after being reelected to the legislature, Lincoln was admitted to the Illinois bar and joined Stuart's law firm. As soon as the legislative session was over, he returned to New Salem, said a few hasty good-byes, and moved to Springfield for good. Within another three years, New Salem would become a veritable ghost town, most of its remaining residents relocating two miles downriver to the new town of Petersburg, which Lincoln had surveyed and carved into lots. When Petersburg defeated New Salem to become the seat of newly drawn Menard County, the once-flourishing community that had welcomed the strange-looking flatboatman into its bosom six years earlier died an ignominious, unlamented death.[34]

+ + +

One of Lincoln's new neighbors in Springfield was Douglas. The election of Martin Van Buren as president over a trio of Whig opponents in the fall of 1836 had brought the twenty-three-year-old first-term state legislator a plum appointment as register of the Springfield Land Office. The predictably hostile *Sangamo Journal* greeted his appointment with a mocking broadside: "We are told the *little man* from Morgan, was perfectly astonished, at finding himself making money at the rate of from one to two hundred dollars per day!" The new office was indeed profitable. Douglas was permitted by law to receive $3,000 in interest and fees, while at the same time double-dipping as state's attorney for the

First Judicial District. Even more valuable, from Douglas's point of view, was his increased exposure to potential voters.[35]

Thanks to intraparty backbiting and some adroit wire-pulling by Douglas, that exposure came in handy sooner than expected. A Democratic convention meeting in Peoria in November 1837 bypassed incumbent congressman William L. May, whose increasing criticism of Van Buren's economic policies had raised hackles among the party faithful, and chose Douglas to run in his place. May complained, with some justice, to Treasury Secretary Levi Woodbury that Douglas had been "engaged in a political electioneering tour through my district, getting up meetings of the voters to organize a Convention of Delegates . . . who are pledged against me." When questioned by Woodbury, Douglas professed innocence, but brashly maintained his freedom "to mingle with my fellow citizens and express my opinions of men and measures (not excepting Mr. May) as I should if I have never received an Office at the hands of the Government."[36]

The Whigs, who had chosen Lincoln's law partner, Stuart, as their candidate for Congress, were quick to charge that a "corrupt bargain" had been struck between Douglas and certain unnamed Sangamon County politicos. A series of anonymous letters, signed "A Conservative," appeared in the *Sangamo Journal* alleging that Douglas had been tricked into running for a seat he could not win by an older Democrat who wanted the younger man's position in the Springfield Land Office. The trickster was thought to be John Calhoun, Lincoln's old surveying boss. Douglas angrily denied that he had entered into any sort of bargain and demanded to know the name of the "infamous, villainous liar" and "cowardly scoundrel" who had written the letters. The villainous scoundrel was probably Lincoln, who was in the best position to know what, if anything, Calhoun had told Douglas, and who already had authored a number of anti-Democratic letters for the *Journal* under the various pen names "Madison," "Citizen of Sangamon," "John Bubberhead," and "Sampson's Ghost." Lincoln, for his part, denied it. "We have adopted it as part of our policy here, to never speak of Douglas at all," he joked. "Isn't that the best mode of treating so small a matter?"[37]

The entire campaign was fought on a similarly low plane, with the diminutive Douglas, the "Peoria Bantling," being compared endlessly to the strapping Stuart, widely reputed to be the handsomest man in Illinois. Douglas was accused falsely of being against the popular Illinois and Michigan Canal project, and when he took his campaign into the labor camps of the Irish immigrants who were engaged in gouging the canal out of the Illinois earth, he was called a "radical mobocract" and a "loco foco" by the Whigs. They charged that the candidate's idea of democracy "means Douglas mounted on the shoulders of two Irishmen, addressing a Chicago rabble upon the glorious privilege of a free country, and the right of unnaturalized foreigners to control the elections of Illinois." The fact that the state constitution permitted men to vote after only six months' residence (construction on the canal had begun two years earlier) was conveniently forgotten. Douglas was not above a little demagoguery himself, telling the credulous workers that he, too, was Irish, descended from a long line of phantom McDouglasses. "I expect to get all their votes," he whispered to a friend.[38]

The growing unpopularity of Van Buren, coupled with the recent downturn in the national economy, grievously hurt Douglas's chances in the election. Nevertheless, he campaigned tirelessly, debating Stuart throughout the state. Once, when Stuart was ill, his law partner Lincoln supposedly stood in for him at Bloomington, vigorously contesting the issues with Douglas on the steps of the courthouse. (No account of the meeting exists, and it may be apocryphal.) The two also faced each other in a Springfield court a few days before the election, finding themselves on opposite sides of a sensational murder case stemming directly from Douglas's nomination for Congress. Henry L. Truett, the son-in-law of deposed congressman William May, was on trial for murder. The facts were not in dispute: Truett had accosted fellow Democrat Jacob M. Early, Lincoln's first captain in the Black Hawk War, at Spottswood's Hotel in Springfield and demanded to know, at the point of a gun, if Early had written the resolutions calling for Mays's ouster. When Early raised a chair to shield himself, Truett shot him dead. Douglas acted as second for newly elected state's attorney Daniel Woodson, while Lincoln represented Truett. In an imaginative defense, Lincoln convinced the jury that Early, in picking up the chair, had forced Truett to fire in self-defense. The jury, to both sides' consternation, concurred, and Truett was acquitted.[39]

Douglas and Stuart had a violent confrontation of their own, three days before the election, at a Springfield market. Enraged by a Douglas remark, Stuart grabbed the smaller man in a headlock and dragged him around the store. Douglas responded by biting Stuart on the thumb, leaving a scar that he carried for the rest of his life. "They both fought till exhausted," an eyewitness reported, "grocery floor slippery with slop." The election itself was no less hard fought. When it ended, no one was sure who had won. For weeks both sides claimed victory, and Douglas took a jaunty victory lap, riding atop a stagecoach from Chicago to Springfield, smoking a cigar and claiming to have "used up Mr. Stuart to the tune of 2,000!" The elation was premature. The final tally gave Stuart a razor-thin margin of 36 votes out of a total of 36,495 cast.[40]

Reports of widespread voting irregularities tainted Stuart's triumph. Whig campaign officials had purposely misspelled Douglas's name on some poll books, refused to record Douglas votes at other places, and, posing as Democrats, had urged voters to support "John A. Douglas" or "James A. Douglas," with the resultant mismarked ballots being thrown out as irregular. Democratic investigators were denied access to the official records, but there was good reason to believe, as the *Illinois State Register* proclaimed, that "Mr. Douglas was elected by the people." Douglas announced his intention to formally challenge the election, but backed off after the Whigs, led by Lincoln, formed a committee of their own to investigate alleged Democratic abuses among Irish canal workers. "Douglas has not been here since you left," Lincoln crowed to Stuart, who by then had left for Washington to claim his somewhat tainted seat. "A report is in circulation . . . that he has abandoned the ideas of going to Washington; though the report does not come in a very authentic form. . . . Speaking of authenticity, you know that if we had heard Douglas say that he had abandoned the contest, it would not be very authentic."[41]

As leaders of the young Whigs and Democrats in Springfield, Lincoln and Douglas continued to cross swords politically. In November 1839, the two engaged in a three-day debate in the capital over Van Buren's opposition to a national bank, with Lincoln declaring in uncharacteristically purple prose: "I know that the great volcano at Washington, aroused and directed by the evil spirit that reigns there, is belching forth the lava of political corruption, in a current broad and deep, which is sweeping with frightful velocity over the whole length and breadth of the land, bidding fair to leave unscathed no green spot or living thing: while on its bosom are riding, like demons on the wave of Hell, the imps of the evil spirit, and fiendishly taunting all those who dare to resist its destroying course." The quote was picked up by the *National*

Intelligencer in Washington, giving Lincoln his first national exposure.[42]

Despite such overheated rhetoric, Lincoln was judged, and judged himself, to have lost the debate with Douglas. The *Illinois State Register*, not an impartial observer, claimed that Douglas "literally swamped his adversaries. [He] delivered one of the most powerful arguments against an United States Bank that we ever listened to. A settled gloom covered the countenances of the Whigs." Lincoln, said the newspaper, "commenced with embarrassment and continued without making the slightest impression. He could only meet the arguments of Mr. Douglas by relating stale anecdotes and old stories, and left the stump literally whipped off of it, even in the estimation of his own friends." One of those friends, Joseph Gillespie, reported that Lincoln "was conscious of his failure, and I never saw any man so much distressed."[43]

During the ensuing presidential campaign of 1840, Lincoln and Douglas debated each other frequently, from one end of the state to the other. It was part of the famous "Log Cabin and Hard Cider" campaign, a six-month-long orgy of singing, sloganeering, and speechifying that participants long afterward would remember as the most exciting and entertaining election of their lives. Having lost the previous three presidential elections to Andrew Jackson and his handpicked successor, Martin Van Buren, the Whigs were desperate to win at any cost. In the first instance of a truly prepackaged presidential candidate, party leaders bypassed Lincoln's political hero, Kentucky senator Henry Clay, and fixed their attention on William Henry Harrison, the previously undistinguished former territorial governor of Indiana, who had run surprisingly well in the 1836 election as part of a three-headed ticket that attempted unsuccessfully to deny Van Buren an electoral majority and throw the race into the House of Representatives.

Harrison had some political advantages, mainly a potential treasure trove of electoral votes from Indiana and his adopted home state of Ohio, but at the relatively attenuated age of sixty-seven, he was a far from ideal candidate. Despite having been a United States senator, congressman, and foreign minister to Colombia, Harrison had few concrete political achievements to which he could point. That didn't matter to Whig bosses. Taking a page from the hated Jackson's campaign book, they marketed Harrison, the patrician son a former Virginia governor and signer of the Declaration of Independence, as a homespun frontiersman and man of the people. They transformed Harrison's comfortable, sixteen-room farmhouse in North Bend, Ohio, into a humble log cabin, and inflated Harrison's somewhat suspect victory over the Shawnee-led Indian confederation at Tippecanoe Creek, Indiana, in November 1811 into a towering feat of arms comparable to Jackson's defeat of the British at New Orleans. In truth, Harrison had been badly surprised at Tippecanoe, but a last-ditch stand had enabled him to hold off the Indians and claim technical control of the battlefield. With that distinctly unemphatic triumph in hand, "Old Tippecanoe" was put forth as the logical successor to Old Hickory in the White House.[44]

Playing off a Democratic jibe that the aged Harrison would be happier spending his days with a barrel of hard cider in a log cabin beside a fire, the Whigs touted their candidate as "the log cabin and hard cider" candidate. Overnight, makeshift log cabins sprang up across the country, accompanied by barrels of hard cider. The Whigs flooded the country with a deluge of Harrison campaign pins, badges, coins, medallions, handkerchiefs, water pitchers, shaving mugs, and writing paper—all festooned with their champion's unexceptional likeness. The ever-pliable Harrison was presented as being all things to all people. To farmers, he was a farmer; to veterans, he was a veteran; to pioneers, he was a pioneer; to hero-worshipers, he was a hero. Truth was not an issue. As one leading Whig admitted later, "All we wanted was to carry the election."[45]

None too creditably, Lincoln played a part in the sham. Besides helping to found a new Illinois publication, the *Old Soldier*, to inflate Harrison's image, he also published a steady stream of "Lincoln Speeches and Tippecanoe Almanacs" in the *Sangamo Journal*, accusing Van Buren of being, among other things, "effeminate and luxury-loving." Nor was Lincoln too scrupulous to resist playing the race card in one highly publicized debate with Douglas late in the campaign, repeating the charge that Van Buren had once voted in favor of a property requirement for New York voters. Such a requirement, Lincoln said, favored free blacks over poor whites, "even if he should be a Revolutionary War veteran." He produced an old Van Buren campaign biography that purported to document the vote. Douglas ripped the book from Lincoln's hands and sent it skimming into the crowd. "All lies!" he shouted. When the *Alton Telegraph*, a Democratic newspaper, accused the dark-complexioned Lincoln of coming "from Liberia"—meaning he was black—the *Sangamo Journal* shot back that Douglas was "clothed with sable furs of Guinea—whose breath smells rank with devotion to the cause of Africa's sons—and whose trail might be followed by scattered bunches of Nigger wool." It was that kind of campaign.[46]

There was an untypical meanness in much of Lincoln's campaigning that year. In an appearance at the Sangamon County courthouse in Springfield, he tore into local attorney Jesse B. Thomas. After first declaring that he "wanted to whip" Thomas, Lincoln went on to mimic Thomas's gestures and voice so mercilessly that the young man burst into tears. The *State Register* denounced the performance for its "assumed clownishness" and "buffoonery," but there was nothing particularly funny about it. The next day, Lincoln apologized. The ad hominem attack, so out of character for the normally gracious Lincoln, may have reflected the strain in his personal life. He had recently been turned down for marriage by one Kentucky woman, Mary Owens, and had begun a halting courtship with another daughter of the Bluegrass—his friend Ninian Edwards's plump, vivacious sister-in-law, Mary Todd, a cousin of his law partner, John Todd Stuart. In this campaign, too, Lincoln faced a challenge from Douglas, another regular visitor to the Edwards's hilltop mansion. The bright and talkative Mary was actually more compatible with Douglas than she was with the socially awkward Lincoln, but their political differences—she was a flaming Whig, a family friend of Henry Clay—made a serious love affair impossible. Nevertheless, the two amused one another with witty drawing-room repartee and took long walks together on the streets of Springfield. Several years after the fact, Mary supposedly told her friend and confidante, White House seamstress Elizabeth Keckley, that Douglas had proposed to her but that she had turned him down, noting prophetically: "I can't consent to be your wife. I shall become Mrs. President . . . but it will not be as Mrs. Douglas." Despite such claims, their relationship never went beyond mutual flirting. "I liked him well enough, but that was all," Mary shrugged.[47]

Douglas, at any rate, was too busy campaigning to do much socializing. He had resigned his post in the Springfield Land Office and, as chairman of the Democratic State Committee, had taken to the roads in behalf of Van Buren. In the course of the 1840 campaign, Douglas made 207 speeches, including one that took place at a public hanging in Carlinville (contrary to rumor, he did not shoulder aside the condemned man to address the crowd from the gallows). Besides Lincoln, he debated his old rivals Stuart and Hardin, and even took on former Illinois governor Joseph Duncan, an apostate Democrat whom he denounced for engaging in "the slang of a palace, and extravagant furniture, and a hundred other ridiculous charges" against Van Buren. After a particularly bitter exchange of words with *Sangamo Journal* editor Simeon Francis, Douglas met the newsman in open combat on a Springfield street. A gleeful Lincoln recounted the ensuing affray: "Douglas, having chosen to consider himself insulted by something in the 'Journal,' undertook to cane Francis in the street. Francis caught him by the hair and jammed him back against a marketcart, where the matter ended by Francis being pulled away from him. The whole affair was so ludicrous that Francis and everybody else (Douglas excepted) have been laughing about it ever since."[48]

◆ ◆ ◆

Douglas's various combats, verbal and physical, paid handsome dividends on Election Day, when Illinois was one of only seven states to buck the Harrison landslide. As a reward for his services, Democratic governor Thomas Carlin appointed Douglas secretary of state in November 1840, replacing drunken Whig officeholder Alexander P. Field. At the age of twenty-seven, Douglas was the youngest secretary of state in Illinois history, but he did not remain in the post for long. Three months later, with the help of the Democratic-controlled legislature, he was named to fill one of five new seats on the state supreme court. Even among Democrats, there were some misgivings about Douglas's youth and comparatively meager legal qualifications. State senator Adam Snyder, who had sponsored the sweeping reorganization, said bluntly that "Douglas is talented, but too young for the office," but added somewhat backhandedly, "We could not do much better than elect him."[49]

The newly chosen "baby judge" was given charge of the Fifth Judicial District, a nine-county region along the Mississippi River that was the fastest-growing area in the state. Part of the reason for its rapid growth involved one of Douglas's old Canandaigua, New York, neighbors, Mormon religious leader Joseph Smith, who had relocated his followers to Illinois after a brief and stormy stay in Missouri. Both the Democrats and the Whigs actively courted the Mormon vote, and Douglas took care to maintain friendly relations with Smith and his coreligionists. During his brief interim as secretary of state, he had helped push through the legislature an act granting a charter to the new city of Nauvoo and giving it the power to raise its own militia, the Nauvoo Legion, that was independent of the state government and exempt from all non-church-related military duty. He also appointed Nauvoo mayor John C. Bennett, "probably the greatest scamp in the western country," to chancery court in Hancock County. "Judge Douglas has ever proved himself friendly to this people," Smith said afterward, in something of an understatement.[50]

Besides doing favors for the Mormons, Douglas traveled the Fifth Circuit's back roads, hearing a staggering number of cases—nearly 400 in the first two months alone. He was, one lawyer observed, "a perfect steam engine in britches." Chicago attorney Justin Butterfield, a Whig, conceded that "I thought I could handle him, but damn that little squatty Democrat—he is the very best and most acute Judge in all this Democratic State. He listens patiently, comprehends the law and grasps the facts by intuition; then decides calmly, clearly and quietly. . . . Douglas is the ablest man on the bench today in Illinois." He was the certainly the most informal, propping his feet on his desk and leaving the bench frequently to sit on his friends' knees and share cigars. "He is certainly the most *democratic* judge I ever knew," one lawyer noted. Douglas proved his point by removing all Whig circuit court clerks and replacing them with Democrats.[51]

Despite assuring his family that "office and honors have lost their charm" and that he intended "to devote all the energies of my mind to my judicial duties and my private affairs," Douglas could not resist the continuing lure of politics. In 1842, he successfully managed fellow supreme court judge Thomas Ford's election as governor, and later that year he came within five votes of receiving the Democratic nomination for the United States Senate. The next year, an even better opportunity opened up when the Fifth Judicial District was included in the newly drawn Fifth Congressional District. Thanks to his wide exposure as a jurist in the district, Douglas defeated his Whig opponent, Orville H. Browning, by a narrow 461-vote margin.[52]

Ten years to the day after he arrived in western Illinois, a twenty-year-old stranger with less than $5 in his pocket, Douglas headed off to Congress. Behind him he would leave a bevy of friends and supporters—and an equal number of political enemies. One of the latter, Abraham Lincoln, had failed in his own bid for a congressional seat, losing the Seventh District nomination to Douglas's old nemesis, John J. Hardin. While Hardin went to Washington with Douglas, Lincoln stayed behind in Springfield, devoting himself to his legal practice and his new wife, Hardin's third cousin, Mary Todd, in more or less that order. Having resigned his seat in the state legislature two years earlier to concentrate on making a living, Lincoln now seemed a spent force politically, part of the soon-to-be distant past that receded, mile by mile, in the cloud of dust behind Douglas's eastbound stage.

2

Whigs and Polkats

While Stephen Douglas set out for Washington, dreaming of glory on the floor of the House, Abraham Lincoln remained behind in Springfield. For once, he had more important things to worry about than politics—specifically, his young wife and the commencement of their rather complex life together. "Nothing new here except my marrying, which to me, is a matter of profound wonder," he told an acquaintance one week after getting married. At thirty-three, Lincoln was ten years older than Mary Todd, whom he sometimes called, a little dryly, "my child bride." (He also called her "Puss," "Little Woman," or "Molly," as the mood struck him.) Their on-again, off-again courtship had been the talk of Springfield for months. Her sister and brother-in-law had actively discouraged the match, which had begun in their own drawing room. The new couple, they told Mary, "had better not ever marry," noting that "their natures, mind—education—raising etc. were so different they could not live happily as man and wife." Nor did Mary's family back in Kentucky endorse the relationship, believing with some justice that Lincoln came from "nowhere" and had "nebulous" prospects. Lincoln had his own reservations about his patrimony, if not his future, but he still resented the implication that he was somehow socially inferior.

"One *d* was enough to spell God," he observed sourly, "but it took two *d*'s to spell Todd."[1]

There is some evidence that Lincoln also questioned the wisdom of their union. Not only did he abruptly call off their first engagement, but he subsequently fell into one of his periodic depressions, this one so severe that his best friend and roommate, Joshua Speed, felt obliged to remove all razors, knives, and other sharp objects from their room. "I am now the most miserable man living," Lincoln told his former law partner, John Stuart. "If what I feel were equally distributed to the whole human family, there would not be one cheerful face on earth. I must die or be better." Eventually, he snapped out of his funk and began peppering Speed, who in the interim had moved back to Kentucky to get married himself, with questions about matrimony. "Are you now, in feeling as well as judgment, glad you are married?" Lincoln asked. Reassured by Speed's happy reply, Lincoln returned to work and, with the help of *Sangamo Journal* editor Simeon Francis's wife, Eliza, secretly resumed courting Mary, meeting her at the Francis home, safely away from the prying eyes of Mary's disapproving relatives. To mark their reconciliation, he gave her an unusual but not inappropriate gift: the election returns from his last three legislative races, tied in a pink ribbon. Both of them were ardent Whigs, and Mary shared her beau's love of politics. Lincoln, for his part, was intrigued to hear about his hero Henry Clay's frequent visits to Mary's childhood home, including the time her father hosted a dinner for the senator during his unsuccessful presidential campaign in 1832 and thirteen-year-old Mary boldly announced her enduring support for the candidate and her intention to live in Washington herself one day.[2]

The relationship, founded as much on political as romantic grounds, took a potentially dangerous turn in the fall of 1842, following the publication of a series of anonymous letters in the *Journal* attacking Democratic state auditor James Shields as "a conceity dunce" and "a fool as well as a liar." The crux of the letters, at least one of which was written by Lincoln, was a political wrangle between the Democrats and the Whigs over state banking matters. Purporting to be from an uncultured country woman named Aunt Becca, the letters went beyond mere politics to ridicule Shields, a dapper little Irishman, for his pompous airs and self-styled romanticism. Mary Todd and her best friend, Julia Jayne, were the authors of the most offensive letter, one in which Aunt Becca offered to let Shields "come here and he may squeeze my hand as hard as I squeeze the butter," and almost dared him to take offense: "I know he's a fighting man and would rather fight than eat."[3]

Rising to the bait, Shields charged into the *Journal* offices and demanded to know who had defamed him in print. Lincoln gallantly claimed sole authorship of the letters, at which point Shields challenged him to a duel. Lincoln, who towered a good seven inches over Shields, chose broadswords as weapons, and the men agreed to meet on the aptly named Bloody Island, a spit of Missouri land directly across the Mississippi River from Alton, Illinois. At almost the last moment, cooler heads prevailed and the duel was called off, although Lincoln said later, still somewhat combative: "If it had been necessary I could have split him from the crown of his head to the end of his backbone." Years later, when an impertinent army officer brought up the fray, Lincoln responded icily: "I do not deny it, but if you desire my friendship, you will never mention it again."[4]

Touched by his chivalry, Mary accepted Lincoln's wedding proposal a few days later and finally told her sister of their plans. The Edwardses agreed, however grudgingly, to host the wedding, which took place in their parlor on the rain-soaked night of November 4, 1842. Lincoln, dressed in black, "looked and acted as if he were going to the slaughter," best man James Matheny reported later, adding that the wedding was "one of the funniest things to have witnessed imaginable—No description on paper can possibly do it justice." Asked earlier by the young son of his landlord where he was going all dressed up, Lincoln groused, "To hell, I reckon." It was not exactly an auspicious start to a marriage that few people—perhaps not even the bridegroom—expected to last. Neither Mary's father nor Lincoln's attended the ceremony, which had been thrown together so hurriedly that the wedding cake was still warm when it was sliced.[5]

The unlikely newlyweds set up housekeeping in a single room at the Globe Tavern, Springfield's second-best hotel. Most of the Globe's renters were transients, but the hotel also provided room and board for a few regular lodgers. Mary, to her credit, attempted to make the best of the situation, which represented a significant comedown from her accustomed standard of living. Lincoln, who had always lived rough, did not mind the accommodations—he was rarely there. Having lost his law partner, John Stuart, when Stuart went off to Congress in 1839,

Lincoln had entered into partnership with another established Spring-field lawyer, Todd family cousin and fellow Whig Stephen T. Logan. The eccentric Logan, who as circuit court judge had certified Lincoln's enrollment in the Sangamon County bar in 1836, was perhaps the only man in Springfield who cared less about his personal appearance than Lincoln. A wizened little man with a wiry shock of red hair, Logan invariably wore an outfit consisting of baggy pants, too-large jacket, and twenty-five-cent straw hat. He was famous for his compulsive whittling—the local sheriff kept a ready supply of wood shingles in a sack for Logan at the courthouse—and preferred to remain behind the scenes while the better-spoken Lincoln handled their cases before juries.[6]

Business was brisk for the new firm of Logan & Lincoln. On a single day in November 1842, the same month that Lincoln got married, the partners handled seventeen cases before the Sangamon County circuit court. Nor was their practice confined to Springfield. While Mary kept house—such as it was—in their eight-by-fourteen-foot hotel room, Lincoln traveled the legal circuit, sometimes staying gone for a month or more at a time. Riding his favorite horse, "Old Tom," Lincoln accompanied circuit court judge Samuel H. Treat and a vagabond lot of other Springfield lawyers on the judge's semiannual sweep of the fourteen-county Eighth District. Covering as much as thirty-five miles a day, the legal caravan would pitch its tents for a day or two at a time in the widely dispersed hamlets of central Illinois. The circuit system was a holdover from the early days of the Republic, having been adopted by the First Congress in 1789 after the founders recognized the fact that there was not enough regular judicial business to merit placing a full-time judge in every county of the sprawling new nation. Instead, Congress devised a system that was part legal hearing, part traveling minstrel show. (The always irreverent Gouverneur Morris observed drolly that judges now would have to combine the legal learning of a scholar with the physical endurance of a postman.)[7]

Lincoln, with his rangy physique and wealth of stories, excelled at the often-exhausting practice. More than that, he enjoyed it. What was drudgery for many of his fellow attorneys was fun for Lincoln. He liked being out in the fresh air, swapping yarns with other lawyers as they traveled between towns, and he relished arguing cases—no matter how trivial—before a countrified jury of his peers. At night, he sat up late while the judge presided over a kangaroo court, convicting the lawyers for their earlier sins in the courtroom. On at least one occasion, Lincoln was fined for the "crime" of charging his client too small a fee. While not a drinker himself, Lincoln would regale a table full of rustic taverngoers with his bottomless fountain of jokes and yarns. "Judges—Jurors—Witnesses—Lawyers—merchants—etc etc have laughed at these jokes," one attorney remembered, "till every muscle—nerve and cell of the body in the morning was sore at the whooping and hurrahing exercise." Fellow circuit rider Usher Linder was more concise. "God, he was funny," he recalled. Lincoln even tolerated the gruesome food, which future United States Supreme Court justice David Davis, a fellow traveler, complained "was hardly fit for the stomach of a horse." At one rest stop where the proprietor had run out of meat and bread, Lincoln grabbed a plate and announced cheerfully, "Well, in the absence of anything to eat I will jump into this cabbage."[8]

Besides earning Lincoln a comfortable living while he was out on the road—more than $150 a week during sessions—the circuit court also proved invaluable politically. It enabled Lincoln to maintain contacts with the leading judges and attorneys (who were often the leading politicians, as well) of every small town in the district. He also engendered good will among the many clients he represented in court, people who would vote in upcoming elections. J. H. Buckingham, a reporter for the *Boston Courier*, later accompanied Lincoln on one such trip and recorded his impressions. Lincoln, he said, "knew or appeared to know, everybody we met, the name of the tenant of every farm-house, and the owner of every plat of ground. Such a shaking of hands—such a how-d'ye-do—such a greeting of different kinds, as we saw, was never seen before. It seemed as if he had a kind word, a smile and a bow for everybody on the road, even to the horse, and the cattle, and the swine."[9]

In his careful, plodding way, Lincoln was seeding the ground for a congressional bid in 1843. Stuart was retiring after two terms in office, and the Whig Party was looking around for a suitable successor. Jacksonville attorney John J. Hardin, a veteran of many Illinois political battles, was the favorite, while Springfield Whigs were split evenly between Lincoln and his good friend Edward Baker, Stephen Logan's former law partner. Ironically, Lincoln's recent marriage was used against him. Baker's supporters charged that Lincoln had married into the elite Edwards-Stuart clan and was thus "the candidate of pride, wealth and aristocratic family distinction." He was also accused, more or less accurately, of being a deist if not an atheist, and was criticized for his comic-opera near-duel with James Shields a few months earlier.[10]

The charges stuck and Lincoln lost the local endorsement to Baker, who in turn lost to Hardin at the state convention that May at Pekin. Cannily, Lincoln managed to turn present defeat into future victory. Taking a page from Stephen Douglas's playbook, he convinced the Whigs to endorse the notion of open nominating conventions, something the Democrats had been doing for years. Using for the first time a biblical maxim that he would reuse with great effect a few years later, Lincoln warned that "a house divided against itself cannot stand." He also got the party to agree to a rotating term of office for congressmen in the Seventh District. Baker was anointed to run in 1844, with Lincoln waiting in the wings for his turn. For a third-place finisher who had not even won the support of his hometown district, it was a brilliant feat of political jujitsu. In the meantime, Lincoln went home to Mary and his well-thumbed law books.[11]

◆ ◆ ◆

Outmaneuvered by Lincoln at the very moment of his triumph, Hardin joined Douglas as a freshman legislator in the Twenty-eighth Congress in December 1843. The two formerly bitter enemies, no longer fighting over the same political territory, could afford to be cordial to one another. They were just two new congressmen in an unusually large class of Washington neophytes (the result of a frenzied spate of gerrymandering in the House). Joining them for the ritual swearing-in were such future political stars as Alexander Stephens and Howell Cobb of Georgia, John Slidell of Louisiana, Andrew Johnson of Tennessee, and Hannibal Hamlin of Maine. One of the reigning leaders of the lower chamber was a man long familiar to Douglas, former president John Quincy Adams, who would watch the younger man's progress with gimlet-eyed disapproval from the Whig side of the aisle. Douglas took the lead in organizing a "mess," or dining club, for members of the Illinois delegation, although the lengthy House sessions and late-night caucuses left little time to eat. "Having a seat in Congress is not the thing it is cracked up to be," Hardin complained after a few weeks in Washington. "The hours of eating here destroy all business habits & the hours of the House destroy a man's health."[12]

Douglas's maiden speech to the House, on January 6, 1844, did little to endear him to Adams or to Adams's fellow Whigs. Pennsylvania congressman Charles J. Ingersoll had introduced a bill demanding the return to Andrew Jackson of the $1,000 (plus interest) that Jackson had been fined by United States district judge Dominick Hall for contempt of court after Jackson ignored a court order and instituted martial law in New Orleans during the War of 1812. Calling on his experience—slight though it was—as a lawyer and judge, Douglas delivered an impassioned defense of Jackson's actions. "There are exigencies in the history of nations as well as individuals," Douglas said, "when necessity becomes the paramount law. . . . In case of war and desolation, in times of peril and disaster, we should look at the substance, not the shadow of things. Talk not to me about rules and forms in court, when the enemy's cannon are pointed at the door, and the flames encircle the cupola." It was a politically effective, if legally dubious, defense, and even Adams admitted in his diary that Douglas had made "an eloquent, sophistical speech, prodigiously admired by the slave Democracy of the House." A few months later, when Douglas called upon Jackson at the general's home in Nashville, the Old Hero thanked him in person for his speech and endorsed a copy in his spidery hand: "This speech constitutes my defense; I lay it aside as an inheritance for my grandchildren."[13]

The Jackson refund bill was the first shot in the 1844 presidential campaign. Democrats were determined to recapture the White House after the bizarre four-year interregnum of William Henry Harrison and his successor, Vice President John Tyler, who replaced Harrison after he died of pneumonia one short month into his term. Tyler, an apostate Democrat who had switched parties in protest of Jackson's iron-fisted handling of the nullification crisis in 1832, had spent virtually his entire presidency governing as a Democrat anyway, much to the teeth-grinding chagrin of the Whigs. Derided by opponents as "His Accidency," Tyler hoped to win the Democratic nomination in 1844. To improve his chances, he approved a treaty annexing the eight-year-old Republic of Texas as a U.S. territory. The Whigs, still in control of the Senate, blocked the treaty's passage. In reaction, the Democrats decided to make annexation their main emphasis in the upcoming election. At the party convention in Baltimore, they selected a dark-horse candidate, former Tennessee governor and congressman James K. Polk, as their nominee. Polk, an ardent expansionist, combined the virtues of Andrew Jackson—he was called "Young Hickory" by his admirers—with an even more aggressive approach to expanding American territory. On the floor of the House,

Douglas praised Polk as "emphatically a Young Hickory. No man living possesses General Jackson's confidence in a greater degree, or displayed more zeal . . . in carrying out the great republican principles with which his administration was identified."[14]

After Congress adjourned in mid-June, Douglas returned to Illinois to battle for reelection from the Fifth District. Beating back a party challenge from former governor Thomas Carlin, he faced Whig nominee David M. Woodson, a Greene County lawyer and a former state legislator, in the general election. As a sidelight to the election, Douglas's old New York neighbor, Mormon leader Joseph Smith, had decided to run for president on a platform calling for federal protection of religious minorities. But Smith's belief in polygamy, and his alleged attempts to foist those beliefs onto the dubious wives of some of his fellow elders, caused a rift in the Mormon community at Nauvoo. After Smith's supporters wrecked the offices of the *Nauvoo Expositor*, which had been critical of the prophet, Smith and his brother Hyrum, along with fifteen other supporters, surrendered to authorities at Carthage, Illinois. Charged with treason, a capital offense, the Smith brothers were held without bond. On the afternoon of June 27, a mob of 200 armed men, their faces painted red, yellow, and black, stormed the jail and fatally shot the Smiths.[15]

Douglas, like most Democrats, deplored the killings and used the crime against the Whigs, who were viewed as anti-Mormon and antiforeign (a holdover, perhaps, from Douglas's successful courting of Irish canal builders in the 1837 congressional election). In the aftermath of Smith's murder, the Mormons overwhelmingly backed Douglas in the August election, and he swamped Woodson by more than 1,700 votes, carrying all but one of the Fifth District's twelve counties. All the other incumbent Democratic congressmen were reelected as well, and the party turned confidently to the looming presidential election between Polk and the Whig candidate, Senator Henry Clay of Kentucky. "Gallant Harry" was making his third run for president, having lost narrowly to John Quincy Adams in 1824 and badly to Andrew Jackson in 1832. "I am the most unfortunate man in the history of parties," Clay complained when analyzing his chances, "always run by my friends when sure to be defeated."[16]

That was by no means sure in 1844, but the nomination of James K. Polk added an element of uncertainty to the race, as did the still-minor, if rising, note of antislavery agitation in the North, which the proposed annexation of Texas had struck with abolitionists. Clay, a slave owner himself, attempted to straddle the issue by insisting that he was "decidedly opposed to the immediate annexation of Texas to the United States," but the obvious vagueness of his position managed to please no one. Southern Whigs called him a "nigger-loving abolitionist," while abolitionists castigated him as a "man stealer, slave-holder, and murderer." Democrats, for their part, accused Clay of having systematically broken, one by one, all Ten Commandments. "Clay," said one political pamphlet, "spends his days at the gaming table and his nights in a brothel." His campaign standard was "a pistol, a pack of cards, and a brandy bottle."[17]

With the tide of public opinion running strongly toward expansionism, Clay and his surrogates hoped to switch the subject to the economy, which was still recovering from the Panic of 1837. As usual, the Whigs favored a high protective tariff on imported goods, and they sent out a raft of speakers to make their case. One such speaker was Abraham Lincoln, whose own inchoate views on the subject caused him a noticeable amount of discomfort on the stump. The tariff, he claimed, would not affect the common laborer or farmer "who never wore, nor never expects to wear, a single yard of British goods in his whole life," but only "those whose pride, whose abundance of means, prompts them to spurn the manufacturers of our own country, and to strut in British cloaks, and coats, and pantaloons." Challenged by a voter at Sugar Creek, Illinois, to explain why that was the case, Lincoln "said he could not tell the reason, but that it was so." At that point, "Lincoln came near having a chicken fit, and choking to death," reported a skeptical observer, "but fortunately some water was procured and he got over it." Dissatisfied with his stumbling answer, Lincoln spent hours boning up on the issue while he continued to denounce "the absurdities of loco focoism" on the campaign trail.[18]

◆ ◆ ◆

As a measure of their growing national prominence, both Lincoln and Douglas made campaign swings outside of Illinois for their parties' presidential candidates in 1844. Following his reelection victory in August, Douglas traveled to Polk's home state for a mass meeting of Democrats at a campground in Nashville. It was during this visit that Douglas paid a courtesy call on his hero, Andrew Jackson, at the Hermitage, where

Jackson thanked him again for supporting the refund bill. Other encomiums also came Douglas's way on the trip. The *Nashville Union* praised him "as a popular debater . . . equaled by few men," and the *Illinois State Register* reported that Douglas had held a large St. Louis audience "in a breathless silence" for three hours while he denounced the tariff as "an act for the oppression and plunder of the American laborer for the benefit of a few large capitalists." The "Young Giant of Illinois," said the newspaper, "was an intellectual giant indeed."[19]

Meanwhile, Lincoln traveled to Indiana on horseback to address Clay rallies at Vincennes and Rockport, repeating his support for the tariff and contrasting it adversely to a direct system of taxation that he warned would "cover the land with assessors and collectors, going forth like swarms of Egyptian locusts, devouring every blade of grass and other green thing." The desolate imagery was in keeping with Lincoln's mood that fall. His swing through Indiana brought him back to Gentryville, where he had spent his boyhood on the banks of Little Pigeon Creek and buried his mother, Nancy, and his older sister, Sarah. A chance encounter with Matthew Gentry, a former classmate who had suddenly and unaccountably gone insane at the age of nineteen, further darkened Lincoln's mood. Gentry, he wrote in a bit of lugubrious verse, had become "a human form with reason fled," a howling madman whose nighttime screams were "the funeral dirge/Of reason dead and gone." Brooding somewhat self-consciously on "things decayed and loved ones lost," Lincoln tramped the old cornfield where his father had sent him to work as a boy: "I range the fields with pensive tread,/And pace the hollow rooms;/And feel (companion of the dead)/I'm living in the tombs."[20]

Part of Lincoln's gloom, no doubt, was a reflection of the dire political landscape. Henry Clay was headed for a third and last defeat in his quarter-century pursuit of the presidency. No amount of halfhearted campaign literature likening "Ol' Coon" Clay to "Old Tippecanoe" Harrison could recapture the magic of four years before. Nor could the song-happy Whigs make much music from the party ticket of Henry Clay and Theodore Frelinghuysen. "Hurrah! Hurrah! The country's risin'/For Henry Clay and Frelinghuysen" did not exactly evoke the alliterative power of "Tippecanoe and Tyler, too." Symbolic of the Whigs' futility was a highly publicized effort to outdo the Democratic "Polkats" by raising an ashen pole that was higher than their opponents' 150-foot-tall hickory pole. When the Whigs' 214½-foot-high pole was raised at a rally in Springfield in August, it immediately toppled over, crushing two members of the Mechanics Union. Whigs charged that Democrats had cut the ropes; Democrats countered that the Whigs had callously ignored the injured mechanics and continued their ceremonies. When other mechanics began to fall ill with intestinal complaints, *Sangamo Journal* editor Simeon Francis accused the Democrats of literally poisoning the public well (it was later determined that a boy had accidentally dropped a package of horsefly salve into the water).[21]

In the end, Polk won the election, although by a surprisingly narrow margin of 38,175 votes out of a total of 2.7 million cast. A shift of some 2,106 votes in New York, where antislavery candidate James G. Birney won nearly 16,000 votes to his Liberty Party standard, would have made Clay president. (New York Whigs did their best—or worst—by urging Irish voters to back "Patrick O'Clay," but it was not enough to carry the state.) Lincoln, always an acute analyzer of elections, agreed with *New York Tribune* editor Horace Greeley that the Liberty Party, by splitting the Whig vote, had "carried all these votes obliquely in favor of Annexation, War, and eternal Slavery." Arguing that "union is strength," Lincoln warned that unless the Whigs stood together, they would continue to see "the spoils chucklingly borne off by the common enemy." By refusing to support Clay, Lincoln said, the abolitionists had played into the Democrats' hands. "If the fruit of electing Mr. Clay would have been to prevent the extension of slavery," he wrote, "could the act of electing have been *evil?*" Along with the need to maintain party discipline, Lincoln took another lesson from Clay's defeat. The growing strength of the abolitionist movement was something that future candidates must keep in mind. He filed it away in that part of his brain that never forgot anything.[22]

◆ ◆ ◆

A few weeks after the 1844 election, Lincoln dissolved his lucrative legal partnership with Logan. Having recently purchased a house on the corner of Eighth and Jackson streets in Springfield, Lincoln was feeling sufficiently flush to strike out on his own and take on a junior partner. His choice was a surprising one. Twenty-six-year-old William "Billy" Herndon had been studying law with Lincoln and Logan for the past two years, and had just received his license to practice. A small, excitable young man who dressed like a dandy in a tall silk hat, patent-leather shoes, and kid gloves, Herndon was as talkative as Lincoln was quiet. He fancied himself something of a philosopher, and had a library full of the works of Hegel, Kant, Bacon, and Emerson. He tried unsuccessfully to get Lincoln to read the weighty tomes, but Lincoln preferred reading the daily newspapers, which he frequently quoted aloud, thereby irritating Herndon. His mind, he explained to the younger man, was like an old jackknife: "It opens slowly and its points travel through a greater distance of space than your little knife: it moves slower than your little knife, but it can do more execution." Still, Lincoln considered his new partner "a laborious, studious young man . . . far better informed on almost all subjects than I have been," and he depended on Herndon to keep him in touch with the other "shrewd, wild boys about town" who were making inroads into local politics.[23]

The partners moved into a second-floor office in the dingy, brick Tinsley Building overlooking an alley behind the courthouse square. They furnished it with two desks, six cane-bottom chairs, a bookcase, a table, and a dilapidated old sofa upon which Lincoln liked to recline while pondering a case. Neither Lincoln nor Herndon was particularly neat, and legal papers and documents soon piled up about the office in dusty heaps. Lincoln kept handfuls of his records stuffed into his trademark stovepipe hat, which functioned, Herndon said, as "his desk and memorandum book." In one corner was a capacious heap of papers, topped by a note in Lincoln's handwriting: "When you can't find it anywhere else, look in this." Despite the haphazard filing system, the partners had more than enough cases to keep them busy. In a work-sharing arrangement that suited them both, Herndon usually stayed behind in Springfield, while Lincoln continued riding the legal circuit in the countryside.[24]

As always, Lincoln combined the practice of law with the practice of politics. It was necessary for him to do so—1845 was shaping up as a crucial year in his political career. In accordance with the agreement worked out two years earlier at the Whigs' state convention in Pekin, Lincoln's friend Edward Baker had been elected to the Seventh District seat in Congress. By rights, the next term should belong to Lincoln, but an unexpected complication had arisen. The previous occupant of the seat, Mary Lincoln's cousin John Hardin, had decided that he liked Washington so well that he wanted to return. Hardin tried to convince Lincoln to agree to a new set of ground rules, doing away with the rotation system. Unsurprisingly, Lincoln rejected the notion, telling Hardin that he was "entirely satisfied with the old system under which you and Baker were successively nominated and elected to Congress." Lincoln wrote to various newspaper editors, reminding them of the earlier agreement: "I want a fair shake and I want nothing more. Turn about is fair play." Most Whigs agreed, one telling Hardin that "it is Abraham's turn." Hardin eventually pulled out of the race and enlisted in the army, which was mobilizing for an incipient war with Mexico. He would die at the Battle of Buena Vista in 1847, conveniently and permanently removing himself as a future rival.[25]

Having dispensed with Hardin, Lincoln faced off against his Democratic opponent in the general election. This time it was an easy race. Despite being a well-known circuit-riding Methodist minister and a former member of the Illinois legislature, Peter Cartwright was no match for Lincoln's years of political experience. In desperation, he fell back on an old charge—that Lincoln was an infidel. Lincoln was sufficiently worried to print, at his own expense, a "Handbill Replying to Charges of Infidelity." In the only public statement of faith he ever made during his more than three decades in politics, Lincoln conceded: "That I am not a member of any Christian Church is true; but I have never denied the truth of the Scriptures; and I have never spoken with intentional disrespect of religion in general, or of any denomination of Christians in particular." Moreover, said Lincoln, "I do not think I could myself be brought to support a man for office, whom I knew to be an open enemy of, and scoffer at, religion." In the end, Lincoln won a decisive victory, outpolling Cartwright 6,340 to 4,829.[26]

◆ ◆ ◆

By the time the congressional elections were held in August 1846, the long-expected Mexican War had begun. Except for one brief statement in the *Sangamo Journal* calling for the nation's "citizen soldiery to sustain her national character [and] secure our national rights," Lincoln had ignored the war during the campaign. That was not the case, however, with the region's leading Democrat. From the time of his first term in Congress, when President Tyler had proposed annexing Texas to the United States, Stephen Douglas had been an enthusiastic expansionist. One of his first major speeches in the House had been a historical critique of the nation's sinuous dealings with Mexico over the future of Texas, from the 1803 treaty with France that cemented the Louisiana

Purchase to the "fatal" 1819 treaty with Spain that his newfound enemy John Quincy Adams, then secretary of state, had helped to broker. The United States, Douglas maintained, had an obligation to the people of Texas to honor their request for annexation.[27]

When Congress declared war on Mexico in May 1846, Douglas took the floor of the House to defend the right of the United States to intervene in Texas's behalf. Responding to a charge by Ohio Whig Columbus Delano that the war was "illegal, unrighteous, and damnable," Douglas accused the critics of being "traitors in their hearts. . . . [H]onor and duty forbid divided counsels after our country has been invaded, and American blood has been shed on American soil by a treacherous foe." Disputing the Whigs' contention that the Rio Grande was not the proper northern boundary between Texas and Mexico, Douglas cited an 1819 dispatch written by Adams maintaining that it was. When Adams protested that he had never intended to claim the full extent of the Rio Grande for the border, Douglas challenged him to name the exact spot where the border diverged. Adams could not say. For once, "Old Man Eloquent" was at a loss for words. "It was a bombshell," Pennsylvania newspaper editor John W. Forney said of Douglas's speech. "It was a new thing to see John Quincy Adams retreating before anybody."[28]

Back home in Illinois, patriotic hysteria gripped the populace. Congressmen John Hardin and Edward Baker and Abraham Lincoln's old dueling opponent, Land Office commissioner James Shields, accepted generals' commissions, and Douglas himself gave serious consideration to an invitation from Hardin to "go along with us" to Mexico. Only the last-minute intercession of President Polk, who urged Douglas to remain in place as one of his strongest voices in Congress, prevented the Little Giant from succumbing to a potentially fatal case of war fever. He settled instead for a new post as junior senator from Illinois, winning election by the state legislature in December 1846. The night before he returned to Washington, Douglas hosted the most lavish party ever held in Springfield, a blowout that set him back $1,500—a considerable sum for the time.[29]

Douglas's strong support for the war brought him the approval of southern legislators, who saw the annexation of Texas as a way to add another state—perhaps several states—to their ranks. Since the end of the Revolutionary War, four new slave states had been added to the republic; Texas would make the fifth. During that same period, only Iowa had come into the Union as a free state. When Polk sent a special message to the House of Representatives requesting an additional $2 million to compensate Mexico for her lost territory, the abolitionists (or Free-Soilers, as they styled themselves) balked. Pennsylvania congressman David Wilmot introduced an amendment to the funding bill that would prohibit slavery in any territory acquired forcibly from Mexico. The Wilmot Proviso, as it became known, lit a long-simmering fuse in American politics. Polk, a slaveholder himself, denounced Wilmot's amendment as "mischievous and foolish," adding, "What connection slavery had with making peace with Mexico it is difficult to conceive." The House passed the amendment along sectional lines, with northern Democrats joining northern Whigs to support the provision, while southern Whigs crossed party lines to unite with southern Democrats in opposition to it.[30]

Douglas, one of only four northern Democrats to vote against the Wilmot Proviso, attempted to broker a workable compromise. As chairman of the House Committee on Territories, he was equally concerned with organizing the recently acquired Oregon territory along the 54°40' boundary line with Canada. He proposed a new amendment prohibiting slavery in Oregon under the existing terms of the 1820 Missouri Compromise, which had set the 36°40' parallel as the dividing line between free and slave states. This was "the most proper arrangement" for all concerned, Douglas argued. Free-Soil advocates disagreed. The Missouri Compromise, said Maine congressman Hannibal Hamlin, "had no more application to the Territory of Oregon than it had with the East Indies." Douglas's amendment was defeated, but it marked him in the eyes of the abolitionist press as one of the "betrayers of freedom" who had stood with the South on the issue of slavery. Douglas, said the editor of the *Chicago Western Citizen*, was "the most servile tool that has crawled in the slime and scum of slavery at the foot of the slave power." It was Douglas's introduction to "the vexed question of slavery in new territories," one that would come to dominate the political landscape for the next dozen years.[31]

Douglas took time away from his congressional duties in April 1847 for a more pleasant task. At the age of thirty-three, he was getting married. His bride, twenty-two-year-old Martha Martin of Rockingham County, North Carolina, came with a somewhat troublesome dowry: the deed to a 2,500-acre cotton plantation on the Pearl River in Mississippi and the approximately 150 slaves who worked it. Martha's father, Colonel Robert Martin, who owned a similar plantation in North Carolina, offered the Mississippi holdings to the happy couple as a wedding present. Douglas tactfully declined, urging the colonel to retain the property until he died, at which time it could be disposed of quietly in his will. It would not look proper for Douglas, a newly elected senator from a northern state, to be seen owning slaves. Under the terms of his father-in-law's will, duly enacted after the colonel died fourteen months later, Douglas was named manager of the property, with a 20 percent commission on all profits. Dowry aside, it was a happy marriage. In time, Martha would give Douglas two sons, Robert Martin, named for her father, born in January 1849, and Stephen, Jr., called "Stevie," born in November 1850.[32]

◆ ◆ ◆

When Abraham Lincoln reached Washington in December 1847 with his own wife and growing family (two sons, Robert and Edward, had been born between 1843 and 1846), the war with Mexico was nearly over. En route to Washington, the Lincolns spent three weeks in Lexington visiting the Todds. While there, they attended a massive antiwar rally at which a grieving Henry Clay, who had lost a son at Buena Vista, denounced the conflict as one of "unnecessary and offensive aggression." Lincoln was quickly coming around to the same view. He assured Herndon that "as you are all so anxious for me to distinguish myself, I have concluded to do so, before long." Mary and the boys settled into a shabby boardinghouse favored by congressional Whigs a stone's throw from the Capitol, while Lincoln worked on a series of lawyerly resolutions demanding to know the exact spot where Mexican troops had first attacked American forces and made the war (in President Polk's view, anyway) inevitable.[33]

Lincoln posed his maiden speech to Congress in the form of a series of legal interrogatories for his fellow lawyer, the president. "Let him answer, fully, fairly, and candidly," Lincoln demanded. "Let him answer with facts, and not with arguments." What he wanted to know, said Lincoln, was "whether the particular spot of soil on which the blood of our citizens who so shed, was, or was not, our own soil." He had his doubts, since both countries conceded that the initial attack had occurred in the area of the Rio Grande valley long settled by Mexicans. If that was the case, then Polk had voluntarily started a war for "military glory—that attractive rainbow, that rises in showers of blood—that serpent's eye, that charms to destroy." Polk's attempts to blame Mexico for the war, Lincoln said, were nothing more than "the half insane mumbling of a fever-dream" from the mind of a man who was "bewildered, confounded, and miserably perplexed . . . running hither and thither, like an ant on a hot stove."[34]

It was a provocative speech, particularly for a freshman congressman, and it marked Lincoln's return to the sort of virulent partisanship he had practiced during the 1840 presidential campaign. Then he had been distracted by his on-again, off-again courtship of Mary Todd; now, perhaps, he was unsettled by her obvious unhappiness with their new living arrangement in Washington. Their boardinghouse, run by Mrs. Ann Sprigg, was known locally as "Abolition House" because it had sheltered, at one time or another, such antislavery zealots as Ohio congressman Joshua Giddings and other Free-Soil Whigs. (No self-respecting Democrat would rent there.) Mary was the only wife on the premises, and the rather Spartan one-room accommodations were all too redolent of their early married life at the Globe Tavern in Springfield. While Lincoln worked late at the Capitol or took his ease at James Casparis's nearby bowling alley, Mary stayed in the room with their two young sons. The boys were the only children in the house, and the other guests apparently resented their presence. (After Mary and the boys returned to Lexington that spring, Lincoln wrote to her that "all the house—or rather, all with whom you were on decided good terms—send their love to you. The others say nothing.") The front of the boardinghouse looked out at the Capitol, whose graceful iron railing was only fifty feet away, but the rear provided a dismaying view of weather-beaten shanties and slouching lean-tos inhabited by "a loathsome community of the debauched, debased and drunken." A few blocks away, the infamous "Georgia pen" housed hundreds of slaves, whose bodies were for sale to the highest bidder.[35]

Washington in the late 1840s was a city in transition. With a population of about 38,000 (not counting slaves), it was smaller and less cosmopolitan than New York, Philadelphia, or Baltimore. An untended menagerie of pigs, cows, and chickens still wandered the streets. Only the lower part of Pennsylvania Avenue, near the White House, was paved, and the unfinished streets overflowed during rainstorms with a foul stream of mud and human waste. For a time, Mary made a brave

45

show of adapting—"You know I enjoy city life," she told a friend back home in Springfield—accompanying her husband and children to a performance of the blackface minstrels, the Ethiopian Serenaders, and to open-air concerts by the Marine Band on the grounds of the White House. But the one-room accommodations were entirely too small, particularly when one of the four people crowded inside them was six feet four inches tall, and soon Lincoln was complaining that Mary "hindered me some in attending to business." The couple argued, and it was mutually decided that Mary and the boys would move back to Lexington. Once there, she bombarded Lincoln with long, complaint-filled letters, asking to return, and her husband at length relented, with a pointed stipulation: "Will you be a good girl in all things, if I consent?" In the end, Mary remained in Lexington, where she and her stepmother grated on each other's nerves like a couple of untuned fiddles.[36]

Along with Mary's manifest unhappiness, Lincoln had to contend with the surprisingly harsh reaction his "spot resolutions" had provoked back home. The ever-loyal Herndon warned Lincoln that he was committing "political suicide" by taking such a bitterly antiwar stand, and noted ominously that there had been "substantial defections" and "murmurs of dissatisfaction" among local Whigs. The *Illinois State Register*, dubbing him "Spotty Lincoln," contrasted his finicky opposition to the war with the "gallantry and heroism" of the fallen Hardin, and a public rally in the martyred politician's home county denounced Lincoln's "base, dastardly, and treasonable assault upon President Polk" and predicted that "henceforth will this Benedict Arnold of our district be known here only as the Ranchero Spotty of one term." It was the last dig that hurt the most. Lincoln had found, to his surprise, that he rather liked Washington, telling Herndon, "If it should so happen that nobody else wishes to be elected, I could not refuse the people the right of sending me again." That was now unlikely, and Lincoln might have done well to ponder the hard-won wisdom of fellow Whig Justin Butterfield of Chicago, who refused to condemn the Mexican War (as he had the War of 1812) with a trenchant observation: "I opposed one war, and it ruined me. From now on I am for war, pestilence, and famine."[37]

Lincoln's opposition to the war did not extend to its most successful practitioner, Brigadier General Zachary Taylor. Eighteen forty-eight was an election year, and the Whigs were casting about again for a plausible presidential candidate. With the Mexican War drawing to a triumphant close, the party's critics, Lincoln included, needed to find a way to dem-onstrate their patriotism without alienating the so-called Conscience Whigs who had opposed the war from the start. The party's solution was an old one: it nominated a hero-general, gave him a catchy nick-name, and fudged the details of his personal characteristics and qualifica-tions for the presidency. Zachary Taylor, "Old Rough and Ready," had won a series of battles during the opening campaign of the war before clashing openly with Polk and leaving the rest of the fighting to his fellow general Winfield Scott. A career soldier for forty years, Taylor was a much more accomplished military man than the late, lamented Wil-liam Henry Harrison. He was also probably the least educated candidate since Andrew Jackson, and, unlike Jackson, he had never taken the least interest in politics—he had never even voted. Other than his battlefield triumphs, Taylor's chief recommendations for the presidency were that he had quarreled with the current occupant of the White House and had never registered as a Democrat. In some circles that made him a Whig, although Taylor was careful to add the qualifying clarification that he was "not an ultra Whig," whatever that meant.[38]

Lincoln, like other Whig leaders, was under no illusions about Tay-lor's fitness to be president. Personally, he would have preferred Henry Clay, but as he explained to Herndon, "Mr. Clay's chance for an election is just no chance at all." Instead, he would work for Taylor as he had worked for Harrison, from a strictly partisan political stance. "I am in favor of Gen. Taylor," he told party activist Thomas Flournoy, "because I am satisfied we can elect him, that he would give us a Whig administra-tion, and that we cannot elect any other Whig. Our only chance is with Taylor."[39]

Whether or not he truly believed that to be the case—he had never met the man—Lincoln jumped into the race wholeheartedly once Taylor received the party nomination. He made a humorous, well-received speech on the floor of the House in which he lampooned Democratic candidate Lewis Cass's comparatively slight military service (he had fought briefly under Harrison during the War of 1812) by likening it to his own modest stint of soldiering in the Black Hawk War. Alluding to the claim that Cass had broken his sword in anger after Detroit was surrendered to the British, Lincoln clowned, "It is quite certain I did not break my sword, for I had none to break; but I bent a musket pretty badly on one occasion." He had never seen any "live, fighting Indians," he continued, "but I had a good many bloody struggles with the mosquitoes; and, although I never fainted from the loss of blood, I can truly say I was often very hungry." By the time he finished his speech, even the Democratic congressmen were laughing along with Lincoln and shouting, "We give it up!"[40]

✦ ✦ ✦

Stephen Douglas, who had supported Cass for the nomination four years earlier on the geographical grounds that "we must have a Western President," now took to the stump for the more narrowly partisan reason of enforcing party loyalty. Douglas's travels carried him through the South, which he had not visited prior to his marriage the previous year. He stopped first in North Carolina, where he endorsed the gubernatorial campaign of his friend and in-law David S. Reid, who had introduced Douglas to Reid's cousin Martha on the floor of the House. Reid won the nomination with the help of a stirring address from Douglas that praised "the seven thousand brave men sent by his own beloved state to the fields of Mexico, to meet the diseases of the climate and the balls and bayonets of the common foe." The *Raleigh Register*, not entirely swayed by Douglas's visit, wondered aloud why a congressman from Illinois had come down to North Carolina to tell the people there how to vote.[41]

Douglas's politicking was cut short by a sudden attack of "bilious fever and ague," and he spent the rest of the summer and fall recuperating with his wife's family. Meanwhile, Abraham Lincoln was electioneering in New England. It was his first foray on the national scene, and Lincoln took Mary and their sons along with him on the trip. They rattled across central Massachusetts by train, stopping in Worcester, New Bedford, Dedham, Taunton, Lowell, Cambridge, and Boston, where Lincoln shared the stage at Tremont Temple with another rising star of the Whig Party, former New York governor William Seward. Lincoln's stump speech was largely an amalgam of broadly humorous jabs at Cass and pointed warnings that apostate Free-Soilers were in danger of helping to elect a Democrat president. He agreed with them that slavery was evil, but added, "We were not responsible for it and cannot affect it in the states of this Union where we do not live."[42]

Seward was more forceful in his opposition to slavery, predicting that "the time will soon arrive when further demonstrations will be made against the institution of slavery" and hoping aloud that the party would come around to nominating a northern abolitionist for president rather than a southern slaveholder like Taylor. Years later, Seward remembered—a little conveniently—that Lincoln had told him: "Governor Seward, I have been thinking about what you said in your speech. I reckon you are right. We have got to deal with this slavery question, and got to give much more attention to it hereafter than we have been doing." Perhaps Lincoln said it, but no one else heard him, and Lincoln's most vivid memory of the trip was not of a conversation with Seward, but of a gala dinner hosted by former Massachusetts governor Levi Lincoln (no relation), to which "I went with hayseed in my hair to learn deportment in the most cultivated state in the Union. It was a grand dinner, a superb dinner; by far the finest I ever saw in my life. And the great men who were there, too! Why, I can tell you just how they were arranged at table."[43]

Keeping an eye on the local races in Illinois, Lincoln urged Herndon to organize a Rough and Ready Club among Springfield's other young Whigs and "let everyone play the part he can play best—some speak, some sing, and some holler." As Lincoln realized all too well, it would take a fair amount of hollering to elect his designated replacement in Congress—his old law partner Stephen Logan. Saddled with Lincoln's unpopular opposition to the war and his own votes in the Illinois legislature against a resolution supporting the war effort, Logan had little chance to win the election. The Democrats had nominated a real, live hero, Major Thomas Harris, to run against him. When the prickly Logan, as expected, went down to defeat, he ungenerously blamed his defeat on "Lincoln's unpopularity, among other things."[44]

Lincoln predicted accurately that Taylor would carry the district and win the election. For the second time in eight years, the party elected a war-hero president—not that it did Lincoln any good personally. He returned to Washington to serve out the remainder of his term, leaving Mary and the boys back in Springfield. Settling in at Abolition House, Lincoln pondered the slavery issue, particularly as it applied to the District of Columbia. After consulting with various leaders on all sides of the issue, Lincoln prepared a compromise resolution, one that called for a referendum on slavery in the district, followed by the voluntary release of slaves by owners who would be paid "full cash value" for their property. Meanwhile, authorities would strengthen their efforts to round up fugitive slaves inside the district and return them to their owners.[45]

The fugitive-slave provision induced abolitionist firebrand Wendell Phillips to hyperbolically label Lincoln "that slave hound from Illinois." Southerners, for their part, also failed to support the measure. South Carolina senator John C. Calhoun, without addressing Lincoln by name, warned that any emancipation of slaves would lead to "the prostration of the white race" and render the South "the permanent abode of disorder, anarchy, poverty, misery, and wretchedness." In the end, Lincoln withdrew his resolution, and Congress enacted no antislavery measures whatsover during the session. Meanwhile, the firm of Franklin & Armfield, the nation's largest slave traders, continued peddling their wares within sight of the Capitol. The firm's swarming slave pen, said Lincoln, functioned as "a sort of Negro livery-stable, where droves of negroes were collected, temporarily kept, and finally taken to Southern markets, precisely like droves of horses."[46]

Lincoln was no more successful at arranging his postcongressional career than he was at putting a stop to the slave trade inside the District of Columbia. Having worked hard to get Taylor elected, he felt entitled to some influence over the president's patronage appointments in Illinois, specifically the lucrative post of General Land Office commissioner, which had been held in the Polk administration by Lincoln's erstwhile dueling opponent, James Shields. When party regulars could not decide between two competing candidates, Lincoln applied for the job himself. To his bitter disappointment, Taylor chose Chicago attorney Justin Butterfield instead, even though Butterfield had supported Clay in the election and, in Lincoln's words, "never spent a dollar or lifted a finger in the fight." No reason was given for the mystifying decision, but it is likely that Taylor passed over Lincoln because of his all-too-public opposition to the war. Whatever the case, the selection left Lincoln angry and confused. As a consolation prize, Taylor offered Lincoln the post of territorial governor of Oregon. For a number of reasons, including Mary's firmly stated opposition, Lincoln declined the appointment and returned to Springfield and his neglected law practice, having completed a single congressional term that he glumly conceded had been a comprehensive failure.[47]

◆ ◆ ◆

For Douglas, too, the second session of the Thirtieth Congress proved to be frustrating. As a two-term senator and chairman of the powerful

Committee on Territories, he operated at a somewhat more exalted position than a lame-duck congressman from Illinois' Seventh District, but that merely served to highlight Douglas's own legislative failures. Chief among them was the ringing rejection of his proposal to create the huge state of California out of the territory won from Mexico. The recent discovery of gold at Sutter's Mill had brought a torrent of gold rushers flocking to the West Coast, hastening the pressure for immediate territorial status or statehood. Douglas's proposal, which left open the right to carve additional states from the land east of the Sierra Nevada, was intended to get around the Wilmot Proviso. Under existing laws, Douglas maintained, the residents of a territory automatically had the power to include or exclude slavery when they applied for statehood; there was no need to impose another stage to the process. As with Lincoln's District of Columbia compromise, Douglas's plan pleased neither abolitionists nor southerners. Lincoln's adamantine housemate, Joshua Giddings, termed the proposal "one of the grossest frauds perpetrated upon a free people," while John C. Calhoun told Douglas bluntly that his bill "would never do." As expected, the bill failed after a raucous, all-night debate in the Senate.[48]

Clearly, Douglas's persuasive powers were not yet as effective on the national scene as they were back home in Illinois. Mary Lincoln, one of his old flames, seconded that assessment, telling someone who dared to compare Douglas to her own husband: "Mr. Douglas is a very little, little giant by the side of my tall Kentuckian, and intellectually my husband towers above D just as he does physically. Mr. Lincoln may not be as handsome a figure, but the people are perhaps not aware that his heart is as large as his arms are long." At the moment, the rest of the country remained generally unpersuaded that either man was a giant, however warm his heart might be. But times were changing, and so were the political statures of both Lincoln and Douglas. In the tempestuous decade to come, both men would stand very tall, indeed.[49]

3

A Hell of a Storm

The new decade found Abraham Lincoln back home again in Springfield, while Stephen Douglas reclaimed his place in the United States Senate. His own lamentable term in Congress now behind him, Lincoln entered a period of self-imposed political exile, one that would last for the next four years. For both men, the years ahead would bring great and often painful changes in their lives and would be attended, as such transformations often are, by a series of deaths and aftershocks.

The winter of 1849–50 was particularly hard on Mary Lincoln. In the space of a few months, she lost both her father and her grandmother; then her younger son Eddie fell gravely ill with pulmonary tuberculosis. For fifty-two days, Mary nursed Eddie through a series of fitful rallies and heartbreaking declines before the boy died on February 1, 1850, not yet four years of age. The grieving parents dealt with their loss in character-istic ways: Mary took to her bed, weeping inconsolably and refusing to eat, only rousing herself periodically to berate the servants, her husband, and their surviving son. Lincoln internalized his grief, saying only, "We miss [Eddie] very much." He lost himself in his work, returning to the paper-strewn law offices of Lincoln & Herndon. "From 1849 to 1854, both inclusive, he practiced law more assiduously than ever before,"

Lincoln wrote of himself in the third person a few years later. With Eddie's death clearly on his mind, he turned down a lucrative offer to join a Chicago law firm on the grounds that "he tended to consumption" and the lakefront weather "would kill him." There is no evidence that Lincoln ever suffered from consumption—the nineteenth-century word for tuberculosis—and the arduous hours he habitually kept belied any trace of physical illness, but his highly susceptible imagination may have transferred Eddie's symptoms to himself. While Lincoln worked hard at rebuilding his legal practice, Mary became pregnant again almost immediately and bore their third son, William, inevitably nicknamed "Willie," on December 21, 1850.[1]

As they had done previously, Lincoln and Herndon divided their duties. Herndon researched cases at the state supreme court library, while Lincoln interviewed prospective clients, drafted briefs and declarations, and argued cases in the various courts. While always imminently logical and clear-eyed in the courtroom, Lincoln nevertheless nursed some peculiar preconceptions with regard to juries. Fat men, he believed, made the best jurors, since they were naturally jolly and easily swayed. Men with high foreheads had already made up their minds and could not be "argufied" into agreement. Blue-eyed blonds were inherently nervous and tended to side with prosecutors. Whatever the makeup of the jury, once he accepted a case, Lincoln pursued it with bulldog determination, whether it was a $2.50 lawsuit over a herd of cattle trampling someone's cornfield or a capital murder trial involving the wastrel son of his old New Salem friends, Jack and Hannah Armstrong, which he would take up in 1857. The young man, called Duff, was charged with killing an acquaintance in a drunken brawl. He was acquitted after an emotional closing argument by Lincoln, who cited the couple's many kindnesses to him and accepted no fee for his services.[2]

Lincoln continued to ride the circuit in the Eighth Judicial District, this time with a new presiding judge. Samuel Treat had moved up to the state supreme court while Lincoln was in Washington, and his replacement, Bloomington lawyer David Davis, quickly became one of Lincoln's closest acquaintances. The rotund Davis easily topped 300 pounds—it was said that he had to be surveyed for a new pair of trousers. Too heavy for any one horse to bear, he rode to court in a specially designed two-horse carriage. A graduate of Yale Law School, Davis had made a fortune in real estate while serving in the Illinois legislature. A

Whig like Lincoln, he, too, favored a moderate stance toward slavery, an outgrowth perhaps of his boyhood in Maryland. Davis came to value Lincoln's levelheaded approach to the law, often appointing him a substitute judge in his absence. The two traced the roughly rectangular circuit from Springfield to Metamora to Danville to Shelbyville, some 12,000 square miles that, as the weary Davis was always pointing out, was equal in size to the state of Connecticut. In the course of their travels, they shared hotel rooms, meals, stories, and jokes (but not beds; Davis was so large that he required his own). At no time, however, did Davis consider himself Lincoln's intimate. "Lincoln never confided to me anything," he observed, adding that his friend "was not a sociable man by any means," and that he had "no strong emotional feelings for any person—mankind or thing." Still, Davis thought, Lincoln was happy riding the Eighth District, or at least "as happy as *he* could be."[3]

Although he later claimed that "his profession had almost superseded the thought of politics in his mind," Lincoln did not entirely forgo politics—he was too much of a party man for that. Stretched out on the sofa in his office, Lincoln pored over the current issues of the *Congressional Globe* and the *Illinois State Journal* (formerly the *Sangamo Journal*), following the ongoing debate over the Wilmot Proviso, California statehood, and the ever-vexing problem of slavery. In July 1850, he was stunned along with the rest of the nation by the sudden death of President Zachary Taylor, who had sickened and died after eating a bowl of cherries and chugging down a pitcher of ice-cold milk—a double mistake in a city whose poor sanitation made it perilous to consume raw fruit or dairy products during the sweltering summer months. The president died of cholera morbus, the same illness that had carried off Mary Lincoln's father at a still-vigorous fifty-nine a few months earlier. (Long-held rumors of assassination by arsenic poisoning were not put entirely to rest until Taylor's body was exhumed in 1991 and found to be poison-free.)[4]

Putting aside his lingering resentment at being passed over for Land Office commissioner, Lincoln agreed to deliver a public eulogy for the second straight Whig president to die soon after taking office. The invitation came from the Common Council of Chicago while Lincoln was presenting a case to the U.S. district court, and he accepted with the reservation that "the want of time for preparation will make the task, for me, a very difficult one to perform." He was right. The eulogy he gave was an oddly—or perhaps, given their recent history, not so oddly—impersonal address. "The death of the late president may not be without its use," Lincoln said, "in reminding us that we, too, must die. Death, abstractly considered, is the same with the high as with the low." Even given the traditions of the moment, Lincoln stepped a little over the line when he fulsomely praised the leading general of a war he had lost his congressional seat denouncing. Seeking to impart a sense of patriotic drama to the rather lifeless speech, Lincoln apostrophized Taylor's victory at Palo Alto: "And now the din of battle nears the fort and sweeps obliquely by; a gleam of hope flies through the half imprisoned few; they fly to the wall; every eye is strained—it is—it is—the stars and stripes are still aloft!. . . . [T]he heavens are rent with a loud, long, glorious, gushing cry of victory! victory!! victory!!!"[5]

There was no eulogy—grandiloquent or not—for Lincoln's father, Thomas, when he died in January 1851. Lincoln, in fact, did not attend the funeral, and declined to visit the dying man beforehand. When his stepbrother John Johnston wondered why Lincoln would not even write to their father, Lincoln responded tersely that "it appeared to me I could write nothing which could do any good." Citing the pressure of work and the recent birth of his new son, Lincoln stayed home in Springfield while his father worsened. In response to another plea from Johnston, he piously advised the dying man "to remember to call upon, and confide in, our great, and good, and merciful Maker; who will not turn away from him in any extremity. He notes the fall of a sparrow, and numbers the hairs of our heads; and He will not forget the dying man, who puts his trust in Him." Coming from someone who rarely if ever darkened the doors of a church, it was less-than-persuasive advice. The heart of the matter came later, when Lincoln admitted that "if we could meet now, it is doubtful whether it would not be more painful than pleasant." The memories of his straitened childhood, which sometimes overtook him during his notorious bouts of melancholy, were best kept at a distance along with the rest of his hardscrabble past. In his own mind, at least, he had buried his father several years before he died.[6]

◆ ◆ ◆

Taylor's death presented a much-needed political opening to Stephen Douglas and other leaders in Congress who were wrestling with the issue of slavery. Missouri senator Thomas Hart Benton, evoking the Bible, spoke for many when he compared the current political situation in the United States to the plague of frogs that had infested Egypt during the days of Moses. "We can see nothing, touch nothing, have no measures proposed, without having this pestilence thrust before us," Benton complained. "Here it is, this black question, forever on the table, on the nuptial couch, everywhere!" Reflecting the heightened sense of urgency, all three of the so-called Great Triumvirate in the Senate— Henry Clay, John C. Calhoun, and Daniel Webster—gave major speeches in the winter of 1850 on the crisis facing the nation in the toxic wake of the Mexican War. Clay, who spoke first, typically sought to conciliate pro- and antislavery factions by introducing a group of resolutions dealing with the disposition of territory acquired in the Mexican Cession. Under Clay's plan, California would be admitted to the Union as a free state, while the rest of the new lands would be organized without reference to slavery. Describing himself as depressed, appalled, and anxious, Clay warned that the nation stood "at the edge of the precipice, before the fearful and disastrous leap is taken in the yawning abyss below, which will inevitably lead to certain and irretrievable destruction."[7]

Clay was followed, in turn, by Calhoun and Webster. Calhoun, suffering from a soon-to-be-fatal case of tuberculosis, was carried into the chamber swathed in flannel blankets from his feet to his shoulders. His face, gaunt and fever-ridden, stared out at his colleagues like a wraithlike apparition—what his fellow southerners called a "ha'nt." Unable to speak above a whisper, Calhoun had Virginia senator James Mason read his speech for him. In it he placed the lion's share of blame for sectional tensions on the federal government, which he said had consistently favored the North at the expense of the South. His own region, he cautioned, could no longer remain in the Union "as things now are, consistently with honor and safety." Calhoun wanted a constitutional amendment enacted immediately to allow the South "to protect herself."[8]

Webster, in his address, presented himself "not as a Massachusetts man, not as a northern man, but as an American." He renounced his earlier support for the Wilmot Proviso, which he now saw as a gratuitous measure designed to "taunt or reproach" the South, one rendered unnecessary by the natural habitat of the desert Southwest and "the law of nature" that made slavery unfeasible there. Instead, he urged northerners to support the Clay proposals, including a provision strengthening the Fugitive Slave Law. At the same time, Webster chastised southern hotheads who were threatening secession. "I would rather hear of natu-

ral blasts and mildews, war, pestilence, and famine, than to hear gentlemen talk of secession," he sighed.[9]

Having made their curtain calls, so to speak, on the congressional
stage, the members of the Great Triumvirate withdrew for good from
the national spotlight. Calhoun died on cue four weeks later, supposedly breathing out a last theatrical lament for "my poor South." Clay,
suffering from steadily worsening tuberculosis, returned to his summer
home at Newport, Rhode Island, in a vain attempt to recuperate. Webster, although in better physical health than his two wasted colleagues,
found his political career fatally injured by his speech. Abolitionist poet
John Greenleaf Whittier dashed off a poem suggesting that Webster had
become a foil of the great "Tempter," and his co-transcendentalist Ralph
Waldo Emerson fumed that Webster had permanently removed his name
"from all the files of honor." The strongest denunciation came a few
days later, when New York senator William Seward unleashed an incendiary address defying the Fugitive Slave Law and calling for the Wilmot
Proviso to be extended to the new western territories. "There is a higher
law than the Constitution," Seward declared. Putting the abolitionist movement on the side of the angels, Seward anointed himself and
his followers as stewards of the Lord, entrusted with safeguarding "the
common heritage of mankind." The unreligious Clay fired back: "Who
are they who venture to tell us what is divine and what is natural law?
Where are their credentials of prophecy?"[10]

With the departure of Clay and his cohorts, it remained for the
younger leaders of the Senate to hash out a workable compromise. As
chairman of the Committee on Territories, Stephen Douglas took a leading hand. He began with a ringing endorsement of popular sovereignty,
"the great and fundamental principle of free government, which asserts
that each community shall settle this and all other questions affecting
their domestic institutions by themselves." Douglas rejected Calhoun's
notion of southern grievances, saying that "the territories belong to the
United States as one people, one nation, and are to be disposed of for
the common benefit of all, according to the principles of the Constitution." Douglas opposed spreading the Wilmot Proviso over the new
western territories, calling it "a dead letter upon the statute book," while
noting, in a nod to Webster, that freedom was naturally on the march
in the West, "for the area was already free by the laws of nature and of
God."[11]

It took six months of tedious and occasionally violent debate before the Senate was able to hammer out a compromise proposal. The new bill, dubbed the Compromise of 1850, brought California into the Union as a free state, organized New Mexico and Utah into territories under popular sovereignty, settled the final boundaries of Texas, abolished the slave trade in the District of Columbia, and strengthened the Fugitive Slave Law. Throughout the deliberations, Douglas was tireless in his leadership, to the point of eating his meals at his desk and developing a painful abscess on his hip from sitting so long in one spot. Mississippi senator Jefferson Davis, no admirer of Douglas, nevertheless praised his northern colleague for his labors. "If any man has a right to be proud of the success of these measures," Davis said, "it is the senator from Illinois." On the night of the bill's passage, Douglas was serenaded by bandsmen in a wildly celebrating Washington. Bonfires, fireworks, and spontaneous marches took place throughout the city, and cries of "The Union is saved!" echoed off the torchlit facades of the Capitol. Douglas, called from his home, responded with a brief but optimistic speech, maintaining, "We are united from shore to shore." He apparently took to heart the advice of one supporter that it was the duty of every patriot to get drunk—the next day, Douglas was one of several senators who missed the opening roll call in the Senate, sending word that he was prostrated with a "cold."[12]

◆ ◆ ◆

Douglas's dogged leadership in passing the Compromise of 1850 brought him increased national renown. A delegation of grateful Californians presented him with a jewel-encrusted gold watch inscribed "California knows her friend," and the *New York Herald* included him in a list of possible presidential candidates in 1852. He further raised his profile by championing a north-south railroad linking the upper Midwest to the Gulf of Mexico. The Illinois Central Railroad bill, passed in May 1850 during the height of the compromise debate, pledged the federal government to granting land and rights-of-way to the states of Illinois, Alabama, and Mississippi for construction of a railroad connecting Chicago to Mobile. It was all part of Douglas's sweeping vision of a truly transcontinental country, linked by railroads and riverboats, which would complete the Manifest Destiny vision of James K. Polk and other expansionists. His own adopted home region would be the hub. "There is a power in this nation greater than either the North or the South," Douglas said, "a growing, increasing, swelling power, that will be able to speak the law to the nation. That power is the country known as the great West."[13]

Douglas's visionary zeal, along with his comparative youth (he was thirty-eight), won him the support of the "Young America" wing of the Democratic Party, which was casting about for a presidential candidate to back in 1852. The leading candidates, besides Douglas, were all antiquarian in their appeal. Michigan senator Lewis Cass, the unsuccessful nominee in 1848, was joined by former secretary of war William L. Marcy, former secretary of state James Buchanan, Texas senator Sam Houston, and Mexican War general William O. Butler in the top tier of available men. All five had served in the War of 1812; Cass, if elected, would be seventy at the time of his inauguration. Douglas, with his unquenchable vigor and optimism, was a living embodiment of Young America, and his longtime residence on the edge of the frontier gave him added appeal. The next president, predicted the *Herald*, would come from the "great northwest," but would have to appeal to other regions of the country as well. "There is but one man who answers to this description," said the newspaper, recommending Douglas for "his eastern birth, his western residence and his southern marriage."[14]

Despite disavowing any interest in the nomination—"I am young and can afford to wait," he magnanimously told a Boston editor in September 1851—Douglas in reality campaigned avidly, perhaps too avidly, for the job. He was aided and abetted by a motley crew of Young Americans, led by George N. Sanders, the perfervid editor of the *Democratic Review*. Sanders, a native Kentuckian, had run guns to revolutionaries during the 1848 uprisings in Europe, and was said to have mounted the barricades in Paris that bloody and quixotic June. With Douglas's support, Sanders acquired the *Review* "for the purposes of controlling its columns until after the presidential election." That was all well and good, but the first issue of the journal sounded a truculent tone that alarmed Douglas and other professional politicians. "The statesmen of a previous generation," warned Sanders, "must get out of the way" and stand aside for someone who could bring to the table "young blood, young ideas, and young hearts to the councils of the Republic." Ensuing issues attacked the other candidates by name. Butler was "a good example of a no-policy statesman," Marcy was "spavined, wind-blown, strained, ring-boned,"

Cass was "a human contradiction," and Buchanan was—cruelest gibe of all—"an old fogy."[15]

Predictably, the old fogies struck back hard. Tennessee congressman Andrew Johnson led the charge, lambasting Douglas as "a mere hotbed production, a precocious politician, warmed into and kept in existence by a set of interested plunderers that would, in the event of success, disembowel the Treasury, disgrace the country and damn the party to all eternity that brought them into power." The whole group, Johnson groused, was nothing more than "miserable banditti, much fitter to occupy cells in the penitentiary than places of state." Douglas's new home at the intersection of New Jersey Avenue and I Street in Washington was nicknamed "Mount Julep" for the copious amounts of whiskey, brandy, cognac, and champagne that were said to be quaffed by the senator and his brain trust.[16]

The Democratic nominating convention in Baltimore quickly devolved into a three-way race among Douglas, Cass, and Buchanan. After three days, forty-eight ballots, and untold amounts of hard liquor and soft promises, the convention was hopelessly deadlocked. A true dark-horse candidate, New Hampshire politico Franklin Pierce, suddenly bolted to the front and captured the nomination. The blazingly handsome Pierce, generally considered the best-looking man ever to run for the White House, was a college friend of author Nathaniel Hawthorne, who contributed in turn the best-written campaign biography of any presidential candidate. A former congressman and senator, Pierce had rushed to defend the colors in the Mexican War, but his military career was snakebitten. He crushed his testicles against the pommel of his saddle at the Battle of Contreras, was thrown from his horse at the Battle of Churubusco, wrenched his knee en route to Mexico City, and came down with dysentery at the Battle of Chapultepec. The Whig Party, as was its wont, nominated yet another general for president, Winfield Scott. The Whigs gleefully contrasted their candidate's sparkling war record with that of Pierce, whom they dubbed "the Fainting General." In a witty if cruel bit of campaigning, they passed out a miniature book, one-inch-high and one-half-inch-thick, entitled *The Military Services of General Pierce*. Jabbing at his widely known weakness for alcohol, the Whigs mocked Pierce as "the hero of many a well-fought bottle."[17]

Douglas, no mean drinker himself, shook off his disappointment over losing the nomination and promised to campaign vigorously for

Pierce in the fall. He was true to his word, giving speeches in Richmond, Cleveland, Indianapolis, Cincinnati, Columbus, and Chicago. In New York, he gracefully buried the hatchet with Lewis Cass, who in a speech preceding Douglas's appearance referred to himself self-deprecatingly as "an old fogy." Not so, said Douglas, declaring that Cass could "not be an old fogy even should he live a thousand years." In a nice bit of one-upmanship, he praised Cass for giving "a pure young American democratic speech." Douglas reserved his heavy artillery for Scott, a political neophyte widely seen as the tool of William Seward and the antislavery wing of the Whig Party. Warning direly that the previous general-turned-president, Zachary Taylor, "had already committed himself to steps which would have led inevitably to a civil war," Douglas worried that "it was only the hand of providence that saved us from our first and only military administration." He wondered aloud how wise it was to convert "a good general into a bad president."[18]

✦ ✦ ✦

Douglas's jibes eventually roused Lincoln from his political slumbers. In June, immediately after the nominating convention had chosen Scott for president, an exhausted and dispirited Henry Clay died in Washington at the age of seventy-five. Lincoln was one of many delivering eulogies for the man he called "my beau ideal of a statesman." Perhaps because he could identify with his fellow Kentuckian Clay more readily than he could with a professional soldier like Taylor, Lincoln's second public eulogy was considerably warmer than his first. Appearing at a public gathering at the House of Representatives in Springfield, Lincoln praised Clay for his eloquence, judgment, and will, adding: "The spell—the long enduring spell—with which the souls of men were bound to him, is a miracle." Clearly thinking of his own self-educated rise, Lincoln noted that "Mr. Clay's lack of a more perfect early education . . . teaches at least one profitable lesson; it teaches that in this country one can scarcely be so poor, but that, if he *will*, he *can* acquire sufficient education to get through the world respectably."[19]

Clay's moderate stance on slavery drew Lincoln's strongest approbation. Clay, he said, "did not perceive, that on a question of human right, the Negroes were to be excepted from the human race." Lincoln set himself squarely on Clay's side, even to the point of supporting the absurd notion put forth by the American Colonization Society to buy back the freedom of 3 million southern slaves and exile—one could scarcely say repatriate—them to Africa. There was no way that southern slaveholders would willingly countenance such a plan, or that northern taxpayers would pay for it if they did. Still, Lincoln claimed, the movement was gaining strength and "may it indeed be realized! Pharaoh's country was cursed with plagues, and his hosts were drowned in the Red Seas for striving to retain a captive people who had already served them more than four hundred years. May like disasters never befall us!"[20]

Lincoln failed to work up comparable enthusiasm for the Whigs' wheezy presidential candidate. He made few campaign speeches, the most memorable being a two-part address to the Scott Club in Springfield in which he sought to rebut Douglas's charges that Scott was a lackey of Seward and the abolitionists. Tiresomely and ostentatiously referring to Douglas as "Judge" throughout the speech, Lincoln spent more time assailing Douglas than he did extolling Scott. Specifically, he accused Douglas of stealing both the idea and credit for the Compromise of 1850 from Henry Clay, Daniel Webster, and other Whigs. He also mocked him for his "wonderful acumen . . . on the construction of language" and for "fall[ing] into a strain of wailing pathos which Jeremiah in his last days might envy, for the old soldier democrats to be turned out of office by Gen. Scott." It was a strained performance, reflecting perhaps Lincoln's growing sense that Douglas had left him behind.[21]

Lincoln did have Douglas to thank for one thing—a substantial increase in his income. The Central Illinois Railroad bill that Douglas had shepherded through Congress brought with it a golden shower of work for lawyers across the state, and Lincoln was not shy in seeking his share, writing to the railroad's chief solicitor in the fall of 1853: "I am now free to make an engagement for the Road; and if you think fit you may 'count me in.'" He received a $250 retainer fee, and subsequently handled some forty cases for the railroad, including eleven appeals that he presented before the Illinois Supreme Court. Besides his obvious political connections, Lincoln had recommended himself to the railroad through his adroit handling of a lawsuit two years earlier between the Alton & Sangamon Railroad and a local landowner, James A. Barret, who had refused to pay the railroad his original subscription price after the line changed its route to bypass his property. Lincoln argued successfully that a railroad had the right to amend its plans. It was an important precedent for railroad companies throughout Illinois and the rest of the country, and it solidified Lincoln's reputation as a skilled practitioner of railroad law.[22]

The most lucrative case of Lincoln's career came via the Illinois Central Railroad. Officials in McLean County, disputing the tax exemption granted the railroad by the state legislature, levied their own tax on the company's real estate within the county. The railroad argued that such a tax would practically force it out of business (and also open it up to similar taxation in other counties). The case eventually came before the Illinois Supreme Court in the spring of 1854. Lincoln's former law partners, John T. Stuart and Stephen Logan, represented McLean County, while Lincoln cochaired the railroad's case with lead attorney James F. Joy. Lincoln argued that the legislature was well within its rights to grant a tax exemption to the railroad; he cited rulings to support his argument from the states of New Jersey, Maryland, Alabama, Indiana, Mississippi, and South Carolina, along with a previous decision in Illinois itself. After nearly two years of arguments and counterarguments, the high court ruled in favor of the railroad. Lincoln submitted a bill of $2,000 for his and Herndon's services. Remarkably, the railroad balked at paying, complaining that "This is as much as Daniel Webster himself would have charged." Undeterred, Lincoln submitted a revised bill for $5,000. At a hearing before his friend David Davis, Lincoln argued that he had saved the railroad over half a million dollars a year in local taxes. Davis ruled in Lincoln's favor.[23]

Other than his anti-Douglas tirade in Springfield, Lincoln campaigned very little for Scott in the fall of 1852. Sensing the electoral debacle to come, he "did less in this Presidential struggle than any in which he had ever engaged," author William Dean Howells later noted in a campaign biography of Lincoln. As it turned out, Lincoln was right. Scott lost to Pierce in a landslide, carrying only four states and losing in the Electoral College 254 to 42. Democrats were exultant, making good on their campaign boast: "We Polked 'em in '44; we'll Pierce 'em in '52." The party gained seventeen seats in the House of Representatives, won nine of twelve governorships, and strengthened its hold on state legislatures, which still elected U.S. senators. In Illinois, Douglas swept to reelection, winning seventy-five of ninety-five votes. The obligatory victory party, held in the statehouse for 1,500 supporters, was another "brilliant levee," even if the honoree was forced to pay for a new carpet in the Senate chamber.[24]

Returning to Washington, Douglas was confident of playing a large role in the new Pierce administration—there was even talk of a cabinet appointment. He drew up a list of friends he wanted to see rewarded with government posts currently held by Whigs. "Reform must begin with the incumbents in office," he growled. "I shall act on the rule of giving the offices to those who fight the battles." The president-elect did not share Douglas's priorities. If anything, Pierce went out of his way to ignore Douglas and his supporters. Douglas watched in disgust as Pierce filled his cabinet with a number of the senator's bitterest enemies, including Jefferson Davis, who was named secretary of war, and James Buchanan, who was appointed minister to Great Britain. Douglas had to content himself with delivering the keynote address at the January 1853 unveiling of the equestrian statue to his hero, Andrew Jackson, in Lafayette Square, directly across from the White House, where his past and future enemies would sit.[25]

As it turned out, political appointments were soon the least of Douglas's worries. His wife, Martha, had just given birth to the couple's third child, a daughter, in Chicago, but the initial elation over the new arrival quickly gave way to despair. Martha developed serious postnatal complications, and Douglas rushed to her side. On January 19, she died at the age of twenty-eight; their daughter died a month later. Douglas, "more depressed in feeling than I ever saw him before," in the view of kinsman David Reid, brought Martha home to North Carolina to be buried in the Martin family plot. The Senate adjourned to allow members to attend the funeral. Douglas returned to Washington almost immediately, leaving his elder son, Robbie, in the care of his grandmother, but it was clear to everyone that Douglas's heart was not in his work. Installing his sister and brother-in-law, Sarah and Julius Granger, in his house to care for his younger son, Stevie, Douglas embarked on a five-month-long tour of Europe. His first stop, in London, created something of a diplomatic stir when he refused to don the appropriate court dress for an audience with Queen Victoria. Douglas insisted, instead, on wearing clothing "appropriate to a visit with an American president." The queen was not amused, and the planned meeting did not take place.[26]

From England, Douglas's journeys took him eastward to France, Italy, Greece, Smyrna, and Constantinople. In Rome, a rumor arose that he was planning to renounce his Protestant faith and convert to Catholicism.

Opposition newspapers rushed to accuse him of cynical political purposes, including a nefarious plan to corner the Catholic vote in the next presidential election. The *Providence Journal* joked that if the rumor were true, the pope would do well to watch Douglas, lest he make "St. Peter's chair elective once in four years, and . . . present himself as a candidate for the next succession." In St. Petersburg, the senator was taken to meet Czar Nicholas I, who was in the midst of secret military maneuvers in preparation for a war with Turkey. The two men hit it off famously. Douglas considered Russia "the most charming country in all Europe," and Nicholas assured his visitor that Russia and the United States were the only two "proper governments" in the world—all the rest were "mongrels" who were destined to be overrun by the younger, more vibrant giants. On his return trip across the continent, Douglas subsequently had an audience with Napoléon III and Queen Eugénie of France, who quizzed him closely about America's possible designs on Cuba but neglected to tell him about their own designs on Mexico. His various meetings with European royalty, while personally gratifying, did not sway Douglas from his democratic tendencies. "We in America," he observed, "are accustomed to spend money for works of utility, not on those of mere ornament, pomp, and show."[27]

Douglas returned in October 1853 to a political party increasingly riven by conflict. Franklin Pierce, after a promising beginning, had run into opposition on all sides for his temporizing and ineffectual leadership. Northern Democrats were unhappy with the large role that proslavery southerners were playing in the administration, while southerners resented Pierce's forgiving embrace of wayward abolitionists. Both factions jockeyed incessantly for position in Washington, and the ever-smiling, ever-affable president met each visitor to the White House with a firm handshake and a twinkling eye, which seemed to suggest approval but in truth represented nothing more than a weak man's need to avoid unpleasantness. Missouri Democrat Samuel Treat (no relation to the Illinois jurist of the same name) complained to Douglas soon after his return "that cowardice, bad advice or something worse renders it impossible for any good to come out of this administration." Another Missourian, Congressman James B. Bowlin, chairman of the House Committee on Public Lands, was even harsher in his analysis. "His efforts have entirely failed to unite the party," Bowlin wrote of the president. "It is torn into shreds and tatters."[28]

Given Pierce's all-too-evident political weakness, Douglas's supporters called on him to reassume a leading role in the Senate and signal his intention to run for president in 1856. The Little Giant at first demurred. "The party is in a distracted condition," he warned Chicago editor Charles Lanphier, "and it requires all our wisdom, prudence and energy to consolidate its power and perpetuate its principles." Having learned a harsh lesson during the previous campaign about seeming too eager to win the nomination, Douglas wanted now to hang back and let events take their course. "I shall remain entirely non-committal, and hold myself at liberty to do whatever my duty to my principles and my friends may require when the time for action arrives," he explained. "Our first duty is to the cause—the fate of individual politicians is of minor consequence. Let us leave the presidency out of view at least two years to come."[29]

Events, however, did not give Douglas the luxury of waiting. After much wrangling, Congress finally approved a measure to fund a transcontinental railroad, and army surveyors branched out to map proposed routes from which the president would select the most suitable. Douglas, favoring the northernmost route, stayed in close communication with Captain Isaac I. Stevens, who was in charge of the mapping expedition from St. Paul, Minnesota, to Puget Sound in Washington Territory. Stevens assured Douglas that the northerly route was imminently feasible, and Douglas quietly purchased 6,000 acres of land at the terminus of the proposed route on the western shores of Lake Superior. Together with other members of a business syndicate, Douglas divided shares in a new township to be named Superior City (now Superior, Wisconsin). The property quickly appreciated in value to $20,000 per lot.[30]

Any route to California across the northern or central part of the country would necessarily pass through unincorporated territory. Douglas, as chairman of the Senate Committee on Territories, understood this; for the past decade he had been attempting to organize the vast area between the Missouri River and the Rocky Mountains into the spread-eagled Nebraska Territory. At the same time, he had also encouraged free homestead policies, a new telegraph line, and overland mail service, as well as the colonization of immigrant trails along the way. "It is utterly impossible to preserve that connection between the Atlantic and the Pacific," Douglas advised, "if you are to keep a wilderness of two thousand miles in extent between you." Southerners, however, were in no hurry to create another territory north of the Missouri Compromise line, particularly one with the prospect of wielding as much political and financial clout as Nebraska. Missouri senator David Atchison, leading the opposition, made his views clear. "I am free to admit that at this moment, at this hour, and for all time to come I should oppose the organization of the settlement of the territory," Atchison said, "unless my constituents and the constituents of the whole South . . . could go into it upon the same footing, with equal rights and equal privileges, carrying that species of property with them." He would see Nebraska "sink in hell," Atchison warned, before he saw it admitted to the Union as a free state.[31]

Faced with such intransigence, Douglas sought to find a workable middle ground. In January 1854 he proposed a bill that would divide the new territory into two parts: Nebraska Territory, west of Iowa, and Kansas Territory, west of Missouri. In theory, this would create a new free state, Nebraska, and a new slave state, Kansas, based on the preferences of their closest neighbors. The ultimate decision, however, would be left in the hands of the residents, in accordance with the popular sovereignty clause of the Compromise of 1850. Grudgingly, Douglas agreed to an eleventh-hour amendment to his bill by Kentucky senator Archibald Dixon, a southern Whig who called for the formal repeal of the Missouri Compromise in the new territories. Douglas tried to talk Dixon out of such explosive language, warning that it would "raise a hell of a storm," but Atchison and other southern senators insisted on the change. Against his better judgment, Douglas yielded the point, although he demanded a personal meeting with President Pierce to ensure White House approval of the bill. Jefferson Davis, whose newfound support of Douglas should have raised warning hackles on the Little Giant's neck, pointed out that Pierce did not generally receive visitors on Sunday. Douglas insisted. The president, roused from his self-imposed cloister, listened to the new bill as it was read aloud, pronounced himself satisfied with the language, shook hands all around, and went back to bed, having committed his administration to the most sweeping and controversial change in public law in more than three decades.[32]

✦ ✦ ✦

The storm that Douglas had predicted was not long in coming. The day after he introduced the Kansas-Nebraska bill in the Senate, a small group of abolitionist lawmakers released an incendiary statement of their own to the press. Wordily (and misleadingly) titled "The Appeal of the Independent Democrats in Congress to the People of the United States," the piece appeared first in the *National Era*, the Washington-based mouthpiece for the abolitionist movement. The document was largely the work of Ohio senator Salmon P. Chase, although it was also toiled over by Massachusetts senator Charles Sumner and congressmen Joshua Giddings of Ohio, Gerrit Smith of New York, and Alexander De Witt of Massachusetts. In the overwrought language favored by the antislavery movement, the document began: "We arraign this bill as a gross violation of a sacred pledge; as a criminal betrayal of precious rights; as part and parcel of an atrocious plot to exclude from a vast unoccupied region immigrants from the Old World and free laborers from our own state, and convert it into a dreary region of despotism inhabited by masters and slaves." The appeal went on to accuse Douglas of hatching a "monstrous" and "discreditable" plot to spread "the blight of slavery" across the land and "subjugate the whole country to the yoke of a slaveholding despotism." His opponents said Douglas had sponsored the bill purely to advance his presidential ambitions.[33]

Douglas hit back hard. On January 30, he rose in the Senate to confront his accusers. Before a jam-packed audience of senators, congressmen, journalists, and visitors, Douglas pointed out that he had planned to introduce the bill a week earlier, but that Chase, "with a smiling face and the appearance of friendship," had asked for a postponement, knowing full well that the *National Era* was about to release his anti-Douglas screed. "Little did I suppose at the time that I granted that act of courtesy," said Douglas, "that they had drafted and published to the world a document . . . in which they arraigned me as having been guilty of a criminal betrayal of my trust, as having been guilty of an act of bad faith, and being engaged in an atrocious plot against the cause of free government." Conveniently overlooking the fact that he had called on the president the previous Sunday, Douglas indicted Chase and his "Abolition confederates" for meeting "on the holy Sabbath, while other senators were engaged in divine worship. . . . This was done on the Sabbath day, and by a set of politicians, to advance their own political and ambitious purposes, in the name of our holy religion."[34]

The core of the debate, as Douglas had anticipated, concerned the abrogation of the Missouri Compromise. Artfully, he argued that the earlier agreement had been superseded by the Compromise of 1850, which he called "a great principle of self-government. . . . Let all this quibbling about the Missouri Compromise . . . be cast behind you," he urged, "for the simple question is, will you allow the people to legislate for themselves upon the subject of slavery?" It was a smooth piece of statesmanship, but Douglas undercut his own case by losing his temper and calling Chase and Sumner "pure, unadulterated representatives of Abolitionism, Free Soilism, Niggerism in the Congress of the United States." When Chase attempted to respond, Douglas roared, "I will yield the floor to no Abolitionist!" and accused the Ohioan of attempting to foment "another political tornado of fanaticism."[35]

In that, at least, Douglas was right. The two sides had indeed unleashed a political tornado, and soon the entire country was consumed by the swirling winds. While the Senate debated the Kansas-Nebraska bill, outside events conspired to sharpen—if that were possible—the partisan divide. That March, a slave named Anthony Burns escaped from his master in Virginia and stowed away on a ship bound for Boston. There he found work as a tailor and ill-advisedly wrote to his brother, who was still a slave, to join him. Their owner intercepted the letter and immediately set off to recover his property. Burns was arrested and held at the federal courthouse, where a group of abolitionist vigilantes led by the rather nonpacific Unitarian minister Thomas Wentworth Higginson stormed the building with pistols, axes, and a battering ram and attempted to rescue the fugitive slave. Shots were exchanged and a deputy marshal was killed. President Pierce immediately ordered 2,000 federal troops into the city; a revenue cutter stood ready in the harbor to speed Burns's return to Virginia. While a marine band played "Carry Me Back to Old Virginny," Burns was escorted in chains through the streets of Boston as sullen residents draped their buildings in black crepe, hung American flags upside down, and tolled lugubrious church bells in protest. The $100,000 it cost the government to keep Burns in custody (about $3 million today) made him, Higginson scoffed, "the most expensive slave in the history of mankind."[36]

While the Burns melodrama played out in Boston, lawmakers in Washington thrashed over the details of Douglas's bill. Posturing and demagoguery were the rules of the day. Texas senator Sam Houston warned that a "wall of fire" would descend on the South if the Missouri Compromise was repealed. North Carolina senator George E. Badger wondered plaintively: "If some southern gentleman wishes to take the nurse who takes charge of his little baby, or the old woman who nursed him in childhood, and whom he calls 'Mammy' . . . into one of these new territories . . . why, in the name of God, should anybody prevent it?" Ohio senator Ben Wade responded that he had no objection to Badger immigrating to Kansas with his "old Mammy. We only insist that he shall not be empowered to *sell* her after taking her there."[37]

After his initial combative appearance, Douglas stayed carefully behind the scenes, strong-arming the undecided and shoring up the faithful. Finally, on March 3, he brought the bill to the floor for a final vote. Debate continued for more than ten hours before Douglas rose to make his final argument at 11:30 that night. In a reprise of his earlier assault, the Little Giant pitched into Chase, Sumner, Seward, and other abolitionists who opposed the measure. For over three hours he hotly held forth, liberally spicing his remarks with "By Gods" and "God damns" while supporters such as California senator William Gwin rapped out approval on the wooden floor with their canes. Alluding to the fact that both Chase and Sumner had been elected to the Senate by compromise coalitions, Douglas mocked: "I did not obtain my seat in this body by a corrupt bargain or a dishonorable coalition. I did not enter into any combinations or arrangements by which my character, my principles, and my honors, were set up at public auction or private sale in order to procure a seat in the Senate." When Seward attempted to interrupt, Douglas drowned him out with a scathing "Ah, you can't crawl behind that free-nigger dodge." Seward retorted piously: "Douglas, no man will ever be president of the United States who spells 'negro' with two *g*s."[38]

It was nearly 5:00 a.m. on March 4 when the vote was called. The conclusion was foregone—Douglas's bill passed the Senate, 37–14. It took another ten weeks for the bill to move through the House, where Douglas's protégé William Richardson tenaciously shepherded its advance. Georgia congressman Alexander Stephens, who at five feet tall was even shorter than Douglas, assisted manfully in the proceedings. On May 22, the House passed the Kansas-Nebraska Act by a comparatively narrow margin of 113–100. Eight days later, the president signed the bill into law. Initially, Douglas was happy to take full credit for the bill. "I passed the Kansas-Nebraska Act myself," he said immodestly. "I had the authority and power of a dictator throughout the whole controversy in both houses." Soon he would have reason to wonder about the efficacy, if not the wisdom, of that claim.[39]

Every action, large or small, has unintended consequences, and the Kansas-Nebraska Act was larger than most. For Douglas personally, no single consequence was more significant than the sudden return of Abraham Lincoln to politics. With the exception of his lukewarm appearances for Winfield Scott during the 1852 presidential campaign, Lincoln had been content to mind his legal career and leave the politicking to others. Still, he followed the debate intently in the newspapers, and one morning friends found him sitting distractedly before a guttering fireplace in a hotel lobby, having stayed up all night pondering the increasingly parlous state of affairs. Lincoln was in Urbana handling a case when news flashed across the telegraph wire that the Senate had passed the Kansas-Nebraska bill. "We were thunderstruck and stunned," he recalled a few months later. Typically, Lincoln did not react immediately, but spent several months carefully studying the legal and moral ramifications of the act. When Kentucky abolitionist Cassius Clay came to Springfield that July to call for a new political organization to put down "the gigantic evil which threatened . . . their own liberty," Lincoln lounged noncommittally on the grass, whittling a stick and listening carefully.[40]

Others in the North were not so calm. The Compromise of 1850 had never set well with abolitionists, who feared that the concept of popular sovereignty could be perverted by a handful of temporary immigrants flooding into a territory. Already that seemed to be happening in Kansas, where proslavery advocates called "Pukes" had begun trickling across the border from Missouri. "We are organizing," Senator David Atchison told Jefferson Davis confidentially. "We will be compelled to shoot, burn & hang, but the thing will soon be over. We intend to 'Mormonize' the abolitionists"—a reference to the forcible eviction of Stephen Douglas's old friends from Missouri fifteen years earlier. (Why Davis, as the sitting secretary of war, did not consider this threat alarming is self-evident in retrospect.) Meanwhile, Boston industrialist Amos Lawrence had begun underwriting an ambitious free-soil movement, the New England Emigrant Aid Company, for the purpose of inducing hardy New Englanders to take their families, their plows, and their antislavery values westward to Kansas. In his honor, a new settlement was christened Lawrence. It would soon be heard from on the national scene.[41]

In Washington, Massachusetts senator Julius Rockwell presented a petition signed by 2,900 citizens calling for the revocation of the Fugitive Slave Law. Charles Sumner chimed in with the opinion that "if the Union be in any way dependent on an act so revolting in every regard, then it ought not to exist." Southerners predictably howled in protest. Alabama senator Clement Clay castigated Sumner as "a leper, a serpent, and a filthy reptile." Virginia's James M. Mason observed that Sumner's "reason is dethroned." A nasty clash of words between Sumner and South Carolina senator Andrew P. Butler would plant the seeds for one of the most discreditable acts in Senate history. Meanwhile, Connecticut author Harriet Beecher Stowe's best-selling novel, *Uncle Tom's Cabin,* continued to educate—some said mislead—readers on the evils of slavery.[42]

Douglas, who had hoped to put the issue to rest, was caught off guard by the violent reaction to his bill. Five state legislatures—in Maine, Massachusetts, New York, Rhode Island, and Wisconsin—passed resolutions condemning the act. A Democratic convention in Stowe's Connecticut also opposed the bill, and other party organizations in the East and the Midwest withheld formal support for the measure. The *Detroit Democrat,* in something of a record for personal calumny, slandered Douglas as "the Illinois man stealer—the mean wretch who misrepresents a nominally free state in the American Senate, while upon his southern plantations the bloody scourge is daily falling by his command upon woman's shrinking flesh—who trades in little children, and overtasks and scourges gray-headed men, that the stock of wines and brandies which his depraved appetite demands may be abundant."[43]

Douglas could shrug off such overheated journalistic attacks, but he was greatly alarmed by reports of political defections among the party faithful back home. As early as mid-March, a crowd of young toughs in Chicago had burned him in effigy in the city square. When the Senate adjourned in August, Douglas set out on a brief speaking tour, explaining his views on popular sovereignty in general and the Kansas-Nebraska Act in particular. His reception was decidedly mixed. Opponents of the bill shadowed him at every stop, and in his adopted hometown of Chicago a howling mob heckled him into submission before he had the chance to speak. "Abolitionists of Chicago," he jeered. "It is now Sunday morning. I'll go to church and you may go to Hell." Later, more composed, he remembered: "I could travel from Boston to Chicago by the light of my own effigy." Missouri congressman Thomas Benton, a longtime foe, gleefully summed up Douglas's troubles. "His legs are too short," said

Benton. "That part of his body . . . which men wish to kick, is too near the ground."[44]

One of those waiting to do the kicking, figuratively at least, was Abraham Lincoln. The pro-Democrat *Illinois State Register* reported in August that Lincoln "had been nosing for weeks in the State Library, pumping his brain and his imagination for points and arguments" to use against Douglas. Like old war horses, the two men were gearing up for the state's annual legislative elections. Lincoln, against his better judgment, had been talked into running again for the legislature—a distinct step down after his term in Congress, but one that fellow Whigs believed was necessary to hold on to the seat in Sangamon County. In Bloomington, the old rivals crossed paths for the first time in years. After speaking to a party gathering, Lincoln paid a courtesy call on Douglas, who was convivially sharing a decanter of red liquor with friends in his hotel suite. "Mr. Lincoln, won't you take something?" Douglas asked. "No, I think not," Lincoln replied. "What! Are you a member of the Temperance Society?" Douglas joked. "No, I am not a member of any temperance society," said Lincoln, joining the fun, "but I am temperate, *in this*, that I don't drink anything."[45]

The jokes soon ended, and Lincoln and Douglas resumed their partisan political warfare. For several weeks, Lincoln attempted to engage Douglas in debate, but the Little Giant was understandably reluctant to share a public forum with his old-time rival, whom he termed "the most difficult and dangerous opponent that I have ever met." At the Illinois State Fair in Springfield, however, Lincoln found an opening. On October 3, Douglas arrived to speak at the fair, but a sudden rain shower forced the event indoors at the statehouse. After Douglas spoke for two and a half hours on behalf of the Kansas-Nebraska Act, Lincoln appeared on the stairway outside and announced that he would respond the next day to the senator's remarks. In the spirit of fairness, he invited Douglas to share the stage. October 4 was unusually hot, and Lincoln's face was bathed in sweat as he went to the table at the front of the hall and took out a long, handwritten speech. Douglas sat directly in front of the speaker's stand. After a little banter with "his distinguished friend, Judge Douglas," Lincoln launched into his address. The next stage of his career was about to begin.[46]

For three hours Lincoln unburdened himself of a thoughtful if sometimes rambling analysis of slavery in America, a practice, he said, that the Founding Fathers had kept hidden in the Constitution "just as an afflicted man hides away a wen or a cancer, which he dares not cut out at once, lest he bleed to death." The founders had expected slavery to die out on its own accord, he argued, and they had attempted to hem it into "the narrowest limits of necessity" through such compacts as the Northwest Ordinance of 1787, which prohibited slavery in the Old Northwest, and the Missouri Compromise of 1820. The latter, a "sacred compact," had held the nation together for more than thirty years, until Douglas and his minions had rammed through the Kansas-Nebraska Act. "This took us by surprise," Lincoln said. "We reeled and fell in utter confusion. But we rose each fighting, grasping whatever he could first reach—a scythe—a pitchfork—a chopping axe, or a butcher's cleaver."[47]

The target of all this slashing, Lincoln said, was the concept of popular sovereignty, which he condemned as a fraudulent device intended to spread slavery into "every part of the wide world." It was true that people had the right to decide their local laws, he admitted, whether they were "the oyster laws of Virginia, or the cranberry laws of Indiana." But slavery was another matter altogether—it required deciding nothing less than "whether a Negro is *not* or *is* a man." Douglas, said Lincoln, "has no very vivid impression that the Negro is human; and consequently has no idea that there can be any moral question in legislating about him." But the Declaration of Independence had said that all men were created equal, and "no man is good enough to govern another man, without that other's consent. When the white man governs himself that is self-government; but when he governs himself, and also governs another man, that is more than self-government—that is despotism. If the Negro is a man . . . there can be no moral right in connection with one man's making a slave of another."[48]

Concluding with an emotional appeal to "lovers of liberty everywhere" to readopt the Declaration of Independence and "join the great and good work" of limiting the spread of slavery into new territories, Lincoln ended his speech to a torrent of applause. Men hurrahed and thumped the floor, and women waved their white handkerchiefs in the air. Douglas gave a lengthy rebuttal, but in the admittedly partisan view of Billy Herndon, "Douglas was completely cut down by Lincoln and . . . felt himself overthrown." Emboldened by Lincoln's address, local antislavery radicals Ichabod Codding and Owen Lovejoy announced plans to hold a meeting in Springfield that very night to organize a new

Republican party in the state. (Lincoln did not attend.) The next day, veteran Democratic politician Lyman Trumbull, who was married to Mary Lincoln's best friend, Julia Jayne, publicly denounced Douglas and declared himself a candidate for Congress on the anti-Nebraska ticket. At the urging of other Whigs, Lincoln continued to press Douglas, trailing him across the state for the next two weeks and giving, in essence, the same speech he gave at Springfield. Having been proved right, yet again, in his analysis of Lincoln's effectiveness on the stump, Douglas did not repeat the mistake of sharing the same stage with his rival, even going so far as pleading laryngitis at one point to avoid answering Lincoln's challenge.[49]

◆ ◆ ◆

In the end, the political firestorm that Douglas had feared wound up scorching northern Democrats everywhere. The party's free-state representation in Congress fell from ninety-three to twenty-two seats, and Democrats kept control of only two northern state legislatures. Of the forty-four northern Democrats who had voted for the Kansas-Nebraska bill, only seven were reelected. Antislavery forces, including a crazy-quilt conglomeration of anti-Nebraska Democrats, Conscience Whigs, nativist Know-Nothings, and newly minted Republicans, won nearly half of the seats in the upcoming Thirty-fourth Congress. In Illinois, the Democratic Party lost control of the statehouse, as well as five of nine House seats. Douglas's friend William Richardson, who managed to hold on to his seat, ascribed the party's poor showing to "a torrent of abolitionism, whigism, free-soilism, religious bigotry, and intolerance, all joined in a wild and wicked foray upon the democratic party and the constitution." More to the point, perhaps, Illinois senator James Shields simply noted that "the Anti Nebraska feeling is too deep—more than I thought it was."[50]

Shields had good reason to worry. In February 1855, the newly constituted state legislature met in Springfield to decide his fate. From Washington, Douglas declared that Shields must be supported to the bitter end, despite the fact that pro-Nebraska Democrats were now in the minority. "Our friends in the legislature," he advised, "should nominate Shields by acclamation, and nail his flag to the mast, and never haul it down under any circumstances nor for anybody." Once again, Douglas's oldest enemy reared his head. Lincoln had resigned his new seat in the legislature, which he had not wanted to begin with, in order to qualify for the Senate (no sitting legislator was eligible). For weeks, Lincoln campaigned inexhaustibly for the post, writing letters to potential supporters, buttonholing lawmakers in the halls of the statehouse, and sleeping on the sofa of his office. Counting heads, Lincoln estimated that he had twenty-six sure votes going into the election; he needed twenty-five more to return to Washington. Old friends David Davis, Stephen Logan, and Ward Hill Lamon came aboard to help in the effort, but others abandoned Lincoln in favor of more radical anti-Nebraska candidates. Charles H. Ray, part-owner of the *Chicago Tribune*, dragged Mary Lincoln into the fight, writing: "I must confess I am afraid of 'Abe.' He is Southern by birth, Southern in his associations and Southern, if I mistake not, in his sympathies. His wife, you know, is a Todd, or a pro-slavery family, and so are all his kin."[51]

A brutal snowstorm, the worst since 1831, delayed the vote for twelve days. When it finally took place on February 8, Lincoln came within a whisker of winning on the first ballot, totaling forty-five votes. Shields had forty-one, but the balance of power was held by Congressman-elect Lyman Trumbull, who steadily rose from five votes to thirty-five. Always politically astute, Lincoln could read the handwriting on the wall. Trumbull's supporters, he said, were "men who never could vote for a Whig, and without the votes of two of whom I never could reach the requisite number to make an election." When the Douglas Democrats suddenly switched from Shields to a popular moderate, Governor Joel Matteson, Lincoln threw his votes behind Trumbull to prevent a Democratic triumph. Logan burst into tears when he got the instructions. "Disappointed and mortified," Lincoln told old friend Joseph Gillespie that he would never run for office again, since "he could bear defeat inflicted by his enemies with a pretty good grace—but it was hard to be wounded in the house of his friends."[52]

That night Lincoln attended a reception at the home of his brother-in-law, Ninian Edwards, which had been planned ahead of time to celebrate Lincoln's victory. Instead, he found himself congratulating "my friend Trumbull" and taking wan satisfaction in having frustrated the plans of Douglas and the Democrats. Mary Lincoln, who had watched the catastrophe from the House gallery, was not so gracious. Denouncing Trumbull's "sordid, selfish nature," she snubbed both him and his wife, her old friend Julia Jayne. She would never speak to either of them again. As for Douglas, he greeted the news of Trumbull's victory with pained incredulity. Trumbull's claims to be a Democrat—anti-Nebraska or not—"will be news to the Democracy of Illinois," said Douglas. "How can a man who was elected as an Abolition-Know-Nothing, come here and claim to be a Democrat in good standing?" It was a question that, one way or another, both he and Lincoln would have to answer in the months to come. For the time being, each man licked his wounds and moved on. When next they faced each other in combat, the whole country would be watching.[53]

4

✣✣✣

Defiant Recreancy

ollowing the disappointing outcome of his Senate race, Lincoln avoided politics altogether for the next twelve months, preferring to concentrate on his legal work. "I was dabbling in politics, and, of course, neglecting business," he told an associate. "Having since been beaten out, I have gone to work again to pick up my lost crumbs of last year." In June 1855, he was at home putting up a bed in his shirtsleeves when a flashy young lawyer from Philadelphia knocked on his door. Peter Watson, a junior associate of nationally known patent attorney George Harding, had come to Springfield to retain Lincoln's services on a major copyright-infringement case involving Cyrus McCormick's famous mechanical reaper. The case was scheduled to be heard in federal court in Chicago, and the Philadelphia firm wanted an Illinois attorney to sit with them in court. Watson, taking one look at the lanky, unkempt Lincoln, immediately regretted his choice, but nevertheless handed over a $400 retainer fee. Lincoln was given the impression that he would argue the case and typically went to work researching the particulars, going so far as to visit the Rockford, Illinois, factory of John H. Manny, the defendant in the suit, to study firsthand the intricate workings of his machine.[1]

The case subsequently was transferred to district court in Cincinnati, where Lincoln's old friend U.S. Supreme Court justice John McLean would preside. Lincoln learned of the change in the newspapers—his new employers had neglected to tell him—and arrived in Cincinnati well prepared to present the legal arguments for their side. Paying a courtesy call on Harding at his suite in the Burnet House, Lincoln made a less-than-favorable impression on the elegant Philadelphian, who saw standing before him "a tall rawly boned, ungainly backwoodsman, with coarse, ill-fitting clothing, his trousers hardly reaching his ankles, holding in his hands a blue cotton umbrella." Harding, at least, was civil. His associate, an owlish, balding attorney from Pittsburgh named Edwin Stanton, ignored Lincoln altogether, pulling Harding to one side and asking in a stage whisper: "Why did you bring that damned long-armed ape here? He does not know anything and can do you no good." When Lincoln suggested collegially that they walk over to the courthouse together, the others simply brushed past him and left him standing alone in the hall.[2]

A different man would have gone back home immediately, but Lincoln was used to such slights. Although Harding and Stanton continued to ignore him, never asking him to sit with them in court or share a meal in the hotel dining room, Lincoln attended the trial every day for a week, sitting in the audience and marveling at the suave courtroom manners of his college-trained associates. He returned to Springfield deeply mortified by the affair, and when Watson sent him a check for the rest of his fee, Lincoln sent it back uncashed, saying that he had done nothing to earn it. Only after Watson returned the check with a personal note assuring him that he was entitled to the remainder, did Lincoln consent to cash it. He said little about the case to Herndon, merely that he had been "roughly handled by that man Stanton." The two lawyers would cross paths again, under very different circumstances, a few years later.[3]

◆ ◆ ◆

While Lincoln licked his professional wounds, his old nemesis Stephen Douglas was suffering through a different sort of pain. The 1854 elections had delivered a stinging blow to the Kansas-Nebraska Act, the Democratic Party, and Douglas himself. He preferred to attribute the electoral defeats to the newly empowered Know-Nothing Party, which he depicted on the floor of the Senate as a sinister confederation meeting "at the dark hour of midnight," swearing "most horrible oaths," and plotting the overthrow of the government. It was not that simple, as

Douglas privately understood, but the Little Giant took his case to the public in 1855, traveling widely in support of Democratic candidates. He helped Henry A. Wise win the Virginia governorship, and, in a particularly satisfying contest, he lifted his friend Onias Skinner over Lincoln's friend and former partner Stephen Logan onto the Illinois Supreme Court. A reporter for the *St. Louis Missouri Democrat* pictured Douglas in full campaign mode: "A little man, with a big head, and a tolerable display of abdominal rotundity, [Douglas] did not convey any impression of the terror or senatorial might which he has at certain periods excited in certain portions of the country." Instead, he spoke "with a loud voice and slow accent, shaking his head and forefinger when desirous of being emphatic."[4]

The constant travel and speechifying took a toll on Douglas's health. In Terre Haute, Indiana, he collapsed. Wracked by severe coughing spasms, he was diagnosed with a case of acute bronchitis. Illinois congressman Thomas Harris, a frequent visitor, reported graphically to mutual friend Charles Lanphier that the senator "is still very hoarse, talks with difficulty, and has much soreness in the chest, and at intervals a hard cough. His attack was very severe. There was a general inflammation of the throat and respiratory organs, so much so, that suppuration has taken place, and the membranes sloughed off." Douglas's political enemies, as usual, were unmoved by his suffering. "It is generally believed that Mr. Douglas was confined at Terre Haute by an attack of delirium tremens," the *Cleveland Leader* scoffed. "It is well known in Chicago that he is a drunken little blackguard." In December, Douglas went to Cleveland, where he underwent a painful series of operations on his throat, including the removal of his uvula and tonsils. He was not able to return to Washington until February 1856. By that time, thanks directly to the Kansas-Nebraska Act he had championed, all hell had broken out in the newborn territories.[5]

◆ ◆ ◆

Throughout 1855, pro- and antislavery immigrants had been flooding into Kansas, taking advantage of a loophole in the act that allowed anyone living there to vote in local elections without having to own land or otherwise prove his residency. In March, some 7,000 voters went to the polls to elect a territorial legislature (Governor Andrew Reeder estimated that there were only about 2,900 eligible voters). New York senator William

Seward had thrown down the gantlet during the congressional debate over the Kansas-Nebraska bill the previous year, declaring in his best quasi-religious way: "Come on, then, gentlemen of the slave states. Since there is no escaping your challenge, I accept it in behalf of the cause of freedom. We will engage in competition for the virgin soil of Kansas, and God give the victory to the side which is stronger in numbers as it is in the right." Fellow abolitionists in the New England Emigrant Aid Company took up Seward's cause, organizing with great fanfare in Massachusetts and other free states. Meanwhile, proslavery senator David Atchison urged his fellow Missourians to "meet those philanthropic knaves peaceably at the ballot-box and outvote them." Privately, he played a different game, leading a force of eighty armed men into Kansas on the eve of the election and vowing "to kill every God-damned abolitionist in the Territory." Atchison was joined by up to 5,000 other proslavery militiamen variously calling themselves the Sons of the South, the Blue Lodge, the Platte County Self-Defensive Association, or the South Band. Having the sizable advantage of geography if not necessarily moral fervor, the proslavery side easily won the election and installed a friendly legislature that essentially adopted Missouri's statutes in Kansas and promulgated an even harsher fugitive slave law, making it a capital offense to help a slave escape and setting a ten-year prison term for anyone caught harboring or concealing an escaped slave.[6]

When Reeder voided some of the ballots and called for new elections in six contested districts, he was met by an angry band of pistol-wielding, shotgun-cradling slavers. Hurrying to Washington to confer with Pierce, Reeder made an impolitic stopover in his native state of Pennsylvania, where he warned somewhat hyperbolically that "Kansas has been invaded, conquered, subjugated by an armed force from beyond her borders, led on by a fanatical spirit." At the White House, the president agreed with Reeder that conditions in the new territory were worrisome, but he chastised the governor for his inflammatory remarks and for failing to criticize the Emigrant Aid Company for its own abuses, including—although Pierce may not have known it at the time—a shipment of some 325 Sharps rifles to abolitionist forces in Kansas. Six companies of New England emigrants already had arrived in the territory and, more ominous yet, five brothers named Brown, the sons of a hard-eyed, hot-tongued charismatic from upstate New York, had drifted in from the East to add their malign presence to the antislavery cause.[7]

After Reeder returned to Kansas and resumed his inconvenient practice of siding with the abolitionists, Pierce removed him from office and
replaced him with former Ohio governor Wilson Shannon. Reeder responded by issuing a ringing denunciation of the legislature, declaring,
"We owe no allegiance or obedience to the tyrannical enactments of this
spurious legislature." With his support, a second, shadow legislature was
formed in Topeka, comprised strictly of free-state men, and the two governing bodies settled in for a wary autumn of threats and counterthreats.
John Brown, patriarch of the antislavery Browns, arrived on the scene
and immediately took command of an unsavory company of "Liberty
Guards," who planned but did not have time to carry out a midnight
massacre of proslavery forces outside Lawrence. Soon enough, Brown
would get another chance.[8]

◆ ◆ ◆

Events in Kansas dominated the political landscape in Washington.
Douglas, still feeling the effects of his long siege of illness, chaired a tumultuous meeting of the Committee on Territories, which prepared a
report endorsing the proslavery legislature in Kansas and placing much
of the blame for the ongoing troubles there on the New England Emigrant Aid Company, which had sought "to control the domestic institutions of a distinct political community fifteen hundred miles distant."
Presenting the report to the Senate, Douglas added portentously: "We
understand that this is a movement for the purpose of producing a collision, with the hope that civil war may result if blood shall be shed in
Kansas. Sir, we are ready to meet that issue." Antislavery proponents
lashed out at Douglas, with Horace Greeley's *New York Tribune* setting
a new low for character assassination. "Douglas," said the newspaper,
"has brains, but so has the Devil, so had Judas and Benedict Arnold. His
is a bulldog mentality, a combination of the swineherd and the Caliban.
He can blackguard his betters like a fish-selling harridan. He can run
through the whole diapason of political falsehood with unrivaled skill,
from the delicate note of suggested prevarication down to the double-
bass of unmitigated lying."[9]

Charles Sumner jumped into the fray with a leering, sarcastic, two-
day-long speech on the floor of the Senate that he entitled melodramati-
cally "The Crime Against Kansas." Sumner's performance was over the
top, even by the slashing standards of the day. Salaciously comparing

the events in Kansas to the coercive embrace of a rapist and his victim, Sumner charged: "It is the rape of a virgin territory, compelling it to the hateful embrace of slavery; and it may be clearly traced to a depraved longing for a new slave state, the hideous offspring of such a crime in the hope of adding to the power of slavery in the national government." He described proslavery immigrants to the territory as "murderous robbers, hirelings picked from the drunken spew and vomit of an uneasy civilization" to prey upon unwary travelers like the Assassins and Thuggees of the Middle East. "Even now the black flag of the land pirates from Missouri waves at the masthead," said Sumner, smoothly switching similes. "In their laws you hear the pirate yell, and see the flash of the pirate knife, while, incredible to relate, the president, gathering the slave power at his back, testifies a pirate sympathy."[10]

Sumner saved his most personal attacks for Douglas and fellow senator Andrew Butler of South Carolina, who was home recovering from a semiparalytic stroke at the time of the speech. Butler, said Sumner, was a modern Don Quixote who "has chosen a mistress to whom he has made his vows, and who . . . though polluted in the sight of the world is chaste in his sight—I mean the harlot, slavery." As for Douglas, he was "the squire of slavery, its very Sancho Panza, ready to do all its humiliating offices." Sumner's opening remarks were bad enough, but he soon descended into personal cruelty, mocking the aged Butler for his paralyzed upper lip and saying that he "overflowed with rage, with incoherent phrases, discharged [with] the loose expectoration of his speech." Sumner compared Douglas to "a noisome, squat, and nameless animal" that "switch[es] out from his tongue the perpetual stench of offensive personality." Douglas, feigning indifference, muttered to friends, "That damn fool will get himself killed by some other damned fool," and wondered, "Is it his object to provoke some of us to kick him as we would a dog in the street, that he may get sympathy upon the just chastisement?"[11]

Douglas would get his answer soon enough. The next day Butler's cousin, South Carolina congressman Preston Brooks, approached Sumner as he sat at his desk on the floor of the Senate. "I have read your speech twice over carefully," Brooks said to the puzzled Sumner, who did not know who he was. "It is a libel on South Carolina and Mr. Butler, who is a relative of mine." With that, Brooks suddenly struck Sumner over the head repeatedly with a gutta-percha cane. Sumner, stunned and bleeding, ripped his desk from its foundations and toppled over, "bellow[ing]," said Brooks, "like a calf." Later, either from confusion or malice, Sumner would claim that Douglas had been present during the attack and had stood by, doing nothing, while he was assaulted. In reality, Douglas had been speaking with William Richardson and two other congressmen in a reception room off the Senate floor when news of the attack arrived. "My first impression was to come into the Senate chamber and help put an end to affray, if I could," Douglas recalled, "but it occurred to my mind, in an instant, that my relations with Mr. Sumner were such that if I came into the hall, my motives would be misconstrued, perhaps, and I sat down again." After the attack was over, Douglas rushed onto the floor with others (perhaps that was when Sumner saw him). Douglas's account was verified by other eyewitnesses.[12]

News of the attack electrified the nation. "Violence reigns in the streets of Washington," wrote William Cullen Bryant in the *New York Evening Post*. "Has it come to this? Are we to be chastised as they chastise their slaves? Are we, too, slaves for life, a target for their brutal blows?" Protest meetings took place in Massachusetts and other northern states, where speakers dwelt on the physical assault and ignored completely Sumner's verbal provocations. In the South, newspapers took the opposite tack, applauding the attack and downplaying the difference in ages between Brooks and the unarmed, unprepared Sumner. The attack, said the *Richmond Enquirer*, was "good in conception, better in execution, and best of all in consequence. The vulgar abolitionists in the Senate have been suffered to run too long without collars. They must be lashed into submission." The unrepentant Brooks reported with satisfaction that he had been inundated with requests for pieces of his shattered cane—"sacred relics," he termed them—and showered with new canes, including one inscribed "Hit Him Again."[13]

Horrifying as it was, the attack on Sumner was soon overshadowed by events on the ground in Kansas. The day after Sumner's speech, federal marshals moved into Lawrence, the hotbed of abolitionism, to serve warrants on antislavery agitators and close down the town's two "seditious" newspapers, the *Herald of Freedom* and the *Free Press*. The Free State Hotel, a virtual fortress bristling with cannons and small-arms portals, was another target of the lawmen. Abolitionist leaders fled before they could be arrested, and the marshals, backed by a mob of about 1,000 proslavery supporters, swarmed through the streets of Lawrence, spoiling for a fight. They ransacked the offices of the offending newspapers, threw their printing presses into the Kansas River, and burned down the home of free-state "governor" Charles Robinson. The ever-present David Atchison was on hand, urging the men to shoot anyone, male or female, who dared to defy them. "When a woman takes on herself the garb of a soldier by carrying a Sharp's rifle," said Atchison, "then she is no longer a woman, and, by damned, treat her for what you find her, and trample her underfoot as you would a snake. If a man or a woman dare to stand before you, blow them to hell with a chunk of cold lead!" As it turned out, the only one killed in Lawrence that day was a proslavery supporter fatally crushed by falling debris from the Free State Hotel, which his fellows were in the process of bombarding with four brass cannons.[14]

Lurid accounts of the "sack of Lawrence" filled newspapers back east, jockeying for space with news of Sumner's miraculous recovery and sudden relapse. Back in Kansas, John Brown made his first sanguinary appearance on the national scene. Together with four of his sons and two other supporters, Brown set out on the night of May 24 for the proslavery settlement on Pottawatomie Creek. Barging into various unguarded cabins, the party dragged out five unarmed settlers and, in full view of their families, hacked them to death with razor-sharp broadswords. Defenders tried to justify the cold-blooded murders by claiming that Brown and his men had merely acted to prevent the lynching of a fellow Free-Soiler, but citizens in Kansas knew the true story. While Brown and his cutthroats went on the lam, factions on both sides began arming themselves for full-scale civil war. Kansas had spun out of control, and the American political system seemed powerless to stop it.[15]

◆ ◆ ◆

The worsening crisis in Kansas, coupled with the modest comeback of the Democratic Party nationwide in 1855, spelled an end to the twenty-year-old Whig Party. Anti-Nebraska Whigs in the North flocked to the new Republican Party, which had already won the governorship in Ohio with Salmon P. Chase, while southern Whigs increasingly defected to the Democrats or the immigrant-bashing Know-Nothings. Illinois, with its sharp geographical divide between northern and southern sympathies, teetered uncomfortably between the party of Stephen Douglas and the anti-Nebraska faction—it could scarcely be called a party yet—of new senator Lyman Trumbull and his supporters.

Abraham Lincoln teetered as well. The previous summer he had exchanged letters with his old friend Joshua Speed, now a transplanted southerner in every sense of the word. From his new home in Kentucky, Speed wanted to know where Lincoln stood on the Kansas-Nebraska Act and on the issue of slavery. "I plainly see you and I would differ about the Nebraska law," Lincoln responded. "I look upon that enactment not as a *law*, but as *violence* from the beginning. It was conceived in violence, passed in violence, is maintained in violence, and is being executed in violence." As for his current political thinking, Lincoln continued: "That is a disputed point. I think I am a Whig; but others say there are no Whigs, and that I am an abolitionist. When I was at Washington I voted for the Wilmot Proviso as good as forty times [actually, it was more like five], and I never heard of anyone attempting to unwhig me for that. I now do no more than oppose the *extension* of slavery."[16]

By May 1856, Lincoln was ready to make the jump to the Republicans. On May 29, some 270 anti-Nebraska delegates gathered at Major's Hall in Bloomington, Illinois, to organize the state Republican Party. Lincoln, who had helped draft a platform calling for restoration of the Missouri Compromise and affirming the basic doctrine that the United States was founded on the principle of freedom for all men, gave the closing address at the convention. With the exception of a reporter from the *Alton Weekly Courier*, no one bothered taking notes at the speech, and it subsequently entered Lincoln lore as the "Lost Speech." Billy Herndon, who was there, said he threw away his own pencil "and lived only in the inspiration of the hour." He characterized the speech as "full of fire and energy and force; it was logic; it was pathos; it was enthusiasm; it was justice, equity, truth, and right set ablaze by the divine fires of a soul maddened by the wrong; it was hard, heavy, knotty, gnarly, backed with wrath."[17]

Lincoln, as usual, took a swing at his favorite opponent, claiming that Stephen Douglas and his fellow Democrats had abandoned their belief in "the individual rights of man" in favor of an absurd notion put forth by southern writer George Fitzhugh that slavery should be extended to white laborers. Fitzhugh spoke for few southerners, and certainly Douglas had never advocated any such proposal, but old habits die hard. Lincoln could not resist whacking "Judge Douglas" whenever he got the chance. As for "the bugbear [of] disunion," Lincoln professed the belief that "the Union must be preserved in the purity of its principles as well as in the integrity of its territorial parts." He proposed a party motto based on an old quote by Daniel Webster: "Liberty and Union, now and forever, one and inseparable."[18]

Lincoln's speech, lost or not, rallied the faithful. He turned down an offer to run for governor, preferring to back former anti-Nebraska congressman William H. Bissell. Instead, he made plans to travel widely through southern Illinois to bolster the new party's presidential nominee—whoever that might be. As Lincoln told Trumbull, a delegate to the upcoming national convention in Philadelphia, "I am *in*, and shall go for anyone nominated unless he be *'platformed'* . . . on some ground which I may think wrong." The convention, showing its old Whig origins, nominated another national hero (although not a general) for president—John C. Frémont, the famed "Pathfinder" of western exploration. At forty-three, Frémont was the youngest candidate yet nominated for president, and probably the least prepared. His chief recommendation, beyond his somewhat inflated claims of pathfinding, was his marriage to Jessie Benton, the beautiful and brainy daughter of former Missouri senator Thomas Hart Benton. The handsome Frémont put himself entirely in the hands of political veterans David Wilmot, Joshua Giddings, Henry Wilson, and other abolitionists, who crafted an alliterative if unimaginative slogan: "Free Soil, Free Speech, Free Men, Frémont." Former Whig senator William Dayton of New Jersey was chosen as Frémont's running mate, after a brief boomlet for Lincoln fell flat.[19]

♦ ♦ ♦

The Democrats, meeting two weeks earlier in Cincinnati, had confronted a parlous political landscape blighted by the ongoing slaughter in "Bleeding Kansas." The two leading architects of that domestic debacle, Franklin Pierce and Stephen Douglas, were damaged goods as far as the party was concerned. For all his ingratiating manner and suave good looks, Pierce had pleased no one with his inept, divisive performance as president. As for Douglas, his support of the Kansas-Nebraska Act, his still shaky health, and his earlier disavowal of interest in the 1856 nomination created an opening for one of his least favorite people, American ambassador James Buchanan. "Old Buck," said one Pittsburgh newspaper, was "the most available and unobjectionable" choice, largely because he had been conveniently out of the country at the time of the

Kansas-Nebraska debate. Backed by a formidable quartet of senators—Jesse Bright of Indiana, John Slidell and Judah Benjamin of Louisiana, and James A. Bayard of Delaware—Buchanan led the convention voting through the first fourteen ballots, with Pierce and Douglas jockeying for second. After the fifteenth ballot Pierce dropped out, releasing his delegates to Douglas, but by then it was too late. Bowing to the inevitable, Douglas withdrew after the sixteenth ballot and threw his votes to Buchanan in the interest of party unity. "My heart was with Douglas, but my head was with Buchanan," Indiana delegate John Pettit explained to Douglas after the fact. "I preferred you for President, but him as a candidate."[20]

Once again, Douglas swallowed his disappointment at being passed over for the nomination and campaigned hard for the Democratic nominee. He appeared at massive rallies in Washington, Philadelphia, and New York City, urging the election of Buchanan as the only way to save the Union. Abraham Lincoln also took to the campaign trail, making some fifty appearances across Illinois on behalf of Frémont. The campaign was complicated for both parties by the presence of a third candidate, American Party nominee Millard Fillmore, the former president, who ran on a simple, if not indeed simplistic, platform: "Americans must rule America." Lincoln complained with some logic that any vote for Fillmore was a vote for Buchanan, since it drew from the same anti-Nebraska well. "This is as plain as the adding up of the weights of three small hogs," Lincoln warned. "With the Frémont and Fillmore men united . . . we have Mr. Buchanan in the hollow of our hand; but with us divided, he has us." He failed to mention that his own household was similarly divided. Mary Lincoln was firmly behind Fillmore, explaining to her half-sister Emilie: "If some of you Kentuckians had to deal with 'the wild Irish,' as we housekeepers are sometimes called upon to do, the South would certainly elect Mr. Fillmore." Meanwhile, Douglas fumed at Republican efforts to block the early admission of Kansas to statehood. "All these gentlemen want is to get up murder and bloodshed in Kansas for political effect," he said. "They do not mean that there shall be peace until after the presidential election. An angel from heaven could not write a bill to restore peace in Kansas that would be acceptable to the Abolition Republican party."[21]

With no angels in sight, the Kansas issue stalled in Congress and the presidential campaign became, yet again, a superficial battle of character assassination, mudslinging, and fearmongering. Republicans mocked Buchanan, who at sixty-five had held a number of governmental posts in his career, as "Old Public Functionary," and whispered that his lifelong bachelorhood was somewhat suspicious, to say the least. Political cartoonists, never the subtlest of journalists, regularly dressed him in women's clothes. Fillmore and the Know-Nothings drew scorn as well for worrying obsessively about the supposed swarms of foreign immigrants lusting to come into the country, which one critic said was "as absurd an anachronism as would be the anticipation of a Carthaginian invasion, or the subjection of the country by mail-clad warriors of a descendant of William the Conqueror." Opponents organized tongue-in-cheek Say-Nothing, Do-Nothing, and Owe-Nothing societies, and promised at the first sign of danger to "take up arms, pitchforks, stove pipes, wooden nutmegs, [and] saw logs."[22]

The predominance of criticism fell on the neophyte Frémont, whom Democrats depicted as "a man whose only merit, so far as history records it, is in the fact that he was born in South Carolina, crossed the Rocky Mountains, subsisted on frogs, lizards, snakes and grasshoppers, and captured a woolly horse." Charges of rampant womanizing (more or less true) were joined by charges that Frémont was a secret Catholic (more or less false). Virginia governor Henry Wise mercilessly characterized the Republican candidate as "a Frenchman's bastard [whose] mother was a strumpet in a Richmond brothel." Actually, Frémont's mother had left her much-older husband and run off with her French teacher, whose child, the future presidential nominee, she subsequently bore out of wedlock. Whether that made her a strumpet, or merely a woman who made spectacularly poor choices in her life, depended as always on the eye of the beholder.[23]

Democrats played the race card unremittingly. The *Richmond Enquirer* labeled the Republicans' true slogan as "free niggers, free women, free land, and Frémont." In Indiana, young girls in white dresses paraded behind a banner that read: "Fathers, save us from nigger husbands." Ohio abolitionist Joshua Giddings was quoted—accurately or not—as declaring, "I look forward to the day when there shall be a servile insurrection in the South, when the black man shall assert his freedom and wage a war of extermination against his master." It did not help the Republican cause when speaker H. L. Raymond, appearing at Boston's venerable Faneuil Hall, told his audience, "Remembering that he was a slaveholder, I spit on George Washington." When outraged listeners hissed, Raymond retorted savagely, "You hissers are slaveholders in spirit!"[24]

Aided by such intemperate language on the part of his opponents, Buchanan triumphed over Frémont by carrying every southern state except Maryland (which went for Fillmore) and adding just enough free states to tip the scales in his favor. Frémont, despite the personal pounding, made a credible showing, particularly for the candidate of a first-time political party, winning 33 percent of the popular vote and 114 electoral votes. He carried eleven states, including all of New England, New York, Michigan, Wisconsin, and Iowa. It was, said one supporter, "a victorious defeat." Less-partisan observers read the purely regional results as an ominous sign of the ever-widening national divide. Illinois went for Buchanan, but Douglas's close friend and associate William Richardson lost the governorship to William Bissell—the first time a non-Democrat had ever won the statehouse there. The Republicans also captured four of the state's nine congressional seats.[25]

Douglas eased the pain of Richardson's loss by marrying again two weeks after the election. His new bride was a twenty-one-year-old Washington-bred beauty named Adele Cutts, the daughter of a government clerk and the grandniece of Dolley Madison, who had lived in the Cutts home when Adele was a child. A popular and cultured young lady, "beautiful as a pearl, sunny-tempered, unselfish, warm-hearted, unaffected, sincere," Adele had an immediate softening effect on the frontier-hardened Douglas, beginning with his appearance. His long hair was trimmed, his recently sprouted beard was shaved, and his shabby clothes were replaced with crisp white collars and tailor-fitted frock coats. James Shields, who stood up as best man at the wedding, described the new Mrs. Douglas as "a splendid person and . . . a great benefit to Judge Douglas." Along with domesticating Douglas, Adele took immediate and affectionate charge of her stepsons, seven-year-old Robbie and six-year-old Stevie, placing the boys in a Catholic school in the capital and giving them a stable new home life. The next April, Douglas went in with Vice President John C. Breckinridge and Minnesota territorial representative Henry M. Rice to purchase three adjacent lots on Minnesota Row on which to erect new houses. By the time the next Congress opened for business, the Douglas mansion at the corner of I Street was ready to take its place as one of the social and political centers of Washington. "The White House itself is not more visited," one newspaper correspondent gushed.[26]

◆ ◆ ◆

Lincoln, too, had a newly remodeled home. Mary Lincoln, with the help of a $1,200 windfall from the sale of property left to her by her late father, oversaw the addition of a second floor on their home in Springfield. Working with the contracting firm of Hannon & Ragsdale, Mary transformed the former cottage into a graceful Greek Revival home. A new double parlor was added, with the rear devoted to a study and library for Lincoln, and separate bedrooms were tacked on for the couple and for oldest son Robert, who was away much of the time at Illinois State University studying for his entrance exam to Harvard. Younger sons Willie and Tad, who was born in 1853, shared a fourth bedroom. When Lincoln returned from another three-month ride through the judicial circuit, he paused in wonder on the street before the newly painted chocolate-brown house. "Say, stranger," he called to a neighbor. "Do you know where Lincoln lives? He used to live here." Although he and Mary had discussed the remodeling project before he left, rumors passed through town that she had done it without his knowledge. As ever, a certain number of people were always ready to believe the worst about Mary Lincoln.[27]

Although he grumbled a little at the cost, Lincoln could easily afford the renovation. The months following the 1856 election had been lucrative ones professionally. He finally had managed to get the Illinois Central Railroad to pay him the remaining $4,800 of his fee for the McLean County case, and the publicity from that case had brought him aboard one of the most significant legal cases of the 1850s—*Hurd v. the Rock Island Bridge Co.*, also known as the *Effie Afton* case. The proceedings involved the owners of the *Effie Afton*, a Mississippi River steamboat, and the operators of the bridge company. At stake was nothing less than the future of interstate commerce—waterborne or railroad—and Lincoln, despite his background as an old river man, now represented the railroad interests. The case arose after the *Effie Afton* plowed into the aforementioned bridge, the first railroad bridge spanning the Mississippi River, and burned. Her owners sued the bridge owners for damages, testing whether it was legal for any company to throw a bridge across the river and threaten water traffic.[28]

As was his custom, Lincoln thoroughly researched the case, going to the bridge in person and dangling his long legs over the side while he carefully studied the river currents eddying about the supports. He argued before Justice John McLean in Chicago's circuit court that the currents were so mild—only five miles per hour, he estimated—that they represented no danger to boat traffic. Pilot error or mechanical failure had caused the collision, he said, therefore the bridge company was faultless. The U.S. Supreme Court subsequently upheld Lincoln's argument, which further helped the railroads tighten their stranglehold on the national marketplace.[29]

Lincoln's new home and increased wealth did not distract him from politics. He and Mary combined the two with a "perfectly extravagant" affair on the occasion of Lincoln's forty-eighth birthday in February 1857. Three hundred guests crowded into the house to enjoy a buffet dinner "loaded with venison, wild turkeys, prairie chickens, quails, and other game." Another 200 were prevented from coming by a heavy rainstorm. Lincoln was paving the way for another attempt at the U.S. Senate—this time a direct challenge to his eternal nemesis, Stephen Douglas. Behind the scenes, he urged fellow Illinois Republicans to "do something *now*, to secure the Legislature," but cautioned, "Let all be so quiet that the adversary shall not be notified." Meanwhile, he surrounded himself with a crack team of political operatives, including the ever-loyal Billy Herndon, Judge David Davis, former legislative colleague Joseph Gillespie, and two prominent Chicago politicians—Norman B. Judd and Charles H. Ray—who had opposed him in his earlier race against Lyman Trumbull.[30]

◆ ◆ ◆

Any hope that Lincoln could fly under the radar, so to speak, went by the wayside in early March 1857, when the Supreme Court delivered its highly charged *Dred Scott* decision. That decision, one of the most controversial in American history, upheld the notion that a human slave was mere property, and that slaveholders were free to take said property wherever they wanted, without fear of inconvenient interference from state or local restrictions. Nor could Congress interfere with such rights by passing any laws prohibiting slavery in unincorporated territories. The ruling, which had been leaked to incoming president James Buchanan by Chief Justice Roger Taney in time for Buchanan's overly sunny inaugural address, touched off a tidal wave of protest from antislavery forces throughout the North, who considered it tantamount to legalizing slavery throughout the Union.

By the time of the court's decision, the Scott case had dragged through the legal system for more than a decade. As a slave, Scott had been taken to free territory in Illinois and Wisconsin by his owner, an army physician named John Emerson. After Emerson died, Scott contended that he was entitled to his freedom on the basis of his two-year residency on free soil. A Missouri court agreed, but appeals and counterappeals snarled the case in legal limbo for eleven years. The Supreme Court ruled that whether Scott was still a slave or not, as a black man he had no legal standing to petition the bench. Blacks, said Taney, "were not included and were not intended to be included under the word 'citizens' in the Constitution." According to Taney, the Founding Fathers had regarded blacks "as a subordinate and inferior class of beings, who had no rights or privileges but such as those who held the power and the government might choose to grant them." They were "altogether unfit to associate with the white race" and "had no rights which the white man was bound to respect."[31]

That was bad enough from the abolitionist standpoint, but the high court went even further by ruling that Congress could not make laws prohibiting slavery in new or existing territories—in effect, rendering the Missouri Compromise unconstitutional. Southerners felt vindicated. Their property rights were upheld and so, by extension, was the institution of slavery. Northerners were aghast. "The Constitution of the United States is the paramount law of every state," Wisconsin senator James Doolittle repined. "If that recognizes slaves as property, as horses are property, no state constitution or state law can abolish it." This seemed to render inoperative the whole concept of popular sovereignty, as Stephen Douglas was quick to realize. In June, he returned to Illinois to address the ruling publicly. Speaking at the statehouse in Springfield, he praised the Supreme Court justices as "honest and conscientious men," and denounced Republican vows to ignore the ruling as a mere obiter dictum, an opinion without the full force of law. "Whoever resists the final decision of the highest judicial tribunal," warned Douglas, "aims a deadly blow at our whole republican system of government—a blow which, if successful, would place all our rights and liberties at the mercy of passion, anarchy and violence."[32]

As for the Missouri Compromise, Douglas pointed out that the Compromise of 1850 and the Kansas-Nebraska Act had already rendered the earlier compact null and void. The property right of southern slaveholders was not in question, he maintained, but it remained "a barren and a worthless right, unless sustained, protected and enforced by appropriate police regulations and local legislation. . . . These regulations and remedies must necessarily depend entirely upon the will and wishes of the people of the territory as they can only be prescribed by the local legislatures." The main thrust of the *Dred Scott* decision, Douglas concluded, was the determination that blacks were not citizens, something he said the framers of the Constitution had intended from the start. "They referred to the white race alone, and not the African, when they declared men to have been created free and equal," said Douglas. "The history of the times clearly shows that the Negroes were regarded as an inferior race, who in all ages, and in every part of the globe, and in the most favorable circumstances, had shown themselves incapable of self-government." Any deviation from that view would lead to the "amalgamation between superior and inferior races" and inevitably bring the superior race "down to the lower level of the inferior."[33]

Lincoln was in the audience that day, and two weeks later he gave the unofficial Republican response. Dismissing the concept of popular sovereignty as "a mere deceitful pretense for the benefit of slavery," Lincoln charged Douglas with cynically playing upon the "natural disgust of nearly all white people to the idea of an indiscriminate amalgamation of the white and black races." This was nothing more than "counterfeit logic," Lincoln said, "which concludes that, because I do not want a black woman for a *slave* I must necessarily want her for a *wife*. I need not have her for either; I can just leave her alone. In some respects she certainly is not my equal; but in her natural right to eat the bread that she earns with her own hands she is my equal, and the equal of all others." It came down to a fundamental difference of opinion, he said. "The Republicans inculcate that the Negro is a man; that his bondage is cruelly wrong, and that the field of his oppression ought not to be enlarged. The Democrats deny his manhood; deny, or dwarf to insignificance, the wrong of his bondage; so far as possible, crush all sympathy for him, and cultivate and excite hatred and disgust against him . . . and call the indefinite outspreading of his bondage 'a sacred right of self-government.'"[34]

◆ ◆ ◆

With his speech, Lincoln sharply contradicted Douglas's views and cannily positioned himself as a leading contender for the Little Giant's increasingly warm Senate seat. For the time being, however, Douglas had other battles to fight—specifically, with the new president of the United States. He and Buchanan had never much cared for each other. Douglas believed, with good reason, that the president had been less-than-normally appreciative of his efforts to get him elected to office in the first place. After stepping aside in favor of Buchanan at the Democratic National Convention in Cincinnati, Douglas had received a stiff note of thanks addressed to "the Honorable *Samuel* A. Douglas." Overlooking the perhaps inadvertent insult, Douglas still campaigned tirelessly for Buchanan, helping him carry the crucial electoral votes of Illinois and other states in the Old Northwest. He also opened his purse strings, donating some $100,000 of his personal funds to Buchanan's campaign. In return, Douglas not unreasonably expected a hand in the selection of Buchanan's cabinet and a generous dollop of patronage appointments for his home state.[35]

As it happened, he got neither. Buchanan still remembered being called "an old fogy" by the senator's enthusiastic young backers at the 1852 convention, and he largely ignored Douglas's recommendations for presidential appointments, going out of his way to select politicians who were personally opposed to the senator. Even Buchanan's promotion of Douglas's new father-in-law, James Madison Cutts, to the Treasury Department ruffled feathers between the two. When Douglas complained that people were accusing him of pressing for Cutts's appointment (he had not), the president replied huffily that the appointment had "proceed[ed] entirely from my regard for Mr. Cutts & his family, & not because Senator Douglas has had the good fortune to become his son-in-law." Taking happy note of the contretemps, the Republican-leaning *New York Tribune* joked of Douglas: "He loved not papa less but party more."[36]

Soon there were more weighty matters of disagreement between the two. In Kansas, the antislavery forces won a decisive victory in October 1857, aided by Buchanan's handpicked territorial governor, Robert J. Walker, who threw out enough proslavery ballots—including some 1,600 copied from an old Cincinnati city directory—to ensure a free-state legislature. Not to be outdone, the sitting legislature in Lecompton called for a new referendum, with voters being given the option of voting for slavery or against slavery—the codicil being that slaves already living within the state (and their descendants) would still be slaves in perpetuity. Free-staters boycotted the referendum, which passed by an inflated margin. Walker denounced the proceedings as "a vile fraud," and northern Democrats found common cause with Republicans in opposing the measure. It was widely expected that Buchanan would refuse to recognize the document, which amounted to a petition for immediate statehood.[37]

Remarkably, Buchanan not only recognized the Lecompton Constitution, but sent it along to Congress with his personal endorsement, reporting with a presumably straight face that "Kansas is therefore at this moment as much a slave state as Georgia and South Carolina." At the same time, he characterized antislavery supporters within the state as "mercenaries of abolitionism" who had created "a revolutionary government" of their own and were planning to spread anarchy throughout the territory. Even supporters of the president were dismayed. "I had considerable hopes of Mr. Buchanan—I really thought he was a statesman," said Franklin Pierce's personal secretary, B. B. French. "But I have now come to the settled conclusion that he is just the damnedest old fool that ever occupied the presidential chair. He has deliberately walked overboard with his eyes open—let him drown." Douglas, after meeting with the demoralized Walker upon his return from Kansas, worried that Buchanan "has made a fatal mistake and got us all into trouble."[38]

Douglas, who clearly understood the stakes involved, nevertheless astonished partisans in both regions by coming out against the Lecompton Constitution in late 1857. That "fraudulent submission," he said, had made a mockery of true popular sovereignty by allowing a minority of proslavery voters to ram through a constitution that did not reflect the true feelings of the majority of Kansas voters, who had boycotted the proceedings. "If this constitution is to be forced down our throats, in violation of the fundamental principle of free government," he said, "I will resist it to the last. I have spent too much strength and breath, and health, too, to establish this great principle in the popular heart to see it frittered away."[39]

By breaking with the Buchanan administration, Douglas declared open warfare on the sitting president of his own party. "I have never seen a slave insurrection before," Republican senator Ben Wade snickered from the sidelines. Fellow senator James Dixon of Connecticut joked that Douglas was "finally indulging in the luxury of a conscience." Raising the specter of previous Democratic senators who had quarreled unsuccessfully with Andrew Jackson, Buchanan warned the party apostate: "Mr. Douglas, I desire you to remember that no Democrat ever yet differed from the administration of his own choice without being crushed." "Mr. President," Douglas responded, "I wish you to remember that General Jackson is dead, sir." To an Illinois Republican, he was even blunter. "By God, sir, I made Mr. James Buchanan," he growled, "and by God, sir, I will unmake him."[40]

Douglas, for once, underestimated the coercive power of the presidency. The Buchanan administration lavished money, patronage, and even prostitutes on wavering congressmen, and the bill to admit Kansas to the Union as a slave state passed narrowly on April 30, 1858. "Farewell to state rights, farewell to state sovereignty," Douglas lamented. He was too pessimistic. Despite a promise of massive federal land grants to Kansans if they approved the Lecompton Constitution, the Free-Soilers rejected the offer of immediate statehood and opted to remain a territory. Furious southerners blamed Douglas personally for the defeat. He was accused variously of "treachery without parallel," "patent double dealing," "detestable heresies," and "defiant recreancy." The *Mobile Daily Register* predicted that Douglas's anti-Lecompton stand "will at once sever the ties which have hitherto bound this able statesman and the people of the South together in such a cordial alliance. There must henceforth exist an impassable gulf between the Southern people and the Illinois Senator." The *Washington Union,* a Buchanan administration mouthpiece, remarked with unconcealed satisfaction: "There is no quarter in the South in which he can hope to be regarded in any other character than as a disorganizer and an apostate." Party activist Isaac H. Sturgeon accused Douglas of plotting to join the Republicans and eliminate the institution of slavery altogether. "I tell you sir as sure as the Lord liveth," he informed another Democratic leader, "Judge Douglas is a traitor to the Democratic party as black as hell itself or he is a deceiver of the Republicans."[41]

◆ ◆ ◆

One of those Republicans, Abraham Lincoln, was undeceived as always by Douglas, but he was greatly concerned by the favorable attention the Little Giant was receiving from other Republicans. *New York Tribune* editor Horace Greeley, whose newspaper was read by upward of 10,000 people in Illinois, eulogized Douglas's opposition to the Lecompton bill as "conspicuously, courageously, eminently so." Massachusetts senator Henry Wilson, a leader of the abolitionist wing of the party, flatly predicted that Douglas was about to switch over to the Republicans, where he would immediately add "more weight to our cause than any other ten men in the country." Lincoln, watching the "rumpus" uncomfortably in Springfield, could see his worst nightmare coming true—Stephen Douglas winning reelection to the Senate with the deluded support of Republicans as well as Democrats. Charging that Douglas and his supporters were merely "boys who have set a bird-trap and are watching to see if the birds are picking at the bait and likely to go under," Lincoln fumed to Lyman Trumbull: "What does the New York Tribune mean by its constantly eulogizing, and admiring, and magnifying Douglas? Does it, in this, speak the sentiments of the Republicans at Washington? Have they concluded that the Republican cause, generally, can be best promoted by sacrificing us here in Illinois? If so we would like to know soon; it will save us a great deal of effort to surrender at once."[42]

Thoroughly alarmed, Lincoln sent Herndon to Washington to beard the lion in his lair. Although he was not feeling well, Douglas received Herndon in his sickroom and shared cigars. Lincoln, said Herndon, stretching the truth, "was not in anyone's way, not even in yours, Judge Douglas." Even on his sickbed, Douglas knew that was not the case, but he merely shrugged and sent his old opponent his personal regards. "Tell him I have crossed the river and burned my boat," said Douglas, leaving matters very much up in the air. A second visit by Herndon to Horace Greeley was even more Delphic. "Let the future alone, it will all come right," the editor told Lincoln's partner. "Douglas is a brave man. Forget the past and sustain the righteous." "Good God, *righteous*," Herndon snorted.[43]

By way of compromise, some Illinois Republicans began suggesting that Douglas step down from the Senate and run for the House from Chicago, in return for Republican support of him and other anti-Buchanan Democrats in the state. When Lincoln heard of the suggestion, he angrily opposed it. "We must never sell old friends to buy old enemies," he said. "Let us all stand firm, making no committals as to strange and new combinations." His old friend David Davis was more acerbic. "A penitent prostitute may be received into the church," he said scathingly, "but she should not lead the choir." Eventually, the outside interference by Greeley and other national Republicans had a negative impact in Illinois. "We want no such ominous wooden horses run into our camp," wrote the editor of the *Dixon Republican and Telegraph*. When Illinois Democrats endorsed Douglas for reelection, the brief flirtation between the two parties ended, and the lines were drawn for another clear-cut battle.[44]

Lincoln, having been devastated by his loss to Trumbull three years earlier, left nothing to chance. With the help of his seasoned operatives, he successfully pushed for a nominating convention to be held, conveniently enough, in Springfield. After beating back a last-minute surge by Chicago mayor "Long John" Wentworth, who at six feet six inches tall was one of the few people who towered above Lincoln, the convention formally selected Lincoln to oppose Douglas. Over the course of the previous several weeks, Lincoln had been working on an acceptance speech, one designed to highlight the differences between the Republicans and the Democrats. When he stepped to the front of the statehouse at eight o'clock on the night of June 16, he had firmly committed the speech to memory. For generations to come, untold numbers of northern school-children would be compelled, however unwillingly, to do the same.[45]

It became known as the "House Divided" speech. Echoing the gospels of Matthew and Mark, Lincoln warned: "A house divided against itself cannot stand. I believe this government cannot endure, permanently half *slave* and half *free*. I do not expect the Union to be *dissolved*—I do not expect the house to *fall*—but I *do* expect it will cease to be divided. It will become *all* one thing, or *all* the other." Lincoln derided the concept of popular sovereignty—he called it "squatter sovereignty"—and reduced it to a basic configuration: "If any one man choose to enslave another, no third man shall be allowed to object." As for the *Dred Scott* decision, Lincoln worried that it had created "a nice little niche" for future courts to legalize slavery throughout the Union. "We shall lie down pleasantly dreaming that the people of Missouri are on the verge of making their state free," he warned, "and we shall awake to the reality instead that the Supreme Court has made Illinois a slave state."[46]

Continuing the somewhat labored conceit about house building, Lincoln posited a conspiracy to extend slavery by a quartet of carpenters whom he named "Stephen, Franklin, Roger and James"—meaning Douglas, Pierce, Taney, and Buchanan. These illusive carpenters "all understood one another from the beginning, and all worked upon a common plan or draft drawn up before the first blow was struck." Lincoln rejected the thinking, so dangerous to his own ambitions, that Douglas was "the aptest instrument" to oppose the spread of slavery through his "little quarrel" with the Buchanan administration over Kansas's Lecompton Constitution. "They remind us that he is a great man, and that the largest of us are very small ones," Lincoln said. "Let this be granted. But 'a living dog is better than a dead lion.' Judge Douglas, if not a dead lion . . . is at least a caged and toothless one. How can he oppose the advances of slavery? He don't care anything about it. . . . He is not now with us—he does not pretend to be." The real work of opposing slavery, he said, must be left to the Republican Party's "own undoubted friends—those whose hands are free, whose hearts are in the work—who do care for the result."[47]

◆ ◆ ◆

When Douglas heard that the Republicans had nominated Lincoln, he was not surprised. "I shall have my hands full," he told Pennsylvania editor John W. Forney. "He is the strong man of his party—full of wit, facts, dates—and the best stump speaker, with his droll ways and dry jokes, in the West. He is as honest as he is shrewd, and if I beat him my victory will be hardly won." The first step was to address Lincoln's most recent charges. Speaking from the balcony of the Tremont House in Chicago, Douglas lit into his longtime opponent. "It is no answer to say that slavery is an evil and hence should not be tolerated," he said. "You must allow the people to decide for themselves whether it is a good or an evil." Lincoln, he said, was a "kind, amiable, and intelligent gentleman, a good citizen and an honorable opponent," but he was dead wrong to contend that the nation had to be either all slave or all free. Such a stance, warned Douglas, was nothing less than a call for "a war of sections, a war of the North against the South, of the free states against the slave states." As for Lincoln's criticism of the *Dred Scott* decision, Douglas came down on the side of the Supreme Court, which he said shared his views on race. "I am free to say to you," Douglas boomed, "that in my opinion this government of ours is founded on the white basis. It was made by the white man, for the benefit of the white man, to be administered by white men, in such manner as they should determine." Unlike his Republican counterpart, he was opposed to black equality, "political or social, or in any other respect whatever."[48]

✦ ✦ ✦

Lincoln was encouraged by the overwhelmingly positive response to his "House Divided" speech, both locally and nationally. Many Illinois newspapers published special pocket editions of the speech, and Greeley ran Lincoln's words in the *Tribune* under the headline "REPUBLICAN PRINCIPLES." To maintain the momentum, Lincoln and his handlers hit upon the tactic of following Douglas around the state. "Speaking at the same place the next day after D[ouglas] is the very thing," Lincoln enthused. The night after Douglas's Chicago appearance, Lincoln spoke from the same Tremont House balcony the Little Giant had used. He denied forcefully that he was advocating a war between the regions—he was merely making a prediction. He also denied suggesting that "the people of the free states . . . enter into the slave states and interfere with the question of slavery." With regard to Douglas's views on "the terrible enormities that place by the mixture of the races," Lincoln repeated his quip "I do not understand that because I do not want a Negro woman for a slave, I do necessarily want her for a wife. There are white men enough to marry all the white women, and enough black men to marry all the black women." He urged: "Let us discard all this quibbling about this man and the other man—this race and that race and the other race being inferior. Let us discard all these things, and unite as one people throughout this land, until we shall once more stand up declaring that all men are created equal."[49]

From Chicago, Lincoln literally trailed in Douglas's wake, riding in a public train car behind Douglas's private coach, which was festooned with an enormous banner reading "STEPHEN A. DOUGLAS, CHAMPION OF POPULAR SOVEREIGNTY." In Joliet, a flatcar carrying a brass cannon was added to the procession, periodically blasting away as the train wove its way across the prairie. Adele Douglas joined her husband for the trip as well, adding her "queenly face and figure" to the campaign team. The Democrats were furious at Lincoln for hitching a ride on their express, but they could do nothing to stop him. The *Chicago Times* tried, ridiculing Lincoln as "a poor desperate creature [who] wants an audience. Perhaps he should join one of the two very good circuses and menageries traveling through the state, for they always bring out a considerable audience." Fellow Republican W. J. Usrey warned Lincoln that the perception was growing among voters that "Douglas takes the crowd and Lincoln the leavings."[50]

To combat that unflattering perception, Lincoln wrote personally to Douglas on July 24, proposing that they "divide time and address the same audiences during the present canvass." Douglas had no intention of sharing the same train platform or theater podium with Lincoln for the entire next three months of the campaign, but he reluctantly agreed to meet him formally seven times, in the county seats of all the state's congressional districts except the second (Chicago) and the sixth (Springfield), where in essence they already had debated. "I will, in order to accommodate you as far as it is in my power to do so, take the responsibility of making an arrangement with you for a discussion between us at one prominent point in each Congressional district in the state," Douglas responded, although he grumbled a bit that Lincoln had waited until he had already finalized his campaign schedule. Lincoln, canny lawyer that he was, immediately took yes for an answer, agreeing to the proposed timetable of appearances and promising, for his part, not to attend any more of Douglas's "exclusive meetings." The stage was set for what history would term, with admirable hindsight in reverse alphabetical order, the Lincoln-Douglas debates.[51]

5

Thunder Tones

Under the guidelines Douglas set down, he and Lincoln would meet seven times over the course of the next seven weeks. The first debate was slated for Ottawa, eighty miles southwest of Chicago in the north-central part of the state. It was reliable Republican territory, and as such presented Lincoln with the opportunity to get his campaign off to a running start. On August 20, the day before the scheduled meeting, huge crowds of people began flocking into the little town, which sat between the Fox and Illinois rivers on the Illinois and Michigan Canal. Ottawa's entire population was less than 9,000 people, but the town tripled in size by the time of the debate. It quickly took on the trappings of a giant religious revival. Men, women, and children poured into town on foot, on horseback, in wagons and carriages, by special trains, even aboard canal boats blazing with political banners. Hundreds of tents spread out in the fields outside of town, and by nightfall a spangle of campfires twinkled in the darkness like the picketed bivouacs of an enemy army on the march.[1]

By eight o'clock the next morning, Ottawa seemed like "a vast smoke house," in the words of the *Chicago Tribune* correspondent, cloaked by smothering clouds of dust kicked up by the tramping crowds. Militia companies and marching bands pushed through the throngs and set up a pair of brass cannons that began banging away, unmindful of the civilians swarming around them. The two candidates arrived separately. Lincoln came by train from Chicago, pulling in at noon to the Rock Island Railroad depot, where he was met by Ottawa mayor Joseph O. Glover and escorted to Glover's home by a half-mile-long parade of supporters. Douglas entered town from the west, his elegant carriage drawn by six white horses. Like Lincoln, he opted to freshen up before the debate, checking into the Geiger House while his backers trudged back and forth in front of the hotel, hurrahing their hero and generally raising hell.[2]

The debate was scheduled to begin at 2:00 p.m., and the audience crammed into Lafayette Square an hour ahead of time. There were no chairs and few trees, and the late-summer sun pounded down relentlessly on everyone. Vendors did a land-rush business in water and lemonade; more potent liquids were also available. No one had thought to guard the stage, a simple platform of unfinished wood topped by a flimsy awning from which dangled half a dozen village "clowns." The stage was so crowded that it took a good thirty minutes to clear a space for local dignitaries, who had no sooner taken their seats than the awning gave way, toppling the revelers into their laps. The candidates arrived to loud cheers a few minutes later, climbing with difficulty onto the jam-packed platform. Lincoln sat at the end of the front row, a carpetbag filled with notes and copies of speeches at his feet, while Douglas stepped to the front of the stage. He was dressed, planter-style, in a wide-brimmed white hat, ruffled shirt, light trousers, and dark-blue coat with polished buttons. Under the agreed-upon format, Douglas would speak first for an hour, Lincoln would have ninety minutes to respond, and Douglas would conclude with a thirty-minute rebuttal. The order would alternate at each debate.[3]

Having faced Lincoln many times in the past, Douglas determined immediately to take the offensive. Like a prosecuting attorney confronting a petty sheep stealer, he threw a series of sharp questions at his startled opponent, demanding to know Lincoln's positions on the Fugitive Slave Act, the slave trade in general, the admission of new slave states to the Union, and popular sovereignty in the territories. Beginning a theme that would run through the debates, Douglas raised the doleful specter of black citizenship, charging that the Republicans favored bestowing full civil rights on blacks, a move he warned would "cover our prairies with [black] settlements" and would "turn this beautiful state into a free

Negro colony. I do not question Mr. Lincoln's conscientious belief that the Negro was made his equal, and hence his brother," Douglas continued. "But for my own part, I do not regard the Negro as my equal, and positively deny that he is my brother or any kin to me whatever."[4]

Thrown off balance by the Little Giant's opening gambit, Lincoln began poorly, denying that he had conspired with Lyman Trumbull in 1854 to capture the state's two Senate seats and form a new abolitionist party, and reading a stultifying seven-minute-long excerpt from a four-year-old speech in Peoria. Unsure of his tone, Lincoln wavered between folksy self-deprecation and arcane legalese, noting at one point: "I demur to that plea—I waive all objections because it was not filed until after default was taken." As further evidence of his unsteadiness, Lincoln twice used the word "nigger" at Ottawa, something he rarely did in public or private. Douglas's attempt to twist his views, Lincoln said, was "but a specious and fantastic arrangement of words, by which a man can prove a horse chestnut to be a chestnut horse." As for the charge that he favored black equality, Lincoln asserted: "I have no disposition to introduce political and social equality between the white and the black races. There is a physical difference between the two, which in my judgment will probably forever forbid their living together on terms of respect, social and political equality." Along with Douglas, "I am in favor of the race to which I belong having the superior position," Lincoln said, but maintained that "in the right to eat the bread which his own hand earns, he is my own equal and Judge Douglas's equal, and the equal of every living man." When someone in the crowd shouted out that he was a fool, Lincoln responded dryly, "Well, that may be, and I guess there are two of us."[5]

The candidates presented diametrically opposite images. Douglas was all clenched fists and high dudgeon, shouting out accusations in his surprisingly deep voice. Lincoln with a comparatively higher, shriller voice, presented a more unpolished stage presence, fumbling with his glasses—"I am no longer a young man"—and bending awkwardly at the knees before suddenly springing upward in an ungainly but compelling gesture of emphasis. Three times during Douglas's rebuttal Lincoln attempted to interrupt, creating enough of a scene to cause two Republican committeemen on stage to pull him back and hiss: "What are you making such a fuss for? Douglas didn't interrupt you, and can't you see that the people don't like it?" With some difficulty, the usually placid

Lincoln managed to rein in his temper. Although he had as much experience giving political speeches (and a good deal more in presenting cases in courtrooms), Lincoln gave the appearance of fumbling for the right words, sometimes "stopping for repairs before finishing a sentence." Both he and Douglas, Lincoln said later, were speaking in "thunder tones" for the audience.[6]

After the debate Lincoln was carried off on the shoulders of his supporters, his long underwear showing beneath his pulled-up pant legs. The partisan press judged the outcome along predictable party lines. The Democratic-leaning *Chicago Times* found Douglas's "excoriation of Lincoln" to have been "so severe, that the Republicans hung their heads in shame," while Republican newspapers thought Lincoln appeared "high toned" and "powerful" in the face of the senator's "boorish" assaults. Horace Greeley anointed the debate as nothing less than "a contest for the Kingdom of Heaven or the Kingdom of Satan—a contest for advance or retrograde in civilization."[7]

Lincoln would not have gone that far, and he was sufficiently worried about his performance at Ottawa to convene an unusual meeting of his brain trust in Chicago a few days later. While pronouncing himself reasonably satisfied with the outcome of the debate—"The fire flew some, and I am glad to know I am yet alive"—he invited suggestions on how he could improve. *Chicago Tribune* editor Joseph Medill, a longtime supporter, urged Lincoln to be more aggressive. "Don't act on the defensive at all," he advised; instead, "hold Dug up as a traitor and conspirator [and] a pro-slavery bamboozling demagogue." Fellow staffer Charles Ray told Republican congressman Elihu Washburne, in whose district the next debate would take place: "When you see Abe at Freeport, for God's sake tell him to 'Charge, Chester! Charge!' Do not let him keep on the defensive. We must not be parrying all the while. We want the deadliest thrusts. Let us see blood follow any time he closes a sentence." Medill concluded that Lincoln should "put a few ugly questions" of his own to Douglas. "You are dealing with a bold, brazen, lying rascal and you must fight the devil with fire. Give him h—l."[8]

The second debate was scheduled for August 27 in Freeport, six hours by train from Chicago and a few miles from the Wisconsin border. The candidates arrived to the already standard salvos of cannon fire and parading supporters and set up camp at the Brewster House. It was a damp, overcast day, but 15,000 men and women—twice the town's population—flocked into a vacant lot near the banks of the Pecatonica River, where another crude platform had been erected between two trees. Lincoln arrived atop a Conestoga wagon, accompanied by an honor guard of humble farmers to emphasis his rural roots. Douglas, scorning Lincoln's "burlesque" appearance, walked over to the square unattended from the hotel. Once again, uninvited guests thronged the stage, which was festooned with signs reading "All Men Are Created Equal," "Douglas and Popular Sovereignty," and "No Nigger Equality." A watermelon rind arced through the crowd and struck Douglas in the shoulder as he prepared to speak.[9]

Lincoln, with the opening honors, sought to respond to Douglas's "seven distinct interrogatories" from the previous debate. He denied favoring repeal of the Fugitive Slave Law, the abolition of slavery in the District of Columbia, the prohibition of slave trade between the territories, or the admission of new slave states to the Union. He did not oppose the right of people within a new state to draft "such a constitution as they may see fit to make," but he supported the right of Congress to prohibit slavery in all territories. As for the question of whether he opposed acquiring new territories unless slavery was first prohibited within them, Lincoln waffled, saying, "I would or would not oppose such acquisition, according as I might think such acquisition would or would not aggravate the slavery question among ourselves." Then he put four questions of his own to Douglas, the second of which became instantly famous as the culminating point of the entire series of debates: "Can the people of a United States territory, in any lawful way, against the wish of any citizen of the United States, exclude slavery from its limits prior to the formulation of a state constitution?" This was the reef upon which Douglas had marooned himself with the Buchanan administration over the Lecompton Constitution. After complaining, with some justification, that he had spent the better part of two years already making his position clear on that question, Douglas reiterated his view that the people of a territory "have the lawful means to introduce [slavery] or exclude it as they please, for the reason that slavery cannot exist a day or an hour anywhere, unless it is supported by local police regulations. Those police regulations can only be established by the local legislature, and if the people are opposed to slavery they will elect representatives to that body who will by unfriendly legislation effectually prevent the introduction of it into their midst."[10]

Douglas's response became famous—or infamous, depending upon one's views—as the "Freeport Doctrine." A legend grew in Lincoln circles that their candidate had brilliantly trapped his opponent into making a fatal mistake. Some even claimed that Lincoln was looking ahead to the presidential election two years later and had designed the question as a way of alienating Douglas from southern Democrats and splitting the party. "I am after bigger game," Lincoln supposedly said at the time. Such an overelaborate theory ignores the fact that Lincoln had asked Douglas the same question in Chicago four months earlier, and Republican newspapers had been hammering away at the same point for months. At any rate, Douglas's standing could scarcely fall much lower in the South, and it was the Senate seat in Illinois that he was after. Still, Douglas was sufficiently unnerved by Lincoln's question to fall back immediately on the race card, reminding the audience that the last time he had been in Freeport he had seen black abolitionist Frederick Douglass riding through town in a fancy carriage with a white woman. "If you Black Republicans think that the Negro ought to be on a social equality with young wives and daughters, and ride in the carriage with the wife while the master of the carriage drives the team, you have a perfect right to do so," said Douglas. "All I have got to say on that subject is this, those of you who believe that the nigger is your equal, and ought to be on an equality with you socially, politically and legally, have a right to entertain those opinions, and of course will vote for Mr. Lincoln." Such overt racism was a bit over the top, even for Douglas. It was not so much that he was a racist (by modern standards, anyway), but that, like much of white America a century and a half ago, he simply could not envision blacks in anything like an equal role. Nevertheless, it reflected poorly on what Martin Luther King, in another context, would term "the content of his character." Frederick Douglass, for his part, entertained the opinion that "no man of his time has done more than [Douglas] to intensify hatred of the Negro."[11]

From Freeport, the candidates descended into the southernmost part of the state, nicknamed Egypt after its best-known town, Cairo (pronounced, frontier-style, Kay-Ro). Jonesboro, the site of the third debate on September 15, was safe territory for Douglas and the Democrats—Republican nominee John C. Frémont had won less than 4 percent of the vote in the last presidential election—but it was also so isolated that only 800 people lived there. Further depressing the turnout was the fact that the state fair was under way in nearby Centralia, and many local farmers opted to view giant rutabagas and fattened hogs instead of more prosaic senatorial candidates. Only about 1,500 people turned out to hear the debate, which was heralded by another flamboyant Douglas arrival punctuated by a brass cannon that filled the air, the disapproving *Chicago Tribune* reported, with "a loud noise and a bad smell."[12]

Douglas opened the debate by repeating at tiresome length his already familiar charge that Lincoln, Trumbull, and other like-minded politicians had conspired to subvert the Whigs and Democrats under "the black flag of Abolitionism." With the help of such "high priests of Abolitionism" as congressmen Joshua Giddings and Owen Lovejoy, Douglas charged, the Republicans had deposed his good friend James Shields from the Senate and replaced him with Trumbull. Now they were trying to do the same with Lincoln. "Suppose Mr. Lincoln should die, what a horrible condition would they be in," Douglas ventured—allowing his opponent to steal a laugh from the pro-Democratic crowd by loudly groaning in mock horror at the thought. Quoting Lincoln's House Divided speech, Douglas charged that Lincoln was "inviting a warfare between the North and South, to be carried out with ruthless vengeance." Such language subverted both the meaning and intent of the Declaration of Independence, Douglas said, since it implied that the Founding Fathers had included blacks in their formulations. "In my opinion the signers of the Declaration of Independence had no reference whatever to the Negro, when they declared all men to have been created equal," Douglas said. "The signers of the Declaration were white men, of European birth and European descent, and had no reference either to the Negro or to savage Indians, or the Feegee, or the Malay, or any other inferior or degraded race, when they spoke of the equality of men."[13]

This time Lincoln did not rise to the bait and lose his temper. When he was greeted by a feeble cheer from a handful of Republican supporters, he asked the Democratic majority, "I hope you won't make fun of the few friends I have here." He agreed with Douglas, Lincoln said, that the individual states were free "to do exactly as they please" about slavery. Where he disagreed was in the notion that the framers had intended for slavery to spread into new territories. "I say the way in which our fathers left this subject of slavery was in the course of ultimate extinction." Lincoln finished his brief remarks with ten minutes to spare. "We fancy he has had enough of Egypt," opined the *Chicago Times*, "and certainly Egypt has had enough of him."[14]

Three days later, Lincoln was on friendly soil again when the campaign pulled into Charleston, in the extreme eastern part of the state. Indeed, he was something of a favorite son, having immigrated to Coles County from nearby Indiana with his family at the age of nineteen. His stepmother, Sarah Bush Johnston Lincoln, still lived in a cabin there. An eighty-foot-long banner hanging across Main Street depicted the young Lincoln driving an oxcart into the village. "Abe's Entrance into Charleston Thirty Years Ago," it proclaimed. Other banners hung from doorways, shop windows, and rooftops, including one showing Lincoln clubbing a cringing Little Giant into submission. Douglas threatened to leave at once when he saw the offending poster, but rallying his forces, he moved through town at the head of a brass band and a pulchritudinous parade of thirty-two young women representing each state in the Union. Lincoln's parade also featured a wagonload of pretty girls—it seemed to be the theme of the day—sporting a banner proclaiming "Girls Link-on to Lincoln." One wonders what Mary Lincoln would have made of the spectacle.[15]

The subsequent debate was held at the agricultural society fairgrounds before a huge crowd of nearly 15,000 people. Perhaps provoked by an enormous Democratic banner depicting "Negro Equality" with a drawing of a white man, a black woman, and a mulatto child, Lincoln opened his remarks with an apocryphal question from "an elderly gentleman" who had asked him "whether I was really in favor of producing a perfect equality between the Negroes and the white people." With the unpersuasive disclaimer that he had not intended to say much about the issue, Lincoln proceeded to say too much. "I am not nor ever have been in favor of bringing about in any way, the social and political equality of the white and black races," he said. "I am not, nor ever have been in favor of making voters of the Negroes, or jurors, or qualifying them to hold office, or having them to marry with white people." Physical differences between the races "will forever forbid the two races living together upon terms of social and political equality," he said, "and I as much as any other man am in favor of the superior position being assigned to the white man." In a comment that still lingers unhappily in Lincoln lore like a bad joke told at a funeral, he went on: "I do not understand that because I do not want a Negro woman for a slave I must necessarily want her for a wife. My understanding is that I can just leave her alone." The only person he knew for a fact to favor perfect equality between the races, Lincoln said somewhat snidely, was "my friend Douglas's old friend, Colonel Richard M. Johnson [whose long-standing affair with a mulatto mistress was common knowledge]."[16]

Lincoln couldn't seem to stop himself. Encouraged by laughter from the crowd, he continued to make jokes on the topic of race mixing. "I have never had the least apprehension that I or my friends would marry Negroes if there was no law to keep them from it," he said, "but as my friend Douglas and his friends seem to be under great apprehension that maybe they might, if there was no law to keep them from it, I give him the most solemn pledge that I will to the very last stand by the law in this state that forbids the marriage of white folks with Negroes." He recommended that Douglas be returned to the state legislature, which Lincoln said was the only body that could legally change Illinois's existing miscegenation laws.[17]

Douglas responded drolly that he was "glad to have got an answer from him on that proposition," adding, "I have been trying to get him to answer that point during the whole time that the canvass has been going on." The rest of the debate was spent rehashing the charges and countercharges revolving around Douglas's alleged inconsistency over the issue of popular sovereignty in Kansas. A girl on horseback had trailed Lincoln's parade into town, carrying a banner proclaiming "Kansas—I will be free," and Douglas devoted most of his time to refuting a charge made by Lyman Trumbull that he was conspiring with the Buchanan administration to sneak slavery into the Sunflower State. "I thought I was running against Abraham Lincoln," Douglas complained. "His only hope is that he is going to ride into office on Trumbull's back." Both Lincoln and Trumbull, said Douglas, varied their principles to fit their surroundings. In the northern part of the state, he continued, "their principles are jet black; when you get down into the center they are a decent colored mulatto; when you get down into lower Egypt they are almost white." Having already talked himself into a corner with his opening remarks, Lincoln wisely chose to ignore the charge.[18]

The largest crowd of the debates assembled three weeks later, on October 7, at Galesburg, in the northwestern part of the state. An estimated 15,000 to 20,000 people braved the "Arctic frost" and biting winds that shredded posters and sent signs skidding pell-mell through the streets. Once again the crowds arrived early, pitching tents on the outskirts of town and waiting out the cold rain the day before. The candidates made their usual entrance by train and buggy and were driven to Knox College, the scene of the debate, in side-by-side carriages. The speaker's platform had been moved from the open air to a spot alongside the college building to shield the candidates—but not the crowd—from the wind. The guests of honor had to climb through a first-floor window onto the stage, prompting Lincoln to quip: "Well, at last I have gone through college." Students from Knox and neighboring Lombard University filled the mostly pro-Lincoln crowd. Galesburg was an old stop on the Underground Railroad, and an enormous "Knox College for Lincoln" banner was draped over the building—so much for academic neutrality.[19]

The strong wind made it hard for the speakers to be heard, or even to speak. Before trying, Douglas took out a throat lozenge and politely offered one to his opponent. He reminded the crowd that Lincoln had spoken out against equal rights for blacks at Charleston and scoffed, "His creed can't travel." He charged the Republicans with entering "an unholy and unnatural combination" with the Buchanan administration to defeat his candidacy. The Republicans, he said, were guilty of creating a purely sectional organization. In a prescient bit of political foresight, Douglas looked ahead to another campaign, two years down the road, when the Republicans would "connect the northern states into one great sectional party, and inasmuch as the northern section is the stronger, the stronger section will out-vote and control and govern the weaker section."[20]

Lincoln denied that he had been inconsistent in his earlier speeches. "I have all the while maintained that inasmuch as there is a physical inequality between the white and black, that the blacks must remain inferior," he said, "but I have always maintained that in the right to life, liberty, and the pursuit of happiness, they were our equals." He contrasted his moral opposition to slavery with Douglas's pragmatic approach to property rights. "He insists, upon the score of equality, that the owner of slaves and the owner of horses should be allowed to take them alike to new territory and hold them there," Lincoln said of Douglas. "That is perfectly logical if the species of property is perfectly alike, but if you admit that one of them is wrong, then you cannot admit any equality between right and wrong. I believe that slavery is wrong. . . . There is the difference between Judge Douglas and his friends and the Republican Party."[21]

Six days later, the campaign pulled into Quincy, on the extreme western edge of Illinois, just across the Mississippi River from Missouri. Boats steamed upriver from Hannibal, Samuel Clemens's hometown, and downriver from Keokuk, Iowa, swelling the turnout to nearly 15,000 people. (Clemens, destined as Mark Twain to be dubbed "the Lincoln of our literature," was not there that day; he was off piloting riverboats in New Orleans.) Despite several days of heavy rain, visitors found the day of the debate sunny and cool. Douglas arrived the night before by private railcar, while Lincoln pulled into town on the morning of the debate and was escorted to the debate site by a parade of supporters led by a horse-drawn model of the USS *Constitution*, piloted cartoonlike by a live raccoon, the symbol of the now-extinct Whig Party. The stage in Washington Square was made of large pine boards, and before Lincoln could begin his remarks the railing gave way, sending dozens of dignitaries crashing through the stage to the ground below. No sooner had they been helped to their feet than another bench, this one reserved for the ladies in attendance, also gave way, leaving them to reel dazedly, bonnets and petticoats askew, into the arms of their rescuers.[22]

Future Civil War general Carl Schurz, an important Lincoln supporter among Missouri's large German population, was less than impressed by his first sight of Lincoln. His champion was "lank," "ungainly," "uncouth," and "grotesque," Schurz observed, and toted a gray woolen shawl, a tattered umbrella, and a worn satchel. Speaking in "a shrill treble," Lincoln once again denounced slavery as a spreading evil and repeated his contention that Douglas and the Democrats were conspiring to make the practice both national and permanent. After Douglas criticized him again for alleging that the *Dred Scott* decision was part of a Democratic conspiracy, Lincoln got into a brief shouting match with a *Chicago Times* reporter in the crowd. "I don't care if your hireling does say I did," Lincoln roared, "I tell you myself that I never said the Democratic owners of Dred Scott got up the case." On that less-than-elevated note, the sixth debate came to an end.[23]

The seventh and final debate, on October 15, was notable more for its location than its attendance. Alton, 115 miles downriver from Quincy, was the site of abolitionist newspaper editor Elijah Lovejoy's murder by a proslavery crowd twenty-one years earlier. Despite the beautiful fall weather and a special $1 round-trip fare from St. Louis, only about 5,000 people—the second smallest crowd of the debates—showed up at

Alton's new city hall for the event. Perhaps, as a Cincinnati newspaper reporter observed, "the novelty had worn off" the debates. The candidates arrived together, having steamed downriver from Quincy aboard the *City of Louisiana*. Mary and Robert Lincoln were on hand for the first time, Robert sporting the quasi-military blue-and-white uniform of the Springfield Cadets. Douglas, his troublesome voice reduced again to a ragged whisper, could scarcely be heard over the crowd. He repeated his well-rehearsed litany of Republican conspiracies, sectional animosities, and white superiority, and claimed to have made Lincoln "flinch a little and back down." Quoting Lincoln's earlier statement that he "would be exceedingly sorry ever to be put in the position" of having to vote on the admission of more slave states, Douglas made one of his rare jokes during the debates: "Permit me to remark that I don't think the people will ever force him into a position where he will have to vote upon it."[24]

Buoyed by his family's presence, Lincoln delivered one of his best performances of the campaign. He conceded that Alton had "strong sympathies by birth, education, and otherwise with the South," and admitted that he was "not less selfish than other men" in seeking political office, "but I do claim that I am not more selfish than is Judge Douglas." ("Roars of laughter," the *Chicago Tribune* reported parenthetically.) The chief difference between the two camps, Lincoln said, was that one side considered slavery to be wrong, while the other did not. "That is the real issue," he concluded, "an issue that will continue in this country when these poor tongues of Douglas and myself shall be silent. These are the two principles that are made the eternal struggle between right and wrong . . . one of them asserting the divine right of kings, the same principle that says you work, you toil, you earn bread, and I will eat it. It is the same old serpent, whether it come from the mouth of a king who seeks to bestride the people of his nation, and to live upon the fat of his neighbor, or whether it comes from one race of men as apology for the enslaving of another race of men. . . . It will hereafter place with us all men who really do wish the wrong may have an end."[25]

On that note, the Lincoln-Douglas debates ended. The campaign continued for another two weeks, passing on to other towns, but the candidates made no more joint appearances. Election Day was rainy and cold, but voter turnout was large—more people voted in the various state races than had voted in the presidential election two years earlier. It was a good day for the Democrats. Counting holdovers, the party won fifty-four seats in the legislature to forty-six for the Republicans. Thanks to the split in party ranks between Douglas and Buchanan supporters, the Republicans managed to win the only statewide election, that of state treasurer, by 3,800 votes, but when the legislature gathered on January 5, 1859, to elect a United States senator, Douglas's victory was a foregone conclusion. Even the Buchananites voted for him. Informed of the results by telegram at his home in Washington, D.C., Douglas wired back majestically: "Let the voice of the people rule."[26]

✦ ✦ ✦

Douglas had triumphed. Not only had he bested his most talented and persistent rival in a punishing senatorial race highlighted by their already-famous debates. He had also held off the combined efforts of the president of the United States and his administration to challenge Douglas's place as the leading spokesman for the Democratic Party in the North. It was a doubly sweet victory, but one that came at a heavy cost. During the just concluded four-month-long campaign, Douglas had made well over 100 speeches, all but two in the open air, and traveled more than 5,000 miles by railroad, steamboat, carriage, and horseback. He had been rained on, roasted, chilled, and heckled, and his naturally strong baritone voice had been worn down to a hoarse gasp. A recurrence of bronchitis, coupled with a lack of sleep and a free-flowing whiskey tap in his private train car, added to the physical toll on the never particularly robust senator. His wife, Adele, also suffered a brief illness, and after the election her brother, J. M. Cutts, Jr., felt the need to caution: "I hope you will not find it necessary to be as active & untiring in your exertions to please this winter, and that your good husband will have less to contend with and that you both will pass a more quiet winter than the last."[27]

As always, Douglas was incapable of resting for long. In late November 1858, he and Adele set out from Chicago on a circuitous, six-week-long return to Washington. With his election by the legislature assured, the trip quickly took on the appearance of an extended victory lap. After a two-day celebration in Springfield, complete with a thirty-two-gun salute, the couple boarded the steamboat *City of Memphis* at Alton and headed down the Mississippi River to New Orleans. The first, unscheduled stop was at Memphis, where Douglas was met en route by a chartered steamer filled with local supporters urging him to come ashore and visit. He did so, and was greeted by the sight of an open slave pen filled with newly imported Africans owned by, among others, future Confederate cavalry legend Nathan Bedford Forrest. The next day, speaking to an immense throng at the Exchange Hall, the Little Giant opened with a racist, if crowd-pleasing, observation that "between the Negro and the crocodile, he took the side of the Negro. But between the Negro and the white man, he would go for the white man."[28]

The crux of Douglas's speech at Memphis, which he would repeat wherever he stopped, was the need for southerners to reject extremists in their midst. "If you deem it treason for abolitionists to appeal to the passions and prejudices of the North," he urged, "how much less treason is it, my friends, for southern men to appeal to the passions with the same end?" They should follow his lead in opposing the Lecompton Constitution in Kansas, since "the people have the right to decide the question [of slavery] for themselves. Wherever climate, soil and production combine to encourage the use of slave labor," Douglas said, "the people will accept and protect it, and wherever the circumstances do not exist, the contrary result will follow. It is visionary to talk of planting slavery where it is not wanted, and it is equal folly in the northern fanatic to attempt to exclude it where it is wanted." This was as far as Douglas could go without violating his own principle of popular sovereignty, and southern ultras, or fire-eaters, predictably found his efforts lacking. "Douglas is his name, duplicity is the chief element in his character," the Port Gibson, Mississippi, *Daily Southern Reveille* sniped. "He knows no friendship, no party, no patriotism, nothing but Stephen A. Douglas." The Mississippi Legislature, then in session at Jackson, pointedly declined to invite Douglas to appear before it.[29]

The reception was notably warmer in New Orleans, a city Douglas had visited often in the past. Upon arrival, he and Adele were led by a brass band and a military escort to their rooms at the luxurious St. Charles Hotel. Not all southerners were as welcoming. Douglas's old enemy, Louisiana senator John Slidell, termed him "the king of the thugs," and a letter writer signing himself "A Mississippi Democrat" condemned Douglas for engaging in "the lowest-down electioneering for the presidency." Speaking before a capacity crowd at the Odd Fellows Hall, Douglas clarified his previous remarks regarding the sanctity of property rights (i.e., slave owning). He had never meant to imply that a territory could legally prevent southerners from taking their slaves into it, he explained, but merely that he did not support any special form of protection for it. Perhaps to soften this message, Douglas came out in favor of the annexation of Cuba—a particular dream of southern expansionists in general and New Orleans merchants in particular. "It is our destiny to have Cuba," he said, "and it is folly to debate the question. Its acquisition is a matter of time only." He hinted that further acquisitions might also be possible in Mexico and Central America. The speech was raucously received, and Douglas and Adele were serenaded by cheering crowds and booming cannons as they departed New Orleans for Havana aboard the somewhat unfortunately named *Black Warrior* on December 12. There, Douglas consulted with government officials and placed an order for another 2,000 of his favorite cigars, while Adele luxuriated in the tropical weather. A thousand miles away, in Washington, her husband's enemies were stirring up an altogether less-agreeable climate.[30]

♦ ♦ ♦

While his erstwhile debating opponent was triumphantly touring the South, Abraham Lincoln was coming to terms with what would be his second senatorial defeat in three years. His first reaction, naturally enough, was disappointment. "I feel like the boy who stumped his toe," Lincoln told visitors to his law office in Springfield. "I am too big to cry and too badly hurt to laugh." Still, he tried to take the longer view. Recalling that on election night he had nearly lost his footing on a rain-slick footpath, Lincoln remembered telling himself then, "It's a slip and not a fall." He viewed the campaign in a similar light. "I am glad I made the late race," Lincoln wrote to his physician-friend, Dr. Anson Henry. "It gave me a hearing on the great and durable question of the age, which I could have had in no other way; and though I now sink out of view, and shall be forgotten, I believe I have made some marks which will tell for the cause of civil liberty long after I am gone." Soon, he was finding himself buoying up other disappointed supporters. "You will soon feel better," he wrote to *Chicago Press and Tribune* editor Charles H. Ray. "Another 'blow-up' is coming; and we shall have fun again." And to Henry Ashbury he vowed: "The fight must go on. The cause of civil liberty must not be surrendered at the end of *one*, or even, one *hundred* defeats."[31]

For the time being, Lincoln was unsure what direction to take. His characteristic response to defeat and disappointment was to go back to work immediately. "This year I must devote to my private business," he told Illinois Republican Party chairman Norman Judd. "I have been on expenses so long without earning anything that I am absolutely without money now for even household purposes." He resumed his legal work with Billy Herndon, appearing in the Sangamon County circuit court four days after the election to represent a client who lost a $23 settlement. His most celebrated case, and only the second murder trial he had handled, took place that summer, when Lincoln defended the grandson of his old congressional opponent, Methodist circuit rider Peter Cartwright. His client, Peachy Quinn Harrison, had fatally stabbed fellow Pleasant Plains resident Greek Crafton at a local roadhouse. As he had done in the Duff Armstrong murder case a year earlier, Lincoln won an unlikely acquittal for his client.[32]

In another instance, Lincoln was unwilling to take on a case with overt political ramifications. When former Chicago mayor "Long John" Wentworth, his recent rival for the senatorial nomination, asked Lincoln to represent him in a $100,000 libel suit filed against him by Norman Judd for accusing the chairman of mismanaging the campaign, Lincoln gingerly demurred. He had no wish to get involved in a nasty intraparty scrape between two potentially valuable allies. Instead, he helped mediate a reconciliation that kept the matter from reaching court. The more or less amicable resolution would pay unexpected dividends a few months later, when Judd attended a meeting of the Republican National Committee in New York and convinced his fellow committee members to award the upcoming presidential nominating convention to his hometown of Chicago. No one at the time, neither Judd nor Lincoln, realized quite how significant that decision would prove to be.[33]

His cautious handling of the Wentworth-Judd contretemps underscored Lincoln's inchoate but not entirely absent hopes of seeking an even higher office than the United States Senate. The idea was first broached to him in late December 1858 by Bloomington attorney Jesse Fell, who had just returned from a visit to his home state of Pennsylvania. People back east were asking, said Fell, "Who is this Lincoln we read about in the papers, who ran Douglas such a fine race?" If Lincoln somehow were able to reach such voters, perhaps by highlighting his humble personal background as a self-made man, he might become a real presidential contender. "Fell," said Lincoln, "I admit the force of much of what you say, and admit that I am ambitious, and would like to be president." But he did not see much chance of that happening. As for his background, "There is nothing in my early history that would interest you or anybody else." Nonetheless, at Fell's urging Lincoln did compose a short biographical sketch to send to newspaper editors in Pennsylvania. It was a typical bit of Lincolnian modesty: "If any personal description of me is thought desirable, it may be said, I am, in height, six feet, four inches, nearly; lean in flesh, with coarse black hair, and grey eyes—no other marks or brands recollected." He apologized to Fell for the brevity of the account. "There is not much of it," he said, "for the reason, I suppose, that there is not much of me."[34]

Still, Fell's advocacy spurred Lincoln's never-sleeping ambition. He began collecting a scrapbook of his best speeches, particularly those from the just-concluded campaign against Stephen Douglas, for possible inclusion in a book. Assiduously pasting newspaper accounts of the debates into the scrapbook, Lincoln cast about for a publisher. Initial efforts failed, mainly because Lincoln wanted the book printed in Springfield, which had no local publishing or printing facilities. Eventually, however, the Columbus, Ohio, firm of Follett, Foster & Company showed interest, and he began preparing the first edition of the long-windedly titled *Political Debates Between Hon. Abraham Lincoln and Hon. Stephen A. Douglas in the Celebrated Campaign of 1858 in Illinois.* In time, it would sell over 30,000 copies. Somewhat surprisingly for an attorney, Lincoln did not seek Douglas's permission to publish a book of their combined speeches, although Douglas was later given the last-minute opportunity—he declined—to make corrections to his own remarks.[35]

Douglas was never far from Lincoln's thoughts that winter. Despite the lasting and severe damage Lincoln had inflicted on the Little Giant during their Freeport debate, Douglas remained the strongest candidate for the Democratic presidential nomination in 1860. In his first political speech since the 1858 election, Lincoln warned Chicago Republicans not to fall victim to errant "Douglasism." The senator was playing a double game, Lincoln complained, attempting to win back disenchanted southerners while also positioning himself to appeal to northerners "as the best means of breaking down the slave power. Let the Republican Party in Illinois dally with Judge Douglas," Lincoln warned, "let them fall in behind him and make him their candidate, and they do not absorb him; he absorbs them."[36]

◆ ◆ ◆

Just then, Douglas was not worrying about appealing to Republicans, let alone absorbing them into the amorphous power of his personality. He had more immediate worries. While he and Adele were still in New Orleans, preparing to go to Cuba, the Buchanan administration made its long-anticipated move to punish the senator for his Lecompton apostasy. Senate Democrats, meeting in caucus, stripped Douglas of his chairmanship of the Committee on Territories, which he had led for eleven eventful years. Under his enthusiastic expansionism, the states of Texas, Iowa, Wisconsin, California, Minnesota, and Oregon had been admitted to the Union, and the territories of Washington, Utah, New Mexico, Kansas, and Nebraska had been organized for admission. The size of the nation had more than doubled. Nevertheless, Buchanan and his southern backers took advantage of Douglas's absence and gave his place to Missouri senator James S. Green, a well-known defender of slavery. Douglas supporters quickly denounced the move as a "piece of low flung meanness and malevolence," instigated by "the old fossil that presides at the White House," but for the time being there was nothing they or Douglas could do about it.[37]

Continuing northward, Douglas and Adele arrived in New York City on December 30. They were met by another large and affectionate crowd, and the next day thousands braved a cold, driving rain outside City Hall to cheer the senator. "There can be no doubt," observed the *New York Tribune*, "that Mr. Douglas is now, *par excellence*, the representative man of the Democracy of the Free States." As if to underscore that judgment, thousands more turned out to greet the Little Giant in Philadelphia, where he was the guest of honor at a dinner held in Independence Hall (Douglas took the opportunity to creatively describe the American Revolution as a struggle for popular sovereignty). Finally, on January 6, 1859, the Douglases pulled into Washington, and a bevy of supporters escorted them to their brightly lit mansion. In response to rumors that southern ultras were planning to assassinate him, Douglas had taken the prudent step of hiring a professional bodyguard, Major Tom Hawkins of Kentucky, reputed to be one of the best pistol shots in the country. Whether or not he told Adele about the threats is doubtful.[38]

Advisers urged Douglas to treat his removal as chairman of the Committee on Territories "with dignified contempt." His brother-in-law Julius Granger cautioned: "Do not come here and pitch into all those that deserve it. You are great in a row, but your rows are so devilishly magnificent that you can't get over them the same day." Ohio editor James B. Steedman concurred. "For God's sake, Judge," he wrote to Douglas, "don't evince any feelings about the petty persecution of the Senate in deposing you from the head of your committee. Bear it with Christian resignation." It was good advice to give, but hard advice to follow. When Douglas set foot in the newly remodeled Senate chamber on January 10, he was met with a "studiously cold and distant" reception from many Democrats. Southern senators Jefferson Davis of Mississippi and Clement Clay of Alabama wanly offered their hands, but most Buchanan supporters treated Douglas with icy contempt.[39]

Indiana senator Graham Fitch, another Buchanan loyalist, quickly jumped on Douglas, taking studied umbrage at Douglas's statement that the current slate of federal officeholders in Illinois was both incompetent and corrupt. Fitch's son was one such officeholder, and Fitch demanded that Douglas retract the statement. Seven separate notes flew between the senators in four days' time, and seconds were chosen for a possible duel, but at the last minute Fitch pronounced himself satisfied—perhaps because Major Hawkins was Douglas's designated second and had let it be known that he would take the senator's death personally. The various quarrels carried over to the Douglases' social life. That winter Adele hosted a grand ball at the couple's mansion on Minnesota Row. Some 1,200 invitations went out, and most were gladly accepted. But every member of the president's cabinet—to say nothing of the president himself—managed to have other things to do on the night of the ball.[40]

Tensions came to a head during an acrimonious session of the Senate on February 23. Southern ultras pressured Douglas to explain his Freeport Doctrine, which they said put southern property rights—their ownership of slaves—at grave risk in the new territories. Mississippi senator Albert Gallatin Brown, a personal friend of Douglas who professed agreement with him "in all things save niggers," insisted that Congress had an obligation to provide adequate protection to slaveholders in the territories. Fellow Mississippian Jefferson Davis leaped into the fray, charging that Douglas's concept of popular sovereignty was "a delusive gauze thrown over the public's mind." It was, Davis continued, "a siren's song[,] a thing shadowy and fleeting, changing its color as often as the chameleon." Douglas countered that Congress had never passed a criminal or a property code for any federal territory—why should it start with slavery? Furthermore, he warned, no Democratic presidential candidate would carry a single northern state "on the platform that it is the duty of the federal government to force the people of a territory to have slavery where they do not want it." That position, shouted Davis, was "full of heresy."[41]

In the end, the Senate failed to pass a federal slave code of any sort during the session, and a Douglas-sponsored bill to establish land-grant agricultural colleges was punitively vetoed by Buchanan. No measure favored by northern Democrats, whether a bill to fund the transcontinental railroad, improve rivers and harbors, or provide land for western homesteaders, passed the Senate. The *Washington States and Union* complained that "there is no such entity as a Democratic party." As for Douglas, he was unutterably weary of southern efforts to provoke him into making ill-considered and damaging remarks. "I have no taste for this childish amusement," he said with what was, for him, lordly restraint. He refuted continuing rumors that he was planning to leave the Democratic Party and defect to the Republicans. "I have no idea of leaving," he said. "I intend to stand here in my place, for the next six years, battling for those principles to which so much of my life has been devoted, and to which I am ready to devote the balance." That was just what his opponents feared the most.[42]

◆ ◆ ◆

Having painted Douglas into a corner with southerners at Freeport (or induced him to paint himself into a corner, which was equally satisfying), Lincoln watched his old rival's vicissitudes from a distance. "He cares nothing for the South—he knows he is already dead there," Lincoln observed, adding that Douglas, like the inveterate gambler he was, still would "play all his chances" and seek the presidential nomination. Douglas's first step was an open letter to Iowa supporter J. B. Dorr, owner and editor of the *Dubuque Herald and Express*. Dorr had written to ask a clarification of the senator's position with regard to the 1860 race. On June 22, Douglas responded with what was, in essence, a declaration of his candidacy—and a declaration of war on southern extremists. He was willing to accept the Democratic nomination, Douglas said, on a platform supporting the Compromise of 1850, the Kansas-Nebraska Act of 1854, and the somewhat ambiguous endorsement of popular sovereignty contained in the 1856 party platform. He would not accept the nomination on any platform calling for a national slave code, revival of the slave trade, or congressional interference in the rights of territories to permit or prohibit slavery within their own borders.[43]

With the Dorr letter, Douglas staked his hopes for the nomination on his proven support in the North, along with whatever inroads he could make with southern moderates. Ultras, predictably, were furious. The *Weekly Mississippian* editorialized that Douglas "would rather rule in Hell than serve in Heaven." Slidell fumed that the letter "breathes that spirit of intolerable arrogance which has always characterized him." The president agreed. "Like other men who have left the Democratic Party," wrote Buchanan, "he has become bewildered & has involved himself in the most absurd contradictions." The fact that Douglas had not left the party apparently constituted no such contradiction. Supporters rallied to the senator's side, although some cautioned Douglas to leave well enough alone. "You must quit writing letters," Steedman urged from Ohio. "Write no more platform letters. Every man in the nation knows precisely what your platform is."[44]

Douglas, however, was not content to stand on his record. In the September issue of *Harper's Magazine* he published a turgid, 20,000-word article entitled "The Dividing Line Between Federal and Local Authority: Popular Sovereignty in the Territories," in which he laboriously attempted to sketch the historical basis for popular sovereignty. Returning to the theme he had broached first during his dinner at Independence Hall, Douglas maintained that the American Revolution had been fought primarily over the issue of the colonies' right to govern themselves. That would have been news, no doubt, to the Founding Fathers, whom Douglas painted somewhat unconvincingly as resolute states' righters. The patriots, he maintained, had fought the king for the privilege "to make their own local laws, form their own domestic institutions, and manage their own internal affairs in their own way." With the help of friendly historian George Bancroft, Douglas threw in various examples of colonial attempts to reserve rights unto themselves, neglecting to mention that neither the king nor the Parliament had ever recognized such rights in the first place. Once again, southern extremists railed at Douglas. The essay, said the *Richmond Enquirer*, was "an incendiary document" that represented "the most dangerous phase which anti-slavery agitation has yet assumed."[45]

For once southerners agreed with Abraham Lincoln, who termed the essay "errant folly" and described its author as "the most dangerous enemy of liberty, because the most invidious one." In mid-September, Lincoln accepted an invitation from the Ohio Republican Party to visit the state and "head off the little gentleman"—meaning Douglas—who was already stumping Ohio in behalf of Democratic senator George Pugh. "In casting about for some proper person to reply to Mr. Douglas," enthused the *Chicago Daily Press and Tribune*, "the Republicans of Ohio have selected the right man for the right place. Douglas's Popular Sovereignty will not be worth the cost of getting out the patient once ventilated by Lincoln." As he had done prior to the Great Debates the year before, Lincoln shadowed Douglas like a bad conscience, following the advice of *Tribune* owner and editor Joseph Medill to "hit below the belt as well as above, and kick like thunder." The two men made separate campaign appearances at Columbus, Cincinnati, and Wooster, with Douglas propounding his new historical reading of popular sovereignty and Lincoln cross-examining his opponent's claims like the good trial lawyer he was. When Douglas asserted at Wooster that slavery was "a local question," and that he had dealt with it "as a political question involving questions of public policy," Lincoln responded mockingly that it was indeed "one of those little unimportant trivial matters which are of just as much consequence as the question would be to me whether my neighbor should raise horned cattle or plant tobacco." As for the overriding concept of popular sovereignty, Lincoln reduced it to its most basic construction: "If one man chooses to make a slave of another man, neither that other man nor anybody else has a right to object." In the end, Ohio, an important bellwether state for the 1860 presidential election, went overwhelmingly Republican, giving the GOP the governorship and both houses of the legislature and setting the stage for arch-abolitionist Salmon P. Chase's return to the Senate in 1860.[46]

♦ ♦ ♦

By the time Ohioans voted, Douglas was back in Washington, with more important things on his mind than the outcome of a state election. On the last day of September, Adele gave birth to their daughter, Ellen. It was a difficult labor, and Adele, who had suffered a previous miscarriage, fell desperately ill with puerperal fever. Having lost his first wife to childbirth nearly six years earlier, Douglas was beside himself with worry.

For the next six weeks, as Adele struggled for her life, he rarely left her bedside. The new mother eventually recovered, but Douglas fell ill himself with rheumatism and bronchitis, which he attributed to the capital's "nauseating" creeks. There were rumors that he, too, might die—wishful thinking, perhaps, on the part of the president and his acolytes.[47]

Instead, Douglas recovered slowly. In mid-October, he was shaken by news from California that one of his most loyal supporters, Golden State senator David Broderick, had been murdered by a proadministration hothead named David Terry, a former state supreme court justice. Terry, who had been defeated for reelection to the bench, blamed Broderick for his loss. He accused his erstwhile friend of "following the wrong Douglas"—meaning Frederick, not Stephen—and challenged Broderick to a duel. The two men met at Lake Merced, south of San Francisco, where Broderick's pistol discharged prematurely (it had been filed to a hair-trigger's point by Terry prior to the duel). Terry then calmly put a bullet in Broderick's chest, and the senator fell to the sand mortally wounded. Broderick was an avid amateur actor, and his last words were appropriately theatrical. "They have killed me because I was opposed to the extension of slavery and a corrupt administration," he moaned. Suddenly, Douglas's hiring of a bodyguard did not look so paranoid.[48]

Broderick's death, sensational though it was, soon was overshadowed by an even more shocking crime. On October 16, former Kansas troublemaker John Brown descended on the western Virginia town of Harpers Ferry, where he intended to seize the U.S. Army arsenal and use the weapons to arm southern slaves for a full-scale revolt. Kansas had been comparatively quiet since the new antislavery legislature took office earlier that year, and Brown had decided to take the war back east, into the heart of the slaveholders' country. Buttressed by funds from a covey of New England abolitionists known as "the Secret Six," Brown rented a cabin in nearby Maryland and stockpiled a supply of rifles, pistols, and medieval pikes, ten-foot-long barbed poles. The subsequent raid was a fiasco. Brown and his henchmen broke into the armory easily enough, but were surrounded immediately by enraged townspeople. The next day a force of 2,000 federal troops commanded by Mexican War hero Robert E. Lee arrived and fought its way into the arsenal, wounding and capturing Brown and his accomplices. The members of the Secret Six, exhibiting rather less courage than Brown, either fled to Europe or

Canada. One feigned insanity and checked himself into a mental institution while he waited to see if Old Osawatomie would implicate him in the raid.[49]

Brown's raid, as intended, shook the nation. "When I strike, the bees will begin to swarm," he had predicted to Frederick Douglass, who had wisely declined to take part in it. Southerners, their memories still raw from the Nat Turner slave rebellion nearly three decades earlier, were beside themselves with anger and fear. "Defend yourselves!" Georgia senator Robert Toombs warned. "The enemy is at your door." Douglas, still recovering from his recent illness, castigated the raid as "a monstrous and wicked outrage" and "the natural, logical, inevitable result of the doctrines and teachings of the Republican party." He named no names, but the *Springfield State Register* in Abraham Lincoln's hometown had less compunction. Brown and his "black republican marauders," said the newspaper, had undertaken the attack with at least the tacit backing of party leaders. "Their open-mouthed treason, which culminates in precisely such outrages as that at Harper's Ferry, is but the logical sequence of the teachings of Wm. H. Seward and Abraham Lincoln—the one boldly proclaiming an 'irrepressible conflict' between certain states of the Union, and the other declaring from stump and hustings that the Union cannot continue as the fathers made it—part slave and part free."[50]

Lincoln and other Republican leaders found themselves on the horns of a dilemma. They condemned the deranged violence of Brown's act, but they also understood the rationale—at least in the abstract—for such a deed. Lincoln, with perhaps more honesty than tact, described Brown as a man of "great courage [and] rare unselfishness." He rejected Democratic charges that his party was responsible in any way for the raid at Harpers Ferry. "You charge that we stir up insurrection among your slaves," he said. "We deny it; and what is your proof? Harpers Ferry! John Brown! John Brown was no Republican; and you have failed to implicate a single Republican in his Harpers Ferry enterprise." That was technically right, since Brown had refused to divulge his Secret Six backers, but there was a certain disingenuousness to Lincoln's argument. For years, he had been warning that divided houses would fall and charging that slavery was a moral evil. When an extremist such as Brown took such warnings seriously and set out to redress the evil in the best way he knew how—sneaking raids and pitiless murder—neither Lincoln nor any other northern leader could convincingly plead complete innocence.[51]

Brown was hanged on December 2, having never revealed his influential backers. Northern reaction to his execution further enraged southerners. The multiple murderer was apotheosized as nothing less than a martyr and hero. Across the North, church bells tolled the hour of his death, and 100-gun salutes boomed in his honor. Public speeches and prayer meetings drew large, bewailing crowds. The notably irreligious Henry David Thoreau attended a church service in Concord, Massachusetts, with fellow abolitionist Ralph Waldo Emerson and emerged to pronounce solemnly: "Some eighteen hundred years ago Christ was crucified. This morning John Brown was hung. These are two ends of a chain which is not without its links." Emerson, not to be outdone, effused that "the old warrior will make the gallows as glorious as the cross." *New York Evening Post* editor William Cullen Bryant predicted that history would forget "the errors of his judgment" and remember merely "the nobleness of his aims." There was, of course, no comment from the victims of his errors. Southern leaders watched the deification with disgust and wonder. "Disguise it as you will," Albert Gallatin Brown observed, "there is throughout all the non slaveholding states of this Union a secret, deep-rooted sympathy with the object this man had in mind." Fittingly, perhaps, Brown himself had the last word, leaving behind a brief final testament: "I, John Brown, am now quite certain that the crimes of this guilty land will never be purged away but with blood." It was less a prediction than a curse, and it would come true soon enough—sooner, indeed, than anyone expected.[52]

6

⚜

Gentlemen of the South,
You Mistake Us

Lincoln was traveling through Kansas—of all places—when John Brown was executed. The next day he told a crowd at Leavenworth that he believed the hanging was justified, "even though he agreed with us that slavery is wrong. That cannot excuse violence, bloodshed, and treason." But Lincoln denounced any attempt to link Brown's actions to the Republican Party as a mere "electioneering dodge," and he pointedly warned any southerners who might be considering secession after the next presidential election: "If constitutionally we elect a president and therefore you undertake to destroy the Union, it will be our duty to deal with you as old John Brown has been dealt with." Besides Leavenworth, Lincoln also visited Elwood, Troy, Doniphan, and Atchison, Kansas, during the first week in December. While modestly denying any interest in the 1860 presidential nomination, Lincoln, like all good politicians, was keeping his options open.[1]

By far his most important appearance came in February 1860, when he addressed the Young Men's Central Republican Union in New York City. Defining youth rather liberally—members included sixty-five-year-old William Cullen Bryant and forty-nine-year-old Horace Greeley, a comparative stripling by group standards—the committee was actually a front for opponents of New York senator William Seward. Lincoln was unaware of this fact when he accepted the group's invitation in the fall of 1859 (he asked for an extension to give him more time to compose a proper speech). The original invitation called for an address at the Reverend Henry Ward Beecher's Plymouth Church in Brooklyn, the so-called Grand Central Station of the Underground Railroad. For reasons possibly having to do with the weather—New Yorkers might have balked at crossing the ice-choked East River at night in the dead of winter—the speech was moved to the more august and accessible location of the Cooper Union on Seventh Street in Manhattan. Event organizers did not bother to tell Lincoln of the change of venues, and he first learned of it through a notice in the *New York Tribune* after he checked into the Astor House on lower Broadway. He was not amused. Having worked for weeks on an address suitable for a church audience, Lincoln now found himself having to spend all day reworking his speech for a more partisan political crowd.[2]

On the morning of his speech, several members of the Young Men's Central Republican Union called on Lincoln at his hotel. They found him wearing a new $100 black suit he had commissioned specially for the occasion from Woods & Henckle tailor shop in Springfield. Unfortunately, the suit had been badly wrinkled on the three-day train ride, and Lincoln apologized "for the awkward and uncomfortable appearance he made in his new suit." His hosts suavely put him at ease, insisting that he accompany them on a brief sightseeing tour of Manhattan. At the corner of Broadway and Bleecker Street, a few blocks from the Cooper Union, Lincoln was ushered into the studio of the celebrated photographer Mathew Brady. His first impression was scarcely welcoming: one wall of the reception room was dominated by Brady's recent photograph of Stephen Douglas, "looking somewhat fiery and slightly dogmatical."[3]

Undaunted, Lincoln made his way upstairs, where the famous photographer was on hand to take Lincoln's picture. Making a virtue of necessity, Brady decided to photograph his elongated subject standing up. He posed Lincoln in front of a fake Grecian pillar, his left hand resting on a pile of books. The subsequent photograph, later heavily retouched to eliminate Lincoln's sometimes "lazy" left eye and deep wrinkles, became the first iconic image of the prairie politician. Widely reprinted (occasionally with a herd of buffalo added to the background to illustrate the candidate's western roots), the Brady photograph introduced the public to a somewhat idealized version of the real man—tall, stately, and formal, with a firm mouth and a pair of rapier-sharp high cheekbones that many a model, male or female, would have killed to possess.[4]

At precisely eight o'clock that night, Lincoln strode onto the stage at the Cooper Union to "loud and prolonged applause." A little nervous and uncomfortable before a crowd of 1,500 of New York's most urbane and accomplished citizens, Lincoln fidgeted through a brief if fulsome introduction by William Cullen Bryant, who termed the fifty-one-year-old speaker one of the "children of the West." At last gaining the podium, Lincoln allowed the applause to die down, then launched immediately into his speech. For the next hour and a half he laid into his familiar punching bag, Stephen Douglas, mentioning him by name five times. Douglas, said Lincoln, had claimed that the Founding Fathers had never intended to prohibit the spread of slavery into new territories—not so. Citing specific research into their backgrounds, Lincoln maintained that twenty-one of the thirty-nine signers of the Declaration of Independence had gone on record as favoring the prohibition of slavery in new territories, and another fifteen (including such nonserving luminaries as Benjamin Franklin, Alexander Hamilton, and Gouverneur Morris) had also given every indication of supporting that stance.[5]

Stretching out his prairie vowels for comic effect, Lincoln denounced Douglas and "his peculiar adherents" for believing in the "gur-reat pur-rinciple fantastically called 'Popular Sovereignty,'" which Lincoln defined helpfully for his audience as the belief that "if one man would enslave another, no third man should object." He scorned southerners for painting Republicans as "reptiles" and "outlaws," and repeated his debatable contention that "no Republican designedly aided or encouraged the Harpers Ferry affair." He glossed over the raid as "peculiar" and "absurd," and described Brown somewhat leniently as "an enthusiast" who had believed he had a divine commission to liberate the slaves. It was similar to the assassination of kings and emperors throughout history, Lincoln claimed, and southerners should not worry about it, since "in the present state of things in the United States, I do not think a general, or even a very extensive slave insurrection, is possible." Instead, he warned southerners to stop threatening to leave the Union whenever they felt put upon. Northerners would leave slavery alone in the South, he said, but they would "fearlessly and effectively" fight to prevent its spread. Lincoln closed with the most remembered line of his entire ninety-minute speech: "Let us have faith that right makes might, and in that faith, let us, to the end, dare to do our duty as we understand it." He received a rousing—some reports said standing—ovation from the crowd.[6]

The next morning, Lincoln set off, as planned, to visit his son Robert at Phillips Exeter Academy in New Hampshire. He was heartened by the overwhelmingly positive response to his speech in the local media. The *New York Times*, then, as now, the quasi-official voice of the nation, devoted three front-page columns to the speech. "When Mr. Lincoln had concluded his address," the newspaper reported, "three rousing cheers were given for the orator and the sentiments to which he had given utterance." Horace Greeley's *New York Tribune* went even further in its praise. "The speech of Abraham Lincoln at the Cooper Institute last night was one of the happiest and most convincing political arguments ever made in this city, and was addressed to a crowded and most appreciating audience," the *Tribune* recounted. "No man ever before made such an impression on his first appeal to a New York audience." A transcript of his entire speech was printed on page six of the newspaper. Greeley's fellow editor, William Cullen Bryant of the *New York Evening Post*, trumpeted Lincoln's speech in blaring headlines: "THE REPUBLICAN PARTY VINDICATED" and "THE DEMANDS OF THE SOUTH EXPLAINED." Lincoln, said Bryant, had "place[d] the Republican party on the very ground occupied by the framers of our constitution and fathers of our republic . . . it is wonderful how much a truth gains by a certain mastery of clear and impressive statement."[7]

Lincoln was deluged with offers for more appearances, and he accepted nearly every one. En route to Exeter, he delivered speeches in Providence, Rhode Island, Concord, Manchester, and Dover, New Hampshire. At Providence, an overflow crowd of 1,500 people turned out to cheer him from the moment he set foot in the auditorium on the second floor of the town depot. Lincoln, said the *Providence Journal*, "abounds in good humor and pleasant satire, and often gives a witty thrust that cuts like a Damascus blade. But he does not aim chiefly at fun. He strives rather to show the plain, simple, cogent reasoning that his positions are impregnable, and he carries the audience with him, as he deserves to." While repeating essentially the same speech he had given at the Cooper Union, Lincoln took pains to throw in a few new touches. Seeking to explain why he did not support the eradication of slavery in southern states, he drew a folksy parallel for the urbane easterners. "If on the street, or in the field, or on the prairie I find a rattlesnake," he explained, "I take a stake and kill him. But suppose the snake was in bed where children were sleeping. Would I do right to strike him there? I might hurt the children, or I might not kill, but only arouse and exasperate the snake, and he might bite the children."[8]

Everywhere he went, Lincoln was greeted enthusiastically. After speaking at Exeter Town Hall in front of Robert and hundreds of his fellow students, he made appearances at Hartford, New Haven, Meriden, Norwich, and Bridgeport, Connecticut, and Woonsocket, Rhode Island. In eleven days, he gave eleven speeches in three dependably Republican states, while carefully avoiding William Seward's stronghold in Massachusetts and politically "doubtful" New Jersey. It was a physically exhausting but emotionally exhilarating trip, sweetened by the fact that Robert (who had failed his entrance exams to Harvard the year before) was excelling academically and socially at Phillips Exeter Academy. That summer, Robert would retake the exams and gain admittance to Harvard, helped immeasurably by a letter of recommendation that Lincoln personally requested from Stephen Douglas to Harvard president James Walker.[9]

By the time Lincoln returned to Springfield in the early-morning hours of March 14, he had been away from home for exactly three weeks. His speech at the Cooper Union, he modestly reported to Mary, "went off passably well." His law partner caught a new lightness in Lincoln's step. His "dazzling success in the East," reported William Herndon, had convinced Lincoln "that the presidential nomination was within his reach." While downplaying his chances, Lincoln admitted to Lyman Trumbull that "the taste *is* in my mouth a little." He also took studied swipes at the other leading Republican candidates, noting that Seward was "the very best candidate we could have for the North of Illinois, and the very worst for the South of it." The same held true for Ohio's favorite son, Salmon P. Chase. Conditions were reversed for Missouri's Edward Bates, who Lincoln figured would be stronger in southern Illinois, while seventy-five-year-old Supreme Court justice John McLean was a good ten or fifteen years too old for the post. Still, when supporter Edward Stafford suggested that Lincoln raise a campaign war chest of $10,000, the potential candidate was aghast. "I could not raise ten thousand dollars if it would save me from the fate of John Brown," Lincoln replied. Any chance he had for the nomination would have to depend on word of mouth, not depth of pockets.[10]

✦ ✦ ✦

While Lincoln was touring the Northeast in the amber afterglow of his Cooper Union triumph, Stephen Douglas was locked in fierce combat on the floor of the Senate. Once again, popular sovereignty was the wedge issue dividing Douglas from the party's traditional base in the South. Georgia senator Alfred Iverson, who earlier had warned that the election of a Republican president would force the South to secede, now postured violent defiance. "Let those loud-mouthed, blood and thunder, braggadocio Hotspurs assemble their abolition army and come to force us back into the Union," he boomed, "and we should hang them up like dogs to the trees of our forests." Other southerners, including Jefferson Davis, James S. Green, and Clement Clay, added their voices to the rising din. Douglas attempted to placate the ultras, observing that "if I were a citizen of Louisiana I would vote for retaining and maintaining slavery, because I believe the good of that people would require it." He proposed a bill making it illegal for one state to invade another—as though that had been the motivating factor in John Brown's raid—but succeeded only in further enflaming southern sensibilities by calling for a strong federal response to such violations. When the *Richmond Enquirer* charged that his bill amounted to coercion of "the sovereign states of the South," Douglas challenged the assertion that he was "plunging deeper and deeper into the abyss of political error." "I do not admit the fact that there is a better Democrat on earth than I am," said Douglas, "or a sounder one on the question of state rights, and even on the slavery question."[11]

He would soon get the opportunity to prove it. The Democratic caucus, controlled from the wings by President Buchanan, passed a series of resolutions intended to bear on the party platform at the rapidly approaching presidential nominating convention in Charleston, South Carolina. Sponsored by Davis, the resolutions called for a federal slave code for all territories and the prohibition of local ordinances interfering with slaveholders' property rights. Douglas, advised again to ignore southern provocations, adopted a policy of "masterly inactivity" on the Senate floor, while furiously wheeling and dealing at his campaign headquarters in the National Hotel and hosting potential supporters at his home on Minnesota Row. Adele, as always, was by his side, graciously presiding over dinner parties and looking luminous again after her grave illness. Further evincing her loyalty, she stopped attending the White

House teas hosted by the president's niece, Harriet Lane, although the two competing hostesses kept adjoining boxes at Ford's Theatre. One night, when a South Carolina fire-eater entered their box to pay his respects, Adele cut him off at the knees. "Sir, you have made a mistake," she said. "Your visit is intended for next door."[12]

Douglas concentrated on winning supporters outside of Washington. He maintained a voluminous correspondence with would-be backers from New York to California, and sent campaign aide A. D. Banks, a former Petersburg, Virginia, newspaper editor, on frequent forays into the South to contact putative moderates. In the Old Northwest, where he was strongest, Douglas won endorsements from state conventions in Illinois, Ohio, Indiana, Michigan, Iowa, and Wisconsin. He also gained adherents in New England, with delegations pledging their support from Maine, Vermont, Rhode Island, and New Hampshire. The powerful states of New York and Pennsylvania remained split, despite the strong-arming tactics of Douglas's old champion George N. Sanders, who was said to be employing "the moral suasion of stewed oysters, Virginia ham and Bourbon whiskey" on delegates. Much of the South remained out of reach, although individual supporters assured Douglas that he was "stronger, a thousand times, with the southern people, than superficial currents set in motion by politicians would indicate." A last-minute effort to move the convention from Charleston to New Orleans, where Douglas had strong personal and business roots, failed. Douglas supporters would have to make their stand in the home state of the ferocious John C. Calhoun, whose restless spirit, nine years dead, still cast a considerable shadow across the ever-darkening face of the South.[13]

◆ ◆ ◆

The Democratic National Convention opened for business in Charleston on April 23. It was unseasonably hot, and thin columns of steam rose from the cobblestone street outside the South Carolina Institute Hall as the 606 delegates gathered to select their party's next presidential candidate. A brief midmorning shower did little to lower the sweltering heat, and the doors and windows of the two-story wooden building were thrown open in a vain attempt to create a cross breeze in the jam-packed first-floor assembly room. The deafening rattle of horse-drawn carriages on Meeting Street drowned out the brief opening remarks by executive committee chairman Daniel A. Smalley and the less concise invocation by local minister Christian Hanckle, who had conveniently pasted his lengthy prayer to the inside cover of a hymnal. Delegates futilely swished palm-leaf fans, mopped their necks with balled-up handkerchiefs, and squirmed in their hard-backed wooden chairs like restless children on the last day of school. Onlookers in the overhanging balconies added to the general hubbub. No one in the room, either visitor or delegate, could hear himself think.[14]

By any objective measure, Charleston had been a disastrous choice for the party's convention. Not only was it difficult to reach by rail—a wearying thirteen changes of train were required between Washington, D.C., and the Carolina coast—but local hotels were inadequate to house the expected onslaught of delegates. With that in mind, several of the state delegations chartered steamers to use as floating dormitories. Others planned to pitch tents on public property, a plan that was swiftly quashed by local authorities. Many Democrats, particularly those from northern states, simply opted not to attend the convention at all. "Charleston is the last place on Gods Earth where a national convention should have been held," Chicago backer Thomas Dyer told Douglas. Massachusetts delegate F. O. Prince complained to Adele Douglas, "I have never been taught to believe in eternal punishment, but the journey here has led me to recognize the contrary 'platform,' to use the term now current, since it has appeared to me, that those who were instrumental in locating the convention here can only be adequately punished therefore by *Brimstone* and *Caloric ad infinitum*." Curiously, Douglas himself was untroubled by the choice. "There will be no serious difficulty in the South," he assured Albany, New York, delegate Peter Cagger before the convention. "The last few weeks has worked a perfect revolution in that section."[15]

Douglas's supporters on the ground in Charleston were considerably less sanguine. Having spent much of their time arguing with southern delegates on the interminable train ride to the coast, they found themselves outnumbered, outorganized, and outshouted by their angry counterparts, who openly suggested that any Douglas supporters would be better off attending the upcoming Republican Party convention in Chicago alongside their fellow abolitionists. Intended as a reward to the South for helping elect northerner James Buchanan president four years earlier, the selection of Charleston now seemed a monument to unintended consequences and the intrinsic unpredictability of politics. For all its flower-scented gardens and soft sea breezes wafting over the Battery from its famous harbor, Charleston was enemy territory for Douglas and his supporters. Five days before, as conventioneers began arriving, an Alabama newspaper scripted a less-than-encouraging welcome. "This Demagogue of Illinois," thundered the *Opelika Weekly Southern Era*, "deserves to perish upon the gibbet of Democratic condemnation, and his loathsome carcass to be cast at the gate of the Federal City." The *Jackson Mississippian* was equally defamatory, terming Douglas "the most profligate of all political reprobates; the most unbearable of all political bores; a turbulent demagogue; a miserable thimblerigger with a remarkable capacity to betray."[16]

Having spent the last ten years of his political life in a thankless struggle to broker some sort of accommodation between pro- and antislavery forces, Douglas was no longer in a mood to compromise. "I do not intend to make peace with my enemies, nor to make a concession of one iota of principle," he told Illinois ally James W. Singleton, "believing that I am right in the position I have taken, and that neither can the Union be preserved or the Democratic party maintained upon any other basis." Singleton, who had known Douglas since the two served together as young men in the state militia, agreed. "We are not in a condition to carry another ounce of southern weight," he replied. "We have essayed to vindicate their rights under the Constitution, we grant to them all we claim for ourselves, and we must now take our chances alike for the protection which the local laws will extend to our property in the territories; to go further and legislate for one or every species of property in the territories—would be *inexplicable inconsistency*, invoking the fatal acknowledgement *as error* all our preconceived notions of the right and capacity of the people to regulate their domestic affairs in their own way." Efforts were still being made to reach out to moderate southerners—what few there were—but northern Democrats were determined to nominate Douglas. "Rest assured of one thing," one committed delegate told Douglas on the eve of the convention. "There can arise no contingency in the convention when your friends will agree to vote for any other man than yourself. The time for compromise and postponement upon that point has passed." Another supporter vowed that the Douglas men would walk out of the convention if he were denied the nomination. It would prove to be a mordantly ironic threat.[17]

There was no doubt in anyone's mind that Douglas was, as Cincinnati journalist Murat Halstead noted, "the pivot individual" around whom all other Democrats revolved. "Every delegate," wrote Halstead, "was for or against him. Every motion meant to nominate or not to nominate him." Signaling his own inveterate opposition to Douglas's nomination, President Buchanan dispatched more than 500 loyalists, both delegates and lobbyists, to battle the Little Giant. They gathered in a rented mansion on King Street behind a local ice cream parlor to plot strategy, led by a quartet of proadministration senators: John Slidell of Louisiana, Jesse Bright of Indiana, James A. Bayard of Delaware, and William Bigler of Pennsylvania. Meanwhile, Douglas supporters congregated at the luxurious Mills House and the rather less comfortable Hibernian Hall, where hundreds of cots had been crammed together barracks-like on the second floor.[18]

In keeping with long-accepted tradition, Douglas remained in Washington, leaving his campaign in the hands of his trusted lieutenant, former Illinois congressman William A. Richardson, who had run his 1856 campaign in Cincinnati. Described by Halstead as "a fine specimen of a strong, coarse man," Richardson would have his hands full, combating both the Buchananites and the southern ultras who were sworn to resist Douglas to the last. He could not have been reassured by a flaming editorial in the *Charleston Mercury* by radical editor Robert Barnwell Rhett, Jr., who crowed: "The Democratic party, as a party, based on principles, is dead. It exists now only as a powerful faction. It has not one single principle common to its members North and South."[19]

The acknowledged leader of the ultras was forty-five-year-old former Alabama congressman William Lowndes Yancey, whose bland exterior masked a ferocious inner heat. As a young man, Yancey had killed a man in South Carolina during a fistfight. Convicted of manslaughter, he had served three months in jail, during which time he wrote a less-than-contrite letter to his brother describing the fight and noting with unseemly self-approval: "I have done my duty as a man, & he who grossly insulted me lies now, with a clod upon his bosom." Later, while serving a single term in Congress, he fought a duel with fellow congressman Thomas W. Clingman of North Carolina over Clingman's opposition to the annexation of Texas. Like a couple of proper English gentlemen, the two exchanged pistol shots at dawn on the field of honor (each missed). As a delegate to the 1848 Democratic National Convention in Baltimore, Yancey led a two-man walkout after Michigan senator Lewis Cass was nominated on a platform that did not include a plank forbidding Congress from prohibiting slavery in newly acquired territories. For the previous ten years, he had traveled tirelessly across the South, promoting the establishment of southern rights associations and advocating secession from the Union. "We shall fire the Southern heart," Yancey told a fellow believer, "instruct the Southern mind—give courage to each other, and at the proper moment, by one organized, concerted action, we can precipitate the cotton states into a revolution."[20]

Yancey arrived in Charleston with formal instructions from the Alabama Democratic Party empowering him to lead another walkout if the convention did not adopt a platform supporting a uniform federal slave code in the territories. Douglas's men anticipated such a walkout, but regarded it as a positive, not negative, act. "Douglas could ask for nothing better," the *St. Paul Pioneer and Democrat* declared. "This course will throw out of the convention that class of votes which would be cast against him. It will reduce that much the number of delegates, and of course, the number required to make up a two-thirds majority; while it leaves his strength intact." Back in Washington, Douglas instructed his supporters to "make no compromises, ask no favors . . . neither receive nor give quarter."[21]

While northern delegates were alternately arguing with their southern counterparts in hotel lobbies and listening to denunciatory speeches from fire-eating rabble-rousers on street corners, Yancey stayed literally above the fray, occupying a suite of rooms on the upper floor of the Charleston Hotel. His hard-eyed, wig-wearing chief lieutenant, Mississippi congressman William Barksdale, circulated through the crowd, strong-arming delegates who might be wavering in their commitment (and who were well aware of his fearsome reputation as a bowie-knife-wielding duelist). Two days before the convention opened, representatives from seven southern states—Alabama, Arkansas, Florida, Georgia, Louisiana, Mississippi, and Texas—met in Yancey's room and agreed to stand together in demanding a federal slave code plank. If adopted, such a plank would force Douglas to step down as a candidate, since he could never agree to its implicit renunciation of popular sovereignty. If not adopted, the ultras would walk out.

Before anyone else could be nominated, the front-runner had to be defeated, and that looked like a formidable task. The Douglas camp won a pair of preliminary skirmishes before the convention even opened. Douglas's old schoolboy friend from Vermont, Daniel A. Smalley, in his role as chairman of the Democratic Executive Committee, ruled in favor of Douglas supporters in two disputed delegations, New York and Illinois. Despite strong pressure from ultras and Buchananites, the committee refused to overturn Smalley's decision. On the eve of the convention, Halstead reported, the "run of the current is Douglas-ward." At the Mills House, Douglas supporters whooped it up, assuring Halstead that "all that is to be done is to ratify the voice of the people. There is nothing but a few ballots, and all is over—Douglas [is] the nominee." As if to underscore their confidence, a number of them got roaring drunk and "made the night hideous" beneath the journalist's hotel window.[22]

The convention formally got under way at noon the next day. For those who believed in portents, it was a clear sign of Douglas's ascendancy—his forty-seventh birthday. (It was also the day traditionally recognized as William Shakespeare's birthday, but no one was heard to remark on the coincidence.) The first order of business was to rule on the executive committee decision to exclude the anti-Douglas delegations from New York and Illinois. Virginia delegate M. W. Fisher rose to speak in behalf of the contested delegations, which were led respectively by New York City mayor Fernando Wood and Chicago postmaster Isaac Cook, a bitter personal enemy of Douglas. With the horse-drawn carriages still lumbering noisily down Meeting Street, the elderly, thin-voiced Fisher could scarcely make himself heard. He was drowned out, at any rate, by a challenge from New York congressman John Cochrane, a suave parliamentarian whose florid complexion and balding head were topped by an artful comb-over. The New York City resident was known for his high living, and Halstead wittily described him as looking "as though it would require a very strong cup of coffee to bring him into condition in the morning." Cochrane's defense of the Douglas delegations carried the day, and the convention's first vote went overwhelmingly in Douglas's favor, 256–47. An elderly Pennsylvania delegate who attempted to take the floor was rebuffed by cries of "Goddamn you, sit down!" and "What the hell do you want to talk for?"[23]

The convention's second official act was less favorable to Douglas. Massachusetts delegate Caleb Cushing, who had served as Franklin Pierce's attorney general and now was firmly allied with the Buchanan administration, was elected permanent chairman. Despite his New England roots, Cushing was notably pro-southern in his sentiments—one disgusted Ohio delegate later termed him "the veriest toady and tool of the Fire Eaters"—and he accepted the post with an impassioned speech limning the geographical glories of the continent, from the rocky hills of the East to the verdant valleys of the Mississippi basin and the golden shores of the West, concluding with a ringing denunciation of the "traitorous" and "half insane" Republicans who were conspiring "to set region against region."[24]

The Democrats were doing a pretty good job of that themselves, and a momentous decision on the second day of the convention underscored the fact. Following a stem-winding speech by Richardson in behalf of a move to free uninstructed delegates from having to vote as a unit, the assembly agreed to allow the delegates to vote individually. This freed another 30 to 40 votes for Douglas, and the 197 votes in favor of the measure were within a hairbreadth of the 202 he needed to win the nomination. Confident of their power, the Douglas supporters unwisely agreed to southern demands that the convention approve a party platform before selecting the nominee. It was the ultras' trump card, and the Douglas camp blithely allowed them to play it. That decision, made in the first flush of victory, would prove disastrous, not merely to Douglas and the Democratic Party, but ultimately to the nation as a whole.

Party platforms ordinarily were no more than vague documents laying out in general terms the positions a candidate was expected to take during the campaign. But 1860 was not an ordinary year. The decade-long wrangle over such abstract concepts as popular sovereignty and states' rights had ossified around the South's adamantine demand for a federal slave code, which Maine congressman James G. Blaine, himself a future presidential candidate, later characterized as an argument over "an imaginary Negro in an impossible place." The canny Halstead summed up the matter neatly for his readers: "The South makes it a point of honor that the platform shall not be one capable of double construction. . . . The Northern delegates don't care much about the honor of the matter. Their political existence depends absolutely upon their ability to construe the platform adopted here to mean 'popular sovereignty,' which will allow them to declare, in the North, that the officially expressed Democratic doctrine is that the people of the Territories may, while in their territorial condition, abolish or exclude slavery. They cannot, dare not, yield the opportunity for pressing this pretext." Noting that the ultras controlled the platform committee by a bare one-vote margin, Halstead predicted that "the Convention is destined to explode in a grand row. There is tumult and war in prospect." The explosion was postponed, for the time being, when the chairman of the Vermont delegation, John S. Robinson, conveniently dropped dead on the third day of the convention, forcing delegates to suspend business for the rest of the day out of respect.[25]

While the platform committee deliberated behind closed doors at nearby Masonic Hall, delegates tramped the streets in search of much-needed diversion. Some found it on the breezy Battery, where the Boston-based stylings of Gilmore's Brass Band serenaded the crowd free of charge, courtesy of the Massachusetts delegation. As the musicians bleated away at patriotic tunes, delegates looked across the harbor to Sullivan's Island, where Colonel William Moultrie's homegrown militia had successfully held off the flower of the British navy in 1776, thus saving Charleston from near-certain capture. Closer to shore, on a man-made island three miles from the Battery, a cadre of army engineers worked desultorily to complete a new fort. Named after former South Carolina general Thomas Sumter, the fort when finished would boast massive brick walls, forty feet high and twelve feet thick, to protect it from any seaborne invaders. None of the 146 gun ports pointed toward shore, since no danger was expected to come from that direction. Excursion boats sailed past the unfinished fort and up the Ashley and Cooper rivers to neighboring plantations, where the southern delegates were greeted warmly and the northern delegates largely went uninvited.[26]

Other conventioneers found more prosaic amusements inside the city. At the Charleston Theater, a skilled magician named Professor Jacobs, ably assisted by a "goblin" called Sprightly, was said "to do wonderful things with cards, rabbits, and a goose." Less mystically inclined delegates repaired to the various saloons along the waterfront to sample an assortment of exotic drinks served in iced bowls alongside free helpings of green peas and strawberries. Still others took advantage of the hospitality room aboard the Pennsylvania delegation's chartered steamer, *Keystone State*, which was stocked with free liquor and lager beer, or visited the New York delegation's headquarters on the *Nashville*, where with typical big-city urbanity the New Yorkers had obligingly stowed a contingent of "amiable females." Professional gamblers swarmed the hotel lobbies, ever ready to deal a few hands of faro or poker, and world-class pickpockets mingled through the crowd, relieving unwary delegates of their winnings.[27]

The convention got back to business on the morning of the fifth day, when the platform committee, looking like the guests of honor at a mass hanging, trooped into the hall. The weather outside was equally gloomy. The heat wave had broken, and cold rain and gusty winds swept across the city. In the overhead galleries, female visitors dripped disconsolately onto the floor, the feathers in their ruined bonnets drooping along with their spirits. Excited delegates snatched at advance copies of the three committee reports. The majority report, presented by North Carolina delegate William W. Avery, upheld the southern position. Signed by all fifteen southern committee members, it firmly rejected the notion of popular sovereignty and called on the federal government "to protect, when necessary, the rights of persons and property on the high seas, in the Territories, or wherever else its constitutional authority extends."[28]

The minority position, endorsed by all but one of the sixteen eastern and midwestern members of the committee, was presented by longtime Douglas loyalist Henry Payne of Cleveland. Warning the southerners that they were in danger of destroying the party—if not, indeed, the nation—over a mere abstraction, Payne urged them to allow the party's eventual candidate "to run this race unfettered and unhampered" by the demand for a federal slave code. The minority platform repeated the position taken by the 1856 convention, which had endorsed a carefully worded statement on popular sovereignty that both northern and southern delegates could accept. The new platform, as suggested by Douglas, added a codicil pledging to abide by the *Dred Scott* decision and any future Supreme Court rulings on slavery in the territories. It was as far as northern Democrats were prepared to go. "We never will recede from that doctrine, sir; never, never, never," Payne cautioned. "We cannot recede from this doctrine without personal dishonor, and so help us God, we never will abandon this principle. If the majority report is adopted, you cannot expect one northern electoral vote, or one sympathizing member of Congress from the free states." Payne's speech was greeted with tremendous applause from the northern delegations and absolute silence from the southern ones.[29]

Benjamin Butler, a delegate from Lowell, Massachusetts, whose somewhat ridiculous appearance—he was cross-eyed, heavy-lidded, fat-faced, and bald—masked a calculating, lawyerly intelligence, rose next to present a one-man minority report. Butler's solution to the platform controversy was simple—he merely endorsed the 1856 platform as it was.

To those who disapproved of the 1856 platform for being too vague and admitting too many interpretations, Butler responded that both the Bible and the Constitution were also open to interpretation. Furthermore, he said, the majority report's call for the "rights of persons and property on the high seas" might be used to reinstitute the African slave trade, while the minority report's pledge to tie the Democratic Party to any and all future Supreme Court decisions "was enough to make the bones of old Jackson rattle in his coffin." When a Maryland delegate acidly remarked that his state, at least, had never encouraged open resistance to the Fugitive Slave Act, Butler replied that Massachusetts had never kept its voters away from the polls with bludgeons and knives.[30]

On that less-than-collegial note, the convention adjourned for lunch, but the pouring rain kept all but the hungriest delegates inside. The southerners caucused informally, and William Barksdale passed along a handwritten note to Cushing that "Mr. Yancey [is] asking very much to speak." This was the moment all Charleston had been waiting for. An extended ovation greeted Yancey's appearance at the podium, and he began to voice what one observer called "the most uncompromising sentiments in the most musical and ingratiating tones." For the next hour and a half—the convention obligingly suspended its one-hour time limit for his benefit—Yancey held forth on the South's minority status within the Union and the necessity of the North to vouchsafe southern rights, particularly the right to freely take their slaves wherever they wanted. "Ours is the property invaded," he said, "ours are the institutions which are at stake; ours is the peace that is to be destroyed; ours is the honor at stake." While southerners on the floor and in the galleries roared their approval, Yancey urged the convention to "bear with us, then, if we stand sternly upon what is yet that dormant volcano, and say we yield no position here until we are convinced we are wrong. We are in a position to ask you to yield. What right of yours, gentlemen of the North, have we of the South ever invaded? What institution of yours have we ever assailed, directly or indirectly? What laws have we ever passed that have invaded, or induced others to invade, the sanctity of your homes or to put your lives in jeopardy?" No one, he said, had the right to interfere with slavery. "It does not belong to you to put your hands on it," he thundered. "You are aggressors when you injure it. You are not our brothers when you injure us." He urged the delegates to unite behind slavery as a positive good. "If we beat you, we give you good servants for life and enable you to live comfortably," Yancey concluded expansively. All white men should join "the master race and put the Negro race to do the dirty work which God designed they should do." Wild shouts and raucous clapping escorted him from the podium.[31]

It had grown dark while Yancey spoke, and the pale yellow glow of gaslights shimmered in the hall as Ohio senator George Pugh angrily made his way to the stage to speak in rebuttal. He was glad to hear a southern leader speak so plainly and boldly, Pugh noted, since that had not been the case in Cincinnati four years earlier, when southern delegates had supported a platform tacitly calling for popular sovereignty. "Must the Democratic party be dragged at the chariot wheel of three hundred thousand slave-masters," Pugh demanded, while northern Democrats "were thrust back and told in effect they must put their hands on their mouths and their mouths in the dust? Gentlemen of the South, you mistake us—you mistake us! We will not do it!"[32]

It was, said one observer, "a fearless speech," and the convention floor seethed with angry delegates. John Cochrane of New York made a motion to split the difference between the platforms by adding language affirming the property rights of all citizens in the territories and calling any efforts to annul those rights "unwise in policy and repugnant to the Constitution." Connecticut delegate W. D. Bishop said he doubted whether anything new could be added to the debate "if the convention remained in session and debated all summer." Noting that the minds of the southern delegates appeared to be made up, Bishop called for an immediate vote on the platform. The convention exploded. Dozens of delegates jumped up at once, climbing onto their chairs, "screaming like panthers, and gesticulating like monkeys." Reporters climbed atop their writing tables to view the explosion, and visitors in the galleries craned their necks over the balcony to see what was happening below. Cushing pounded his gavel like a hammer, but no one could hear it. A crowd of angry southerners gathered menacingly around Bishop, and impromptu wrestling matches took place throughout the hall. Someone cried out in a strangled voice that—good God!—the Democratic Party was about to die.[33]

Cooler heads eventually prevailed, and the delegates voted to adjourn for the night. It was a long one. Telegrams flew back and forth between Charleston and Washington, asking for instructions from party leaders in Congress and the White House. George N. Sanders, who as master of the New York ports had risked presidential displeasure by attending the convention as a Douglas backer, wired Buchanan, appealing to his patriotism and reminding him of Douglas's selfless withdrawal in Buchanan's favor at the Cincinnati convention. Sanders urged the president to announce his support for Douglas, adding portentously that Buchanan "could not afford to be the last president of the United States." Buchanan was in no mood to endorse his bitter enemy, and the fact that Sanders's telegram was sent collect—it cost Buchanan $26.80 to read it—did nothing to improve the president's state of mind. Meanwhile, southern leaders such as Robert Toombs of Georgia and Jefferson Davis of Mississippi were urging their state delegations to walk out if they did not receive satisfaction. Robert Hunter of Virginia, who retained hopes of being the nominee himself, advised his state not to withdraw—at least, not yet. Douglas's people, on the other hand, continued to exude confidence. C. P. Culver reassured the senator that Yancey's speech had merely been a way for the South to let off steam, and that in the end only Alabama and Mississippi would oppose his platform. The odds were ten-to-one that Douglas would be nominated.[34]

The next day dawned cold and rainy, and the delegates returned to the convention hall in equally foul spirits. Kentucky and Ohio delegates groused that they had run through their liquor supplies, and the men from the Bluegrass State suffered the added ignominy of having to pay for thirty empty hotel rooms out of their own pockets—an additional $125 per man. The Pennsylvania delegation had similar problems. Having chartered the *Keystone State* with the expectation that it would pay for itself by taking visitors on excursions around the harbor, the delegates were faced with a $2,000 shortfall. The ship would return north later that day, bearing with it many of Douglas's most vocal supporters. Henceforth, the visitor's gallery would be filled primarily with southern shouters.

Empty whiskey barrels and deserted poop decks were the least of the convention's worries, as immediately became clear when deliberations resumed in the clammy hall. At the urging of proadministration senator William Bigler, the various platforms were sent back to the committee for further tinkering. The harried members returned with three more platforms, each largely unchanged from the originals. The convention had devolved into a Jesuitical parsing of phrases, the most significant of which was an admission by the Douglas camp that "inasmuch as differences of opinion exist in the Democratic party as to the nature and extent of the powers of a Territorial Legislature, and as to the powers and duties of Congress . . . over the institution of slavery within the Territories," they were prepared to accept any future Supreme Court rulings on the subject, even ones that might limit popular sovereignty. It was a last-ditch effort to reach common ground with the South on the spirit, if not the letter, of the law. But southern delegates were not prepared to place their trust in a Supreme Court whose makeup might change dramatically when pro-southern dinosaurs like Chief Justice Taney inevitably passed away. They filibustered into the night, and the convention adjourned for the Sabbath, still hopelessly deadlocked and increasingly dispirited.[35]

Sunday was no day of rest for the warring delegations. The Buchananite troika of Slidell, Bayard, and Bright met with Yancey deep into the night to plot strategy. They were joined by Louisiana delegate Richard Taylor, son of the late president, who hoped to add a moderating tone to the southern position. Yancey promised to try once more to convince the members of his own delegation not to bolt prematurely from the convention, and the others waited up until dawn for him to return with an answer. He never came. Meanwhile, rampant wheeling and dealing continued on all sides. Halstead reported that one southerner had been approached three separate times by Douglas's people and asked which foreign mission he wanted in return for his support. The Douglas camp, Halstead noted with grudging admiration, was playing "a bold game with enormous force and splendid impudence for an imperial stake," offering ten times the number of patronage posts that actually existed in the government. Other northern delegates did not seem so avid about lining up southern support. Cleveland delegate J. W. Gray candidly told his hometown newspaper, the *Plain Dealer*: "Our only fear is that they will not go. They are a nuisance to the party and the country, and the sooner they get out the better." One exasperated Louisianian was asked so many times when he was planning to walk out that he responded: "Oh, never mind. We won't go out until we are ready. You are too damn keen for us to go."[36]

Not everyone stayed indoors plotting. The rain had finally stopped, and a cool breeze blew in from the Atlantic. Halstead listened to some southern delegates sitting outside at breakfast complaining about the frost and worrying about its effect on cotton-planting efforts back home. A northern delegate whiling away the afternoon saw a sign in a shop window announcing "Slaves for sale." Seriously or not, he inquired within about buying "a nice woman" for his household, and was shown a pretty young mulatto woman who was said to have many sterling qualities as a seamstress. Since he was a convention delegate, he could have her for the bargain price of $1,500. The delegate said he would have to think about it. Other northerners were thinking primarily about getting out of town. Trains, stagecoaches, and boats were packed with gamblers, ward heelers, and disappointed office seekers who could no longer afford the city's exorbitant rates. Since most of them were Douglas supporters, their departure meant that the hall would be filled even more densely with proslavery locals.[37]

On Monday morning, the convention reopened for business. Yancey was observed to be smiling like a child on Christmas morning. He was the only one. The rest of the delegates, northern and southern, were suitably grim. After dispensing with the first item of business, Benjamin Butler's minority report, the delegates took up what Halstead humorously described as the "Douglas-Popular Sovereignty-Supreme Court-ambiguous" report. When a young Maryland delegate moved to reconsider Butler's report, a voice from the Alabama delegation mistakenly seconded the motion. Realizing his mistake, the Alabama delegate shouted, "Mr. President, I don't second the motion of that man down yonder." The Marylander took offense at the tone, and demanded to know the other delegate's name. The man rose from his chair—all 220 pounds of him—and responded, "I intended no disrespect to the gentleman from Maryland—but my name is Tom Cooper of Alabama." The first man smoothly saved face, announcing his own name and declaring that if Tom Cooper wished to call on him later, they would have a drink together.[38]

That was the last note of friendly accord at the convention. The delegates voted to consider the minority report plank by plank, beginning with a bare endorsement of the Cincinnati platform. The first plank passed, 165–138, with all but 12 of the majority votes coming from northern states. A last-minute move by Richardson to placate the South by dropping the resolution pledging the party to abide by future Supreme Court decisions failed miserably, with angry northerners voting against their own proposal when it became obvious that the southern delegates had no intention of voting at all. Halstead caught Yancey's eye, and observed that the Alabaman was now smiling like a bridegroom. One by one, the chairmen of the southern delegations rose to declare their objections to the proceedings. Then they walked out, taking their delegates with them. In a mass exodus, the delegates from Alabama, Arkansas, Florida, Louisiana, Mississippi, South Carolina, and Texas left the hall and retired to St. Andrew's Hall, a few blocks away. Watching them go, the southern ladies in the gallery fluttered their fans, twirled their parasols, and favored them with approving waves.[39]

That night a carnival atmosphere prevailed in Charleston. Residents took to the streets in support of the southern walkout, and a crowd of several thousand congregated in front of the federal courthouse. Cries of "Yancey! Yancey!" filled the air. At 11:00 p.m., their champion appeared and delivered an impromptu speech denouncing the "Rump Convention" that remained at Institute Hall. He would, he said, help organize a "Constitutional Democratic Convention" the next day at Military Hall. "Perhaps even now the pen of the historian is nibbed to write the story of a new Revolution," Yancey added. "Three cheers for the independent Southern Republic," someone called out, as if on cue.[40]

The next day, the remaining delegates reconvened. Douglas supporters, although disheartened by the previous day's events, still looked forward to securing for the Little Giant the prize that had escaped him so narrowly in 1852 and 1856. It soon became apparent that this was not to be. After Georgia spokesman Henry L. Benning read a statement withdrawing twenty-six members of his delegation from the convention, Cushing ruled that the eight Georgia delegates wishing to remain could not vote, since they did not truly represent their state. A series of arcane parliamentary wrangles ensued. The New York delegation, hoping to play kingmaker and possibly nominate one of its own members for president, led the effort to require that the nominee receive two-thirds of the total number of votes at the convention—303—not merely two-thirds of those remaining in the hall. With fewer than 250 voters still remaining in the hall (each delegate cast half a vote), Douglas would have to capture five-sixths of the total votes to win the nomination. It was impossible. Beginning at dusk, twelve separate ballots were recorded, with Douglas receiving between 145½ and 150½ votes. The rest were scattered among favorite-son candidates.[41]

The next day was more of the same. Following an appearance by the Boston Brass Band, which played several patriotic tunes from the gallery, the roll call resumed. Forty-five more ballots ensued, with Douglas never rising above 152½ votes, and no one else getting more than 65½. Maryland delegate William S. Gittings spoke for everyone when he said that it was no use voting over and over again with no change. "If you'll nominate Douglas, we can elect him, by God!" he insisted. Rumors swept the hall that Douglas would withdraw, but he issued a firm denial from Washington, saying that there was "not one word of truth in the report." His supporters would not have withdrawn him, at any rate. "Douglas or nobody," Illinois backer Charles Lanphier reported. "His friends will never yield."[42]

While the national convention slowly ground to a halt, the southern bolters met at Military Hall and agreed to reconvene in Baltimore on the second Monday in June. When the New York delegation announced that it would withdraw its support of Douglas if he was not nominated by the sixtieth ballot, Richardson finally accepted the inevitable and threw his weight behind a similar motion to adjourn the convention and meet again in six weeks, also in Baltimore. Meanwhile, he recommended that the southern states make arrangements to fill the vacancies left by their bolting members. Cushing gaveled the convention to an end, and the delegates—angry, exhausted, disappointed, and broke—hastened to put Charleston behind them. By late afternoon on May 3, the only people left inside Institute Hall were the janitors sweeping up the melancholy remains of a political disaster, the crumpled posters and paper fans that had failed, literally and figuratively, to lower the temperature inside the hall.[43]

A few blocks away, in the middle of Charleston harbor, workers continued mortaring away on the ever-rising walls of Fort Sumter. But for the time being, at least, no one was watching.

7

The Rush of a Great Wind

One week after the Democratic National Convention had adjourned in tatters, the Illinois Republican Party held a nominating convention of its own. The convention, in Decatur, was controlled from the start by Abraham Lincoln's battle-tested political lieutenants—David Davis, Norman Judd, "Long John" Wentworth, Ward Hill Lamon, John M. Palmer, Richard Yates, Joseph Medill, and others. Its primary purpose was to select a candidate for governor, but its larger—if necessarily hidden—agenda was to endorse a candidate for president. For appearances' sake, Lincoln could not be seen openly politicking for such an endorsement. He remained resolutely in the background, tending to his law practice in Springfield, although he did take the time to caution Lyman Trumbull, who was supporting U.S. Supreme Court justice John McLean, to "write no letters which can possibly be distorted into opposition, or quasi opposition to me." Somewhat uncharacteristically, Lincoln included a veiled threat with the message. Should Trumbull continue working for McLean, he said, Lincoln's "peculiar friends" might take offense. Trumbull, who was up for reelection, took the hint and kept his mouth shut. As for his own prospects, Lincoln said with studied modesty that his only concern was "to be placed anywhere, or nowhere, as may appear most likely to advance our cause."[1]

Behind the scenes, however, Lincoln and his troops were carefully laying the groundwork for a much more ambitious role. Judd, as a member of the Republican National Committee, had managed to convince his fellow committeemen to hold the presidential nominating convention in Chicago, an excellent "neutral site," he said, since Illinois had no clear-cut favorite for the nomination—yet. That was about to change. As delegates began assembling in Decatur, local activist Richard J. Oglesby, another Lincoln supporter, had an inspiration. To really catch on with voters, he said, a candidate needed a memorable nickname. "Old Abe" carried potentially negative connotations; besides being undignified, it called attention to its owner's less-than-prepossessing appearance, and it sounded vaguely Jewish as well. Somehow tracking down Lincoln's elderly cousin, John Hanks, Oglesby laid hands on a couple fence rails that Lincoln conceivably could have split as a young man. On the opening day of the convention, Oglesby arranged for Hanks and another man to lug the rails down the center aisle of the meeting hall. A sign proclaimed "Abraham Lincoln/The Rail Candidate/For President 1860," and pointed out helpfully, if erroneously, that the rails had been split by Lincoln and his cousin Thomas Hanks (it was John Hanks who did the splitting), and that Lincoln's father was the first pioneer of Macon County, Illinois (he was not). Factual errors aside, the stunt was a great success. Lincoln, who could not have been completely happy to have his rough-hewn past brought up again at such a pivotal moment in his career, nevertheless played along gamely with the gag, allowing that while he could not vouch for the rails' authenticity, "he had mauled many better ones since he had grown to manhood."[2]

Although not as evocative, perhaps, as "Old Hickory" or "Tippecanoe," Lincoln's new nickname, "the Rail-splitter," would follow him for the rest of his political career. With its deliberate echoes of hardscrabble frontier life, it appealed to the common folk who had settled Illinois and the rest of the Old Northwest, and its image of self-reliant white workmen embodied the free-labor movement that was sweeping the North as a rebuke to black slavery in the South. Further investigation showed that the rails in question actually had been split by one Bill Strickland, a blind man who was safely confined to the Macon County poorhouse, but by then the image had taken hold. The *Chicago Herald* joked that by the age of eighteen Lincoln was splitting an average of 76,000 rails per day; an Indiana newspaper estimated that one could construct a fence of

Lincoln-split fence rails that would stretch all the way from the North Pole to the South Pole. By the time of the convention, "Honest Old Abe" was vowing, in one account, to split 3 million rails before nightfall. "I've only got two hundred thousand rails to split before sundown," he told visitors. "I kin do it if you'll let me alone." Although amused by the stunt, the Rail-splitter's law partner was not fooled by the high jinks. "I began to think I could smell a very large mouse," Herndon remembered, "and this whole thing was a cunningly devised thing of knowing ones, to make Mr. Lincoln President."[3]

While convention delegates were cheering their semifictitious new champion, Lincoln and his brain trust painstakingly handpicked delegates for the national convention and rammed through a resolution requiring the Illinois delegation, voting as a bloc, "to use all honorable means to secure his [Lincoln's] nomination." It was imperative to stop the first-ballot nomination of William Seward, and control of the Illinois delegation was a crucial factor in that effort. As always, Lincoln was undeluded about his personal appeal. "I suppose I am not the first choice of a very great many," he explained to one campaign supporter. "Our policy, then, is to give no offence to others—leave them in a mood to come to us, if they shall be compelled to give up their first love." To his friend Edward Baker, editor of the *Illinois State Journal*, he did impart one brief canister blast at Seward: "I agree with Seward in his 'Irrepressible Conflict,'" wrote Lincoln, "but I do not endorse his 'Higher Law' doctrine." A break with the South might well be coming—he had been predicting as much for years—and Lincoln wanted to make sure that the full power of the Constitution was on his side. Ever the realist, he had no patience with, or else saw no need for, an airy appeal to higher conscience or divine laws. The Constitution, as it was, was good enough for him.[4]

♦ ♦ ♦

While his old rival was maneuvering skillfully back home in Illinois, a distraught and distracted Stephen Douglas was dealing with the fallout from the Charleston debacle. Although he had remained calm—at least outwardly—during the long days and nights of the convention, Douglas had resumed drinking heavily, much to the chagrin of his wife and advisers. The day after the convention adjourned, California senator Milton Latham called on Douglas and found him drunkenly denouncing the "pack of bloodhounds" that was nipping at his heels. In the Senate, he could scarcely sit still, fidgeting in his chair, tattooing the armrests with his stubby fingers, and looking generally "as if he was trying to bite a pin in two." Soon he faced yet another attack from his seemingly indefatigable southern enemies in the chamber. Once again Jefferson Davis was the chief tormentor, demanding a final vote on the federal slave code and denouncing Douglas for "appropriat[ing] to himself exclusively all that belongs to a doctrine which he did not originate." "I never pretended that I originated it," Douglas said, referring to popular sovereignty. "But if one man is not the peculiar guardian of it, it is very evident that one man is the object of attack in regard to it." The debate degenerated from there, with Davis slamming Douglas for his "swelling manner" and "egregious vanity," and Douglas protesting that Davis was "following a mere phantom in trying to get a recognition of the right of Congress to intervene for the protection of slavery in the territories when the people do not want it."[5]

In the course of his three-hour response to Davis, Douglas became ill, his voice reduced to a hoarse whisper, and fellow senator George Pugh had to finish his remarks for him. What Douglas was trying to say was that the slavery code plank had already been rejected at the Charleston convention, and further insistence on government intervention would "bring the two sections into hostile array, render a conflict inevitable, and force them either to a collision or a separation." That was more or less what Davis had in mind. Still, he resented Douglas's insinuation that he did not love the Union, the Mississippian boomed, charging that Douglas was the true cause of the intersectional strife. The South would have no more to do with the party's "rickety, double-constructed platform," Davis said, then immediately contradicted himself by adding, "As for myself, I would sooner have an honest man on any sort of rickety platform than to have a man I did not trust on the best platform which could be made."[6]

Pale, grim-faced, and in obvious discomfort, Douglas shot back: "In regard to the Senator's declaration that he will grant no quarter to squatter sovereignty, I can only say to him that it will remain to the victor to grant quarter, or to grant mercy. I ask none." He withdrew from the floor and immediately took to his bed, gripped by another severe attack of bronchitis. Advice poured in from all sides. "Do not under any circumstances be drawn into a debate which will degenerate below the dignity of your position," William Richardson implored. "For God's sake don't peril interests not only dear to you but to your friends and the country when you have nothing to gain, but everything to lose." He needn't have bothered. Douglas was too ill to return to the Senate; he missed the final vote in which the congressional slave code was adopted, 36–19. Concerned that he might have to endure another operation on his throat, Douglas suffered an unexpected emotional blow when his eight-month-old daughter Ellen suddenly sickened and died in early May. Like Hamlet, he was discovering that "when troubles come, they come not singly, but in battalions."[7]

A rare bright spot came when former Georgia congressman Alexander Stephens wrote to Douglas, reassuring him that the majority of the southern people would stand behind the 1856 platform. At less than 100 pounds, "Little Aleck," stunted and tubercular, was perhaps the only man in politics smaller than Douglas, but he carried real weight among southern moderates. He had been a Douglas ally in Congress, and he pledged now not to accept the top spot on any ticket deposing the Little Giant. A second positive sign—or one that the Douglas camp chose to interpret as positive—was the rather quixotic gathering of old-line Whigs and irredentist Know-Nothings that met in Baltimore on May 9 to form the new Constitutional Union Party. Widely derided as the "Old Gentlemen's Party" for the comparative gray-beardedness of its presidential and vice presidential nominees, former Tennessee senator John Bell (sixty-three) and Massachusetts statesman Edward Everett (sixty-six), the Unionists hoped to peel off enough votes in the Upper South and Lower North to deny either the Democratic or Republican nominee a victory in the Electoral College. The election then would be thrown into the House of Representatives, where a true compromise candidate might be elected—possibly even Bell himself. Douglas's people saw the ad hoc new party as potentially helpful to their cause, feeling that it would draw more votes from the Republicans than the Democrats. That remained to be seen. An out-and-out abolitionist such as Seward might provoke widespread conservative opposition in the doubtful states, cutting into the Republican vote and giving Douglas an opportunity to snatch up the leavings. A moderate candidate—if the Republicans could find one—would make such a division of spoils that much more difficult. Bell's party, immediately dubbed the Do-Nothings by opponents, announced a carefully punchless campaign platform: "The Constitution of the country, the Union of the states, and the enforcement of the laws." Quite intentionally, the platform said nothing at all about slavery.[8]

♦ ♦ ♦

In a spirit of determined optimism, Lincoln's campaign team descended on Chicago in mid-May. Their mood, if not necessarily their preference, was mirrored by other conventioneers. At only their second national convention, the 466 Republican delegates were filled with a burgeoning sense of possibilities. The Democratic disaster at Charleston had underscored the gaping divisions within the opposition, divisions that the ongoing wrangles in the Senate between Douglas and his southern rivals did nothing to conceal. Suddenly, the White House seemed entirely within reach. The task before the delegates was to choose the most readily electable candidate, while retaining the moral high ground that their opposition to slavery gave them, at least in their own minds. Sensing victory, some 40,000 Republican visitors descended on Chicago for the convention, arriving by train or boat on the shores of Lake Michigan, where they were greeted by welcoming volleys of cannon fire unloosed every thirty seconds by members of the Chicago Light Artillery at the foot of Jackson Street. Hotels, boardinghouses, and saloons swelled with new arrivals, and even local pool rooms were pressed into service to accommodate the crowds, their felt-topped playing tables cushioned with mattresses for the weary throng. Civic-minded citizens had raised $5,000 to construct a temporary wooden structure on the corner of Lake and Market streets where the convention would meet. With a 10,000-seat capacity, the "Wigwam"—so called because the chiefs of the Republican Party would gather there—was said to be the largest auditorium in the country. It had a huge rectangular floor, 180- by 100-feet, and a spacious balcony running along three sides. Chicago women had softened the surroundings by wreathing rosettes and evergreens through the uprights and hanging red, white, and blue bunting from the rafters. A giant gilded eagle frowned down from the podium.[9]

The day before the convention opened, the *Chicago Press and Tribune* ran a three-column editorial headlined "The Winning Man, Abraham Lincoln." It was the work of Norman Judd, whom Lincoln had asked personally to "help me a little in this matter, in your end of the vineyard." Despite Judd's determined press agentry, Seward remained the preconvention favorite, the one politician who had most forcefully and frequently articulated the antislavery cause in Congress. Seward also hailed from New York, which had the largest number of electoral votes. But he had certain serious weaknesses as well. To begin with, he was opposed within his own state by reformers such as William Cullen Bryant and Horace Greeley, who complained loudly about his close links to the flamboyant and corrupt political wheeler-dealer Thurlow Weed. Seward was also weakest in precisely those states the Republicans needed to carry to win what was universally expected to be a close election—Pennsylvania, Indiana, and Illinois. Stephen Douglas, if he managed to nail down the Democratic nomination, was historically formidable there, and even old John Bell might siphon off precious votes with his appeal to tradition-minded Whigs. Worse yet, Seward's unwavering and un-compromising espousal of an "irresistible conflict" made many people nervous. It was one thing to draw a distinction between pro- and anti-slavery positions in Congress; but a president would have to find a way to govern the entire country—assuming there was still a country left to govern in 1861.[10]

Besides Seward, there was a notable lack of first-tier candidates. Fellow abolitionist Salmon P. Chase of Ohio also faced in-state opposition, and he was scarcely less conciliatory than Seward when it came to the South. Edward Bates of Missouri was too conservative for radical antislavery proponents, and his link to the Know-Nothings fatally weakened him with the large German population within his own state. Pennsylvania's colorless Senator Simon Cameron had little to recommend him other than his place of residence, and Supreme Court justice John McLean was even older than Bell and Everett. That left Lincoln, although few delegates realized it yet. He was sound enough in his opposition to slavery to appeal to the abolitionists, but moderate enough—at least in theory—to reach Republican conservatives who did not want to confront the South. Above all, Lincoln had fought Douglas and the Democrats within Illinois for more than a quarter of a century, and even though he had lost the 1858 senatorial race, he had made a far better showing than many people had expected. With the crescent of states in the Old Northwest shaping up to be the major battleground of the election, Kentucky-born, Indiana-reared, Illinois-based Lincoln was well positioned to contend for those rustic votes, one hand-split fence rail at a time.

That, at any rate, was what Lincoln's managers were busy telling convention delegates. Establishing their headquarters at the Tremont

House, rotund Judge David Davis and his assistants fanned out to spread the gospel of Abraham Lincoln and his manifest "availability." Their most pressing task was to prevent a first-ballot stampede to Seward, whose wealthy New York backers had dispatched a thirteen-car train-load of boisterous supporters to Chicago to encourage just such a rush. Lincoln's people countered by persuading Illinois railroads to provide free rides to the convention site for Lincoln backers. To further offset Seward's numbers, Jesse Fell, secretary of the Republican State Cen-tral Committee (and the man who first had put the presidential bug in Lincoln's ear), had his office print thousands of counterfeit admis-sion tickets to the Wigwam. When Seward's delegates tried to enter the hall, many of them were turned away. Others were seated intentionally as far away from the front as possible, while the crowd was salted with Lincoln "shouters" whose leather-lunged hurrahs could drown out the distant cheers for Seward. (One renowned stentorian, Methodist min-ister Edward Ames, was said to be able to shout all the way across Lake Michigan.)[11]

It would take more than stump-shouting preachers to stop Seward, of course, and Davis and his helpers worked ceaselessly to broker deals with other delegations. The biggest plum was Pennsylvania, whose forty-eight convention votes were halfheartedly committed to Cameron, a veteran wire-puller credited with the immortal definition of an honest politician as "a man who, when he's bought, stays bought." After the convention opened on May 16, Davis met with Cameron in his room at the Tremont House. Lincoln, already alarmed by a message from backer Charles H. Ray that "a pledge or two may be necessary when the pinch comes," sent firm orders to Davis to "make no contracts that will bind me." Davis shrugged them off. "Lincoln ain't here and don't know what we have to meet," Davis said, "so we will go ahead, as if we hadn't heard from him, and he must ratify it." It is unclear whether Davis made a concrete promise to Cameron of a cabinet post in return for delivering Pennsylvania's delegation, or merely told him that he would recommend Cameron for the job. But ten months later Cameron would find himself sitting behind the secretary's desk at the War Department, from which position he would oversee the mismanagement—willful or not—of hun-dreds of thousands of dollars' worth of faulty equipment and weapons before Lincoln could stop him. For the time being, Davis came bustling down the hotel stairs and told Joseph Medill, "Damned if we haven't got them," meaning either the Pennsylvanians or Seward. Some of the delegates took time off from their horse-trading to attend the opening night of a new play at McVickers Theater, a few doors down from the Wigwam. It was a broadly acted drawing-room comedy about the collision of the New World and the Old, entitled *Our American Cousin*. Widely popular, it would play across the country for the next several years, concluding its run in Washington, D.C., at Ford's Theatre in the spring of 1865.[12]

Other meetings were taking place that night as well. In Seward's headquarters, campaign manager Thurlow Weed addressed the wavering delegations. "Four years ago we went to Philadelphia to name our candidate," he warned them, "and we made one of the most inexcusable blunders. We nominated a man who had no qualification for the position of Chief Magistrate [John C. Frémont]. We were defeated as we probably deserved to be. What this country will demand as its chief executive for the next four years is a man of the highest order of executive ability, a man of real statesmanlike qualities, well known to the country, and of large experience in national affairs. No other class of men ought to be considered at this time. We think we have in Mr. Seward just the qualities the country will need." *New York Tribune* editor Horace Greeley respectfully disagreed. Warning delegates that Seward could not carry Indiana, Iowa, New Jersey, or Pennsylvania, Greeley admonished: "I suppose they are telling you that Seward is the be all and the end all of our existence as a party, our great statesman, our profound philosopher, our pillar of cloud by day, our pillar of fire by night, but I want to tell you boys that in spite of all this you couldn't elect Seward if you could nominate him." A rumor circulated that the Republican gubernatorial candidates in the doubtful states of Indiana, Illinois, and Pennsylvania would all resign if Seward were nominated. Greeley was "a damned old ass," said one Seward delegate—understandably, given the circumstances.[13]

By the time the convention was ready to receive nominations, Lincoln's men had wrapped up the unanimous first-ballot votes of Illinois and Indiana, whose chairman, Caleb Smith, was a former Whig who had served in Congress with Lincoln, as well as second-ballot pledges from Pennsylvania and New Jersey—the four lower northern states that had gone Democratic in 1856. A Republican who could carry those four states, along with the other northern states that Frémont had won four years earlier, could be elected president. It was a powerful argument for Lincoln.

There was a palpable air of excitement as convention marshals opened the doors of the Wigwam on the morning of May 18. Seward's supporters, 1,000 strong, assembled at the Richmond House and marched four abreast to the auditorium behind their scarlet-and-white, epaulette-wearing band. By the time they arrived, bogus Lincoln delegates had taken many of their seats. It was standing room only inside the Wigwam; men were jammed three-deep into every crevice of the hall. After a brief floor fight over the makeup of the Maryland delegation, convention chairman George Ashmun of Massachusetts entertained nominations for president. In short order, Seward, Lincoln, Cameron, Chase, Bates, McLean, and New Jersey favorite-son candidate William L. Dayton were nominated. *Cincinnati Commercial* journalist Murat Halstead, who had just endured the Democratic conflagration in Charleston and the Constitutional Union minuet in Baltimore, was on hand to observe the Republicans in action. "The only names that produced tremendous applause were those of Seward and Lincoln," he noted. Supporters of both men competed for dominance. "The shouting was absolutely frantic, shrill and wild," wrote Halstead. "No Comanches, no panthers ever struck a higher note, or gave screams with more infernal intensity." Hats flew through the air, handkerchiefs waved wildly, and Indiana delegate Henry Lane, a hard-core Lincoln man, leaped onto a table, swinging his hat and cane like an acrobat. "Abe Lincoln has it by the sound!" shouted one man above the din.[14]

Not yet. Seward led the first ballot with 173½ votes, far short of the 233 needed for nomination. Lincoln was second with 102 votes; the rest trailed far behind. In the New England states, where Seward was thought to be strongest, Lincoln managed to win 19 votes, undoubtedly a reflection of his recent speaking tour there. Anxious Seward supporters called for an immediate second ballot. Slowly but unmistakably, votes peeled away from the New Yorker, 48 in one blow from Cameron's Pennsylvania. The totals now stood at Seward 184½, Lincoln 181. The wily Halstead stopped tallying anyone's votes but Lincoln's. At the end of the third ballot, Lincoln had 231½ votes—just one and a half shy of the nomination. Ohio delegate David K. Cartter of Cleveland jumped to his feet. A large, dark-haired man disfigured by smallpox and afflicted with a stutter, Cartter seized his one moment of reflected glory. "I rise (eh), Mr. Chairman (eh), to announce the change of four votes of Ohio from Mr. Chase to Mr. Lincoln" was how Halstead rendered it. There was a moment of silence, a collective intake of breath, and then "there was a noise in the Wigwam like the rush of a great wind in the van of a storm—and in another breath, the storm was there. There were thousands cheering with the energy of insanity." Someone shouted to an observer on the roof: "Fire the salute! Abe Lincoln is nominated!"[15]

Back home in Springfield, the new Republican nominee had spent an understandably restless morning, playing "fives," a sort of rudimentary handball, in the vacant lot next to the office of the *Illinois State Journal*. Unable to relax, he had paced over to the law office of James C. Conkling, the husband of Mary Lincoln's best friend, Mercy Ann Levering, who had just returned from Chicago with the latest scuttlebutt. It was Conkling's considered opinion that Seward could not be nominated—Lincoln would win. Stretched out on Conkling's sofa, Lincoln received the favorable report noncommittally. "Well, Conkling, I believe I will go back to my office and practice law," he said. Restlessly, Lincoln wandered over to his office, then to the telegraph office, and finally back to the *Journal* office. At length, a messenger rushed in and handed him a telegram. "Lincoln opened it," a witness said, "and a sudden pallor came over his features. He gazed upon it intently nearly three minutes." The telegram read: "TO LINCOLN YOU ARE NOMINATED." "Well, we've got it," Lincoln said, then added a characteristic joke: "Gentlemen, you had better come up and shake my hand while you can—honors elevate some men." He left immediately to tell the "little woman at our house" the news.[16]

All across Springfield cannons boomed, church bells tolled, people cheered and danced in the streets. That night, a torchlight parade wound its way to the familiar wooden home at the corner of Eighth and Jackson. Appearing at his front door, the Republican nominee for president said modestly that "he did not suppose the honor of such a visit was intended particularly for himself as a private citizen but rather as the representative to a great party." He would have invited everyone inside to celebrate, Lincoln said, if only he had enough room. "We will give you a larger house on the fourth of next March," someone shouted. The next day, an official delegation from Chicago arrived to formally notify Lincoln of his nomination. He offered the men ice water—he had decided not to break his sixteen-year ban on serving alcohol in his home, much to Mary's evident distaste. Convention chairman Ashmun read the notice to Lincoln who, careful lawyer that he was, asked for more time to go over the document. An awkward silence ensued. Lincoln broke it by picking out the tallest man in the group, Pennsylvania delegate William D. Kelley, and asking his height. "Six feet three," said Kelley. "I beat you," laughed Lincoln. "I am six feet four without my high-heeled boots." "Pennsylvania bows to Illinois," Kelley said suavely. "I am glad that we have found a candidate for the presidency whom we can look up to." Going out the door, a still-glowing Kelley whispered to fellow delegate Carl Schurz: "Well, we might have done a more brilliant thing, but we could hardly have done a better thing."[17]

◆ ◆ ◆

In Washington, Lincoln's oldest rival agreed with that assessment. From his contacts in Chicago, Stephen Douglas had received the news of Lincoln's nomination sooner than anyone. When he announced the news to his Senate colleagues, a great cheer arose from the Republican side of the aisle. Some of his own friends were equally pleased, saying that Lincoln could be beaten easily, but Douglas knew better. Lincoln, he said, was the best debater he had ever faced, and they could expect "a devil of a fight" in the general election—assuming that Douglas could still win his party's nomination, and that it would still be worth something if he did. Douglas spent the next month arm wrestling with southern ultras and Buchanan administration fixers who were attempting to erode his base of support. Former president Franklin Pierce was a particular target. Jefferson Davis, who had been his secretary of war, importuned Pierce to enter the race, saying that he would "as soon have a Free-Soiler as our little grog-drinking, electioneering demagogue." Pierce had no particular love for Douglas, whose Kansas-Nebraska Act had effectively undermined his presidency, but he would not consent to have his name placed in nomination in Baltimore—even his hometown paper, the *Concord Patriot*, was supporting the Little Giant. In Connecticut, a Douglas supporter haughtily turned down a job offer from Buchanan's people, denouncing them as "a class of puppies who are barking at trees they cannot climb." Massive public meetings in support of Douglas were held in Boston, Philadelphia, and New York City, the latter at the site of Lincoln's recent triumph, the Cooper Union.[18]

In the South, Douglas sought to solidify his support with moderates, while at the same time backing new slates of delegates to replace the ultras who had bolted the convention at Charleston. Influential North

Carolina moderate W. H. Holden switched his support to Douglas with a frank assessment of the current situation: "The choice is now between Douglas and defeat and sectional dissolution," he said. "God forbid that the madness of the North and our own blindness, prejudice and folly should ever compel us to this step. I voted fifty-seven times against Douglas at Charleston. I expect to vote for him at Baltimore." At a meeting in Columbia, Tennessee, the chairman of the Volunteer State delegation tore into "honest, deranged Jeff Davis" and "that damned, corrupt, dishonest Slidell," and promised to support Douglas if he was the party's nominee. Douglas was encouraged by the show of support, telling prominent financial backer August Belmont, "All we have to do is to stand by the delegates appointed by the people in the seceding states in the place of the disunionists."[19]

Unfortunately for Douglas, it would not be that simple. Nine southern senators and ten congressmen signed an open letter urging the wayward delegates to reassemble in Baltimore and work together to draft a suitable new platform, whether or not Douglas stood atop it in the end. Louisiana senator Judah Benjamin, not one of the signers, announced defiantly that he and other ultras would go to Baltimore with "unaltered instructions and a firm determination" to force the Douglas Democrats into submission. "Mr. Benjamin is mistaken," retorted Ohio senator George Pugh, "if he supposes that the men who stood there at Charleston for two weeks in that atmosphere voting down your resolutions again and again, and voting for Stephen A. Douglas, are going to be tired when it comes to Baltimore, which is a much more agreeable atmosphere for them." Pugh's statement reflected the determined attitude that the ubiquitous Murat Halstead observed among Douglas's supporters as they reassembled in Baltimore in mid-June. "The friends of Mr. Douglas," he wrote, "assumed an arrogance of tone that precluded the hope of amicable adjustment of difficulties." It would be better for the country, said one Douglas supporter, "to get rid of Yancey, Davis, and Co. They are a curse to us and the Republic and should go with Arnold and Burr."[20]

In that less-than-conciliatory attitude, the Democratic delegates reconvened at 10:00 a.m. on June 18 inside Baltimore's Front Street Theater. Trainloads of Douglas supporters thronged the city, far outnumbering the southern ultras who, by coincidence, had reserved rooms in the same hotel as the pro-Douglas Illinois delegation. Former Massachusetts congressman Caleb Cushing, serving again as convention chairman, immediately reasserted his uselessness, refusing to rule on the admissibility of the seceding delegations. For three long, tense days the credentials committee debated the issue, while special trains sped Douglas loyalists back and forth from Baltimore to Washington for nervous midnight skull sessions. Meanwhile, Baltimore's finest, decked out in broad coats and crinolines, dutifully trooped into the visitor's gallery two or three times each day, only to witness the convention immediately recess again. Alabama fire-eater William Yancey, who had single-handedly disrupted the Charleston convention, was back on the scene and looking for trouble. The northern Democrats, he jeered, were like ostriches, "hiding their heads in the sand of popular sovereignty, all unaware that their great, ugly, ragged, abolition body was exposed." As he had done previously, Yancey played to the crowd outside the convention hall, giving fiery, impromptu street-corner speeches designed to keep everyone on edge.[21]

On the morning of the fourth day, in a piece of political theater that was almost too perfect a metaphor to believe, the stage platform on which the delegates were sitting suddenly gave way, sending 150 startled New Yorkers and Pennsylvanians tumbling through the floor. "New York and Pennsylvania have gone down together," said a wag. New York delegate Isaiah Rynders, one of the fallen, clambered out of the wreckage and announced cheerfully, "Mr. President, the platform has not broken down—only one plank got loose." When someone requested another recess to allow workers to repair the floor, Rynders added the sardonic hope that they should "at the same time repair the injury done to the Democratic Party."[22]

An hour later the floor, if not the party, was repaired, and the convention filed in to hear the credentials committee ruling. The majority report, favored by Douglas, readmitted most of the straying southern delegates, but drew the line at the Alabama delegation, which would have permitted Yancey to stroll victoriously into the hall. A minority report called for the admission of all the seceding delegates, on the questionable grounds that they had not permanently walked out of the nominating process—only that part being conducted in Charleston. Complicating matters even more, the hall was jammed with spectators who had gained entry with bogus tickets. Argumentative as ever, Massachusetts delegate Benjamin Butler complained that "he had not come five hundred miles to attend a mass meeting" and demanded that the floor be cleared at once. The convention adjourned in disarray. Congressman William Montgomery of Pennsylvania, leaving the hall, sniped at fellow delegate Josiah Randall, calling him a "poor old man," at which point Randall's son dashed up and punched Montgomery in the face. Bleeding profusely, Montgomery shook off the blow and knocked the much-smaller man to the ground before onlookers separated them.[23]

The next day, June 22, the convention reassembled to vote on the committee reports. After the minority report was decisively rejected, 150–100½, the delegates approved the majority report piecemeal. Tennessee delegate J. D. C. Atkins, a consistent voice of moderation, rose to request that the proceedings not be delayed any further. He was met with a mixture of "applause and hisses," Halstead noted. After another brief recess, Georgia delegate W. B. Gaulden, a slave trader from Savannah, made a rambling speech on the virtues of slavery, which he said had "done more to advance the prosperity and intelligence of the white race, and of the human race, than all else together." Defining himself proudly as "a slave breeder" and "a nigger man," Gaulden invited the delegates to visit his plantation, where "I will show them as fine a lot of Negroes, and the pure African, too, as they can find anywhere. And I will show them as handsome a set of little children as there can be seen, and any quantity of them, too." This was too much for other members of his own delegation, who publicly censured Gaulden for bringing "mortification and disgust to the delegation from Georgia." On that note, a Douglas delegate moved that they begin the nominations, but Cushing studiously ignored him. Instead, he turned to Virginia delegate chairman Charles W. Russell, who had been monotonously chanting "Mr. President!" over and over for several minutes.[24]

Russell had worked hard to keep the Virginia delegation from bolting the Charleston convention, he said, but now he and his fellow delegates had come to believe that it was "inconsistent with their convictions of duty" to participate any further in the proceedings. He declined to say what those convictions were, noting merely that the delegates were answerable only to "the Democracy of Virginia"—it was unclear whether he meant the party or the state. Twenty-five of the thirty Virginia delegates then rose and left the theater, followed immediately by sixteen delegates from North Carolina, nineteen from Tennessee, nine from Maryland, and all seventeen from the Pacific Coast states of California and Oregon. In properly theatrical fashion, California delegate Austin Smith of San Francisco favored the crowd with a florid valediction full of "melancholy faces," "lacerated hearts," "grinning assassins," and much "bleeding and weeping over the downfall and destruction of the Democratic Party." Smith's performance concluded the evening's dramatics, and the convention adjourned for the night.[25]

Back in Washington, Douglas had been expecting the worst. Two days earlier, he had sent a confidential letter to William Richardson, once again the leader of his efforts, offering to withdraw in favor of "some other Non-intervention and Union-loving Democrat," possibly Alexander Stephens. But Richardson, infuriated by the refusal of southern delegates to compromise on either the platform or the candidate, pocketed the letter and refused even to admit that he had received it. Douglas sent a follow-up telegram to Dean Richmond, chairman of the New York delegation, repeating his offer and inviting Richmond to pick another candidate. There was no one else. Having invested so much time, money, and emotion in the effort to nominate Douglas, the northerners and midwesterners who dominated the convention were unwilling, if not indeed unable, to imagine switching to someone else. As the not unsympathetic Halstead observed, Douglas "had raised a greater tempest than he had imagined. He had stirred up the storm but could not control the whirlwind."[26]

The next morning, the whirlwind broke, or at any rate blew itself out. More states walked out of the convention, including the host state of Maryland and the border states of Kentucky and Delaware. Amid loud, mocking cheers, convention chairman Caleb Cushing also left; his place was taken by Ohio governor David Tod. The inimitable Butler, assuming leadership of the Massachusetts delegation, announced that he and his liberty-loving colleagues were leaving as well, since they had no intention of "sit[ting] in a convention where the African slave trade—which is piracy by the laws of my country—is approvingly advocated." He had taken the precaution of having a "plug ugly" Boston prizefighter named Price watch his back while he made the announcement, but he need not have bothered. Judging by the cheers and handshakes that greeted his announcement, everyone was happy to see Butler go.[27]

With the pro-Douglas Tod now wielding the gavel, the convention turned at last to the matter of choosing a nominee. It was a foregone, forlorn conclusion. On the first ballot, Douglas received 173½ votes, out of a diminished total of 191½ cast. A second vote was taken, and Douglas's strength increased to 181½. Despite the ruling at the Charleston convention that a candidate needed two-thirds of the total delegates to win the nomination, Douglas supporter Daniel Hoge of Virginia moved that since his man had received two-thirds of the vote of all the delegates remaining in the hall, he should simply be declared the nominee. Richardson pointed out that the Charleston convention was the only time in party history that the Democrats had adopted a two-thirds rule. There was precedent, if not necessarily unanimity, for Douglas's nomination, and the hall erupted in a storm of cheers after Richardson's speech. The new chairman called for quiet. "Gentlemen of the convention," said Tod, "as your presiding officer I declare Stephen A. Douglas, of Illinois, by the unanimous vote of this convention, the nominee of the Democratic Party of the United States for president. And may God, in his infinite mercy, protect him, and with him this Union." In a futile bow to the South, Alabama senator Benjamin Fitzpatrick was chosen as Douglas's running mate, despite the fact that he had voted for the fugitive slave code in the Senate and generally had opposed the Little Giant on most other issues as well.[28]

While Douglas was belatedly receiving the prize he had worked toward all his life, his opponents met inside jam-packed Maryland Institute Hall in a spirit of contradictory self-congratulation. Cushing, backed by Butler and his pugilist bodyguard, reassumed the role of convention chairman. Halstead wandered over from the Front Street Theater to watch the proceedings. All the leading ultras were there, including Yancey and Robert Toombs, and Halstead noted that "I had not seen them look so happy during the sixteen weary days of the convention." Yancey, in particular, "glowed with satisfaction." In short order, the session nominated outgoing vice president John C. Breckinridge and Oregon senator Joseph Lane as its standard-bearers. Called on to say a few words in support of Breckinridge, Yancey took the opportunity to bury Douglas "where his friends placed him . . . beneath the grave of squatter sovereignty," but went on at such wearisome length that he drove hundreds of delegates from the hall while Cushing fidgeted unhappily on stage alongside him. A planned seconding speech for Breckinridge was canceled for lack of time.[29]

That evening, both wings of the grievously wounded Democratic Party adjourned unceremoniously and left Baltimore behind them. Halstead shared a train car with some of the northwestern delegates, one of whom complained: "I have been vexed. After all the battles we have fought for the South—to be served in this manner—it is ungrateful and mean." Southerners, he added, "had been ruling over niggers so long they thought they could rule white men just the same." An Indiana delegate chimed in that he "was happy to tell the Seceders that the valley of the Wabash was worth more than all the country between the Potomac and the Rio Grande, niggers included." A separate delegation of Douglas loyalists steamed into Washington by rail, carrying with them the somewhat sodden news of his nomination. At the bravely lighted headquarters in the National Hotel, they were joined by other supporters and marched over to Douglas's home on I Street, where the obviously unwell senator met them with a brief address that contained more warning than warmth. "The Union," he said, "is in great danger. It can only be saved by a strict adherence to popular sovereignty and the defeat of the interventionist extremes. Secession is disunion. Secession from the Democratic Party means secession from the federal Union. Can the seceders fail to perceive that their efforts to divide and defeat the Democratic Party, if successful, must lead directly to the secession of the southern states?"[30]

Two nights later, a similar delegation, this one complete with a brass band, serenaded Douglas's next-door neighbor, Breckinridge, with a similar display of enthusiasm. It, too, was met with a decided lack of excitement from the honoree. "It sometimes happens that men are placed in a position where they are reluctant to act and exposure themselves to censure, if not execration," said Breckinridge. "But we must be prepared for such occurrences in this life. All men can move forward with dignity and purpose, to pursue that course." The Kentucky-born vice president, who had just been elected to the Senate from his home state, was not actually living in the mansion at the time (he would, in fact, never live there). Instead, he had been escorted to the empty residence by Jefferson Davis and Robert Toombs for the sole purposes of making the point to his neighbor Douglas, if one needed to be made, that there were now two Democratic nominees in the race.[31]

Breckinridge's last-minute entry into the presidential contest was a surprise to everyone—himself included. Earlier that month, he had met with a group of northern delegates led by Benjamin Butler, who were en route to Baltimore for the second convention. They sounded him out on the issues—not surprisingly, he was committed to the Union and the Constitution—and heard him denounce southern extremists who were threatening to secede if the Republican nominee, Abraham Lincoln, was elected in November. In Butler's retelling, the northern bolters nominated Breckinridge more as a hedge against secession than a protest against Douglas. Perhaps, but that did not explain the instant support the vice president received from Davis, Toombs, and other ultras. In fact, they were playing a double game, opposing Douglas and the northern Democrats on the one hand, while strengthening the Republicans (and the option of secession) on the other. It is doubtful whether Breckinridge fully understood just how completely and cynically he was being used by the ultras, although Pennsylvania delegate George Nelson Smith warned him that "the nomination of the Seceders' convention . . . will be fatal to the party and ruinous to you. I beseech you to consider well the step you are about to take. Evil will most assuredly follow acceptance." "I trust I have the courage to lead a forlorn hope," Breckinridge observed forlornly.[32]

A halfhearted attempt to reunite the party was put into motion by Jefferson Davis—of all people—who attempted to convince the three anti-Lincoln candidates to withdraw in favor of a fourth candidate, possibly former New York governor Horatio Seymour. In Davis's account, written twenty years after the fact, Breckinridge and Bell readily agreed to drop out, but Douglas refused, calling the idea impractical and saying that he was "in the hands of my friends, and my friends will not accept such a scheme." A second version, which sounds more like Douglas, had him telling Pennsylvania representative Edward McPherson, who had broached a similar scheme: "By God, sir, the election shall never go into the House; before it shall go into the House, I will throw it to Lincoln." In an attempt, perhaps, to force his hand, fellow southerners successfully pressured Douglas's running mate, Benjamin Fitzpatrick, to withdraw from the ticket, but this merely stiffened Douglas's resolve. In place of Fitzpatrick, the Democratic National Committee selected another southerner, former Georgia senator and governor Herschel V. Johnson. It was a better choice, anyway. Not only was Johnson closer to Douglas on the issues, he was also a longtime friend of the Little Giant who had supported his presidential bids in 1852 and 1856—and would have done so in Baltimore as well, had he been allowed to take the place of a Charleston seceder. It was a case of addition by subtraction.[33]

After the conventions, the various nominees began organizing for the fight. Douglas retained his headquarters at the National Hotel, naming Louisiana congressman Miles Taylor, an old friend, as chairman of the campaign. Given the confused state of the Democratic Party, Taylor's first task was to urge state organizations to give their "unequivocal support" to the Douglas-Johnson ticket. In Pennsylvania, where Breckinridge was popular, largely on the basis of being native son James Buchanan's often-ignored vice president, voters were to be given a choice of voting for either him or Douglas, depending on which candidate was thought to have a better chance of winning. This arrangement infuriated Douglas, who warned: "Any compromise with the Secessionists would be ruinous. An amalgamation ticket with the bolters would disgust the people & give every Northern State to Lincoln." Meanwhile, Breckinridge set up camp in the White House, where the president, despite his personal dislike for his old running mate, conferred frequently with Breckinridge's managers—Jefferson Davis, John Slidell, and William Bigler. As always, Buchanan used the power of patronage to cudgel his opponents, removing several pro-Douglas men from government posts, although he was careful to leave Douglas's father-in-law and brother-in-law in their "lucrative offices."[34]

Despite lingering physical and emotional ills, Douglas began making plans for a campaign trip to New York and New England. An inveterate campaigner, he could not envision obeying the genteel tradition of a presidential candidate remaining aloof from the most important campaign of his life. Lincoln, who had been on the road, off and on, for the better part of a year, had no such qualms. He would remain in Springfield and let the campaign come to him. Moving into a small room in the state capitol provided for his use by Governor John Wood, Lincoln and his tireless new secretary, John G. Nicolay, occupied themselves with receiving visitors and opening—but not always answering—the blizzard of letters that arrived each day. *New York Evening Post* editor William Cullen Bryant advised Lincoln in no uncertain terms "to make no speeches, write no letters as a candidate, enter into no pledges, make no promises, nor even give any of those kind words which men are apt to interpret into promises." Given his nearly three decades of political experience, Lincoln needed no such advice, but he took it anyway because it agreed with his own strategic vision. He broke character, so to speak, only once, when he wrote to his old friend Simeon Francis after the Baltimore convention: "I hesitate to say it, but it really appears now, as if the success of the Republican ticket is inevitable. We have no reason to doubt any of the states which voted for Frémont. Add to these, Minnesota, Pennsylvania, and New Jersey, and the thing is done." Another veteran politician shared his view, if not his optimism. Alexander Stephens surveyed his party's dire political landscape. "The seceders intended from the beginning to rule or ruin," Little Aleck observed bitterly. "Men will be cutting one another's throats in a little while. In less than twelve months we shall be in a war, and that the bloodiest in history." His prediction would prove all too accurate, on both counts.[35]

8

⚜

The Prairies Are on Fire

The general election was set, with four exceptionally well-qualified presidential candidates confronting the electorate. On its face, the multicandidate election was not unusual. Five times in recent years there had been third-party candidates. But there was something decidedly different this time around. The election was not among four candidates seeking the national vote, but two separate elections, breaking down sectionally. Four men were running for president in 1860, but only two of them really counted—Abraham Lincoln and Stephen Douglas. Neither John C. Breckinridge nor John Bell could hope to carry any states in the North. By the same token, neither Lincoln nor Douglas could expect to carry any of the southern states—Lincoln, in fact, was not even on the ballot there. The contest would be decided in the northern states, between Lincoln and Douglas, and opening odds favored Lincoln.

Douglas, swept away by the first flush of enthusiasm after his nomination, predicted optimistically that he would carry Alabama, Arkansas, Georgia, Louisiana, Missouri, and Texas, and hoped "to get enough more in the free States to be elected by the people." That was highly unlikely, given the Republicans' strength across the swath of northern states from New England to Minnesota, to say nothing of his ongoing anathematization in the South. Still, Douglas was nothing if not a fighter, and he immediately took to the campaign trail, setting out for New York City in late June to meet with prospective financial backers. En route, he stopped over in Philadelphia, where he declined (for once) to make a speech, saying only, "If my political opinions are not known to the people of the United States, it is not worthwhile for me to explain them now."[1]

Accompanied by Adele, Douglas set up camp in New York at the luxurious Fifth Avenue Hotel. The couple was escorted up Broadway by a boisterous claque of supporters, but once again the candidate declined to make a campaign speech. "It is the first time in my life," he said, "that I have been placed in a position where I had to look on and see a fight without taking a hand in it." That would not last long. "Mr. Douglas has no faith in standing still," observed the *New York Times*. After his New York stopover, he intended to head to the flinty shores of New England, his ancestral home, to see his brother-in-law, James Madison Cutts, Jr., graduate from Harvard and to visit his aged mother in upstate New York. The visit was announced long in advance, and when Douglas failed to appear in Clifton Springs for several weeks, the opposition press had a field day with his continuing absence. "A Boy Lost!" screamed one Republican handbill. "Left Washington, D.C., some time in July, to go home to his mother. He has not yet reached his mother, who is very anxious about him. He has been seen in Philadelphia, New York City, Hartford, Conn., at a clambake in Rhode Island. He has been heard from in Boston, Portland, Augusta, and Bangor, Me. He is about five feet nothing in height and about the same in diameter the other way. He has a red face, short legs, and a large belly. Answers to the name Little Giant, talks a great deal, very loud, always about himself. He has an idea that he is a candidate for President. Had on, when he left, drab pants, a white vest, and blue coat with brass buttons; the tail is very near the ground." Plaintive messages signed "S.D.'s Mother" were published daily in Republican newspapers, appealing for information about her "wandering son."[2]

In fact, Douglas had been caught up in a delusive, if not self-deluding, burst of enthusiasm for his candidacy in the Northeast. At Harvard, he appeared on the same stage with Constitutional Unionist vice presidential candidate Edward Everett and Massachusetts senator Charles Sumner, who was still recovering from his savage beating on the floor of the Senate four years earlier. Neither Douglas nor Sumner alluded to the incident, although Douglas did cross swords with Boston editor Benjamin F. Hallett, author of the ambiguous Cincinnati platform of 1856. The Democrats, said Hallett, would soon unite behind a single candidate. "Never!" shouted Douglas, noting that he could never work with anyone who had "voted against me at Charleston on principle," and "if you voted against me out of personal hatred, I know very well how to act toward you." In keeping with his renewed bellicosity, Douglas toured the Revolutionary War battlefields at Lexington and Bunker Hill, where he compared his fight for popular sovereignty to the patriots' struggle against the British. This was too much for one Massachusetts journalist, who complained that Douglas "has staked so much on the Squatter Sovereignty doctrine that he seems to be falling into a monomania about it, and drags it about the country with him with as much assiduity as if it were a change of linen or a toothbrush."[3]

For nearly two months, Douglas toured New York and New England, describing an erratic loop that followed no discernible pattern. To get to western New York, joked one New Hampshire newspaper, Douglas "naturally came to New Haven, Guilford and Hartford on his way, and at the latter place he was 'betrayed' into a speech. Still bent on his maternal pilgrimage, he goes toward Boston. At Worcester, some Judas 'betrayed' him into a speech. At Boston, 'betrayed' again." Even the folks back home took note of his wanderings. The *Weekly Illinois Journal* printed "A Plaintive Poem" that wondered: "Why did I down to Hartford go?/'Twas not my squatter self to show;/I went to hunt, I told you so,/My mother." Still seeking, however transparently, to make his trip appear nonpolitical, Douglas would feign surprise when the crowd at a railroad station summoned him to speak. At Concord, New Hampshire, he consented to speak "a little, just for exercise." He may have spoken more truly than he meant. Lost in the initial outpouring of support was the fact that the Republicans had carried the entire region, including New York, with the much-weaker, woefully inexperienced John C. Frémont in 1856. Since then, the abolitionist movement there had gotten even stronger, and Abraham Lincoln had made a well-received swing through New England the previous winter following his landmark appearance at the Cooper Union. Douglas could scarcely hope to carry any of the New England states, and he wasted valuable time and energy preaching, in essence, to the choir.[4]

At length, Douglas pulled into Clifton Springs, near Canandaigua, for a brief visit with his mother, who complained in true maternal fashion that "he never writes when we may expect him." Mrs. Granger expressed the odd opinion that her son's presidential campaign would have a good effect on his health by keeping him from making so many speeches. There was not much chance of that. Douglas preceded his visit to his mother with a well-publicized pilgrimage to his father's gravesite in Brandon, Vermont, where virtually the entire town turned out to meet his train. A twenty-one-gun salute heralded his arrival, followed by a prematurely optimistic rendition of "Hail to the Chief." Stopping at the modest two-story house where he was born, Douglas affirmed: "I am proud of being a native of Vermont. Here I first learned to love liberty." Someone in the crowd—probably a Republican—challenged him on his earlier statement that Vermont "was a great state to be born in— provided you left it early in life." Douglas replied smoothly that he had meant that it was impossible to rise above all the "great men with great minds" who lived there, and so he had been forced to make his way west to seek his fortune.[5]

The Douglas express rumbled through Burlington, Montpelier, Concord, Manchester, Nashua, and Providence before rolling to a stop at the upscale resort of Newport, Rhode Island, where the candidate spent the next twelve days relaxing, swimming in the ocean, and attending formal dinners where he and Adele invariably were the guests of honor. It was a good time to rest. "It is not a seemly or a welcome sight to see any man whom a large portion of his countrymen have thought fit for the Presidency, traversing the country and soliciting his own election," sniffed the *New York Times*. The Jonesboro, Illinois, *Gazette* was more dismissive. "Douglas is going about peddling his opinions as a tin man peddles his wares," it reported. "The only excuse for him is that since he is a small man, he has a right to be engaged in small business, and small business it is for a candidate for the Presidency to be strolling around the country begging for votes like a town constable." The *North Iowan* went even further, comparing Douglas to a performing monkey and recommending, "He should be attended by some Italian, with his hand organ to grind out an accompaniment."[6]

Douglas cared little what the opposition newspapers were saying about him, but he was greatly troubled by the dire financial report he received at Newport from his campaign treasurer, August Belmont. The

New York City financier, American representative to the fabulous Roth-schild fortune, was having no luck raising funds for the Little Giant. He had started the bidding, so to speak, by throwing in $1,000 of his own money, but other New Yorkers were loath to contribute funds to what had the unmistakable look of a losing campaign, particularly since many of them had long-standing ties to southern business interests. "If we could only demonstrate to all those lukewarm & selfish moneybags that we have a strong probability to carry the State of New York," said Bel-mont, "we might get from them the necessary sinews of war." As it was, he could not even manage to get a quorum for a called meeting of the Democratic National Executive Committee in early August. Only two members bothered to show up. Belmont appealed to each congressional district to contribute $100 to Douglas's campaign—scarcely a heavy tithe—but by mid-September "not a single cent" had been raised.[7]

Another unpropitious omen for the campaign was the loss of the *Chicago Times*, Douglas's longtime mouthpiece in Illinois, which was purchased by Cyrus McCormick. There was talk of the *Times* throwing its support to Breckinridge. The only prominent northern newspaper supporting Douglas was James Gordon Bennett's *New York Herald,* and that was a decidedly mixed blessing, given Bennett's parlous reputation, both personally and professionally. Even then, Bennett was halfhearted in his backing. Fellow editor Joseph Medill, a Lincoln loyalist, found Bennett willing to bargain. "He is too rich to want money," Medill informed Lincoln. "Social position we suspect is what he wants. He wants to be in a position to be invited with his wife and son to dinner or tea at the White House occasionally. I think we can afford to agree to that much." Lincoln, as always, was noncommittal.[8]

Lincoln, naturally, was much on Douglas's mind. His old debating opponent, said Douglas, "is a very clever fellow—a kind-hearted, good-natured, amiable man. I have not the heart to say anything against Abe Lincoln; I have fought him so long that I have a respect for him." It was obvious, he told one audience, that "you will have to go to Illinois for your next President." While in Boston, he said much the same thing to Massachusetts Republican Anson Burlingame. "Won't it be a splendid sight, Burlingame?" he gushed. "Douglas and Old Abe, all at Washington together—for the next President is to come from Illinois." Burlingame understood him to mean it to be the latter, in which case Douglas had already read the writing on the wall. So, too, had his southern running mate. In a letter to Alexander Stephens in July, Herschel Johnson warned: "I have not much hope for the future. The sky is dark. The fires of sectionalism in the South are waxing hot and Black Republicanism in the North already exhibits the insolence of conscious strength. The South is in peril—the Union is in peril—all is in peril that is dear to freemen." Johnson expected Lincoln to be elected, hoping only that the Democratic Party could be reconstructed "at a future day." It was not much on which to hang a campaign.[9]

◆ ◆ ◆

Lincoln, keeping himself safely under wraps in Springfield, made one early misstep in the campaign. He would like to go into Kentucky to discuss the issues, he told a correspondent, presumably tongue-in-cheek, but "would not the people lynch me?" Somehow the letter got out, making Lincoln look both foolish and timid. Much embarrassed by the ensuing brouhaha, the candidate publicly retracted the statement and took pains to ensure that he would not make the same mistake again. Careful, if not necessarily content, to remain in the background, he dutifully entertained a steady stream of friendly reporters who trooped through his parlor in search of homey details for their readers. "Honest Old Abe," recounted the *Chicago Press and Tribune*, was "always clean . . . never fashionable . . . careless but not slovenly. In his personal habits, Mr. Lincoln is as simple as a child. His food is plain and nutritious. He never drinks intoxicating liquors of any sort. He is not addicted to tobacco."[10]

Lincoln, in their recounting, was as rustic and pure as Natty Bumppo. Not only could he discuss "the great democratic principle of our Government," enthused one Missouri journalist, "but at the same time tell how to navigate a vessel, maul a rail, or even to dress a deer-skin." (Why such frontier-like topics would have arisen in Lincoln's genteel sitting room, the visitor did not say.) Meanwhile, Mary Lincoln graciously welcomed as many as 100 visitors a day into their home. She was a new sort of candidate's wife, more than willing to share her political opinions— she even bet a neighbor a new pair of shoes that her husband would be elected president—but smart enough to do so with a smile. "Whatever of awkwardness may be ascribed to her husband," reported a *New York Evening Post* journalist, "there is none of it in her. She converses with freedom and grace, and is thoroughly *au fait* in all the little amenities of society." Gushed another reporter: "I shall be proud as an American citizen when the day brings Mary Lincoln to grace the White House."[11]

Lincoln's biggest problem was boredom. Herndon found his law partner "bored—bored badly. I would not have his place." Confined to the city limits of Springfield, Lincoln spent most of his time at the capitol, where he and Nicolay labored to answer the mountain of letters that tumbled against the door like a gentle but insistent landslide. Most were either letters of congratulation or requests for autographs. Lincoln answered the latter with a standard, if brief, reply: "You request an autograph, and here it is. Yours truly A. Lincoln." The candidate gave his assistant a detailed checklist of instructions for handling the mail: "Ascertain what he wants. On what subject he would converse, and the particulars if he will give them. Is an interview indispensable? And if so, how soon must it be had? Tell him my motto is 'Fairness to all' but commit me to nothing." To avoid the prying eyes of Democratic postmasters, Lincoln employed a "flying squadron" of friends to hand-deliver especially sensitive letters. Photographers and painters also descended on Springfield, including one painter with the unfortunate name of John Brown, who was given the task of painting a miniature of the candidate that would be "good-looking whether the original would justify it or not."[12]

Besides the normal curiosity raised by a relatively obscure presidential nominee, there was another reason that the public wanted to see what Lincoln looked like. Southern Democrats were spreading rumors that the "sooty" Republican candidate was a mulatto, a "horrible-looking wretch . . . a cross between the nutmeg dealer, the horse swapper, and the night man," who was planning to unleash the horrors of racial amalgamation on white womanhood. "I shudder to contemplate it," one Alabama politician warned. "What social monstrosities, what desolated fields, what civil broils, what robberies, rapes, and murders of the poorer whites by the emancipated blacks would then disfigure the whole fair face of this prosperous, smiling, and happy Southern land." In New York City, Democrats paraded behind a banner showing Lincoln piloting a steamship upon which an insolent-looking black man embraced a white woman. "Free love and free niggers will certainly elect Old Abe if he pilots us safe," read the caption.[13]

Fortunately for Lincoln, given such an ugly climate, he did not have to hit the campaign trail. The well-financed Republican National Committee arranged for a bevy of spokesmen, including several of Lincoln's former presidential rivals, to carry the message for him. William Seward, Salmon P. Chase, Simon Cameron, and Edward Bates all campaigned in their states for Lincoln, along with the usual complement of local gad-flies and mountebanks. The Republicans also organized Wide Awake Clubs for eager young men to march, holler, and sing the praises of Lincoln and his running mate, former Maine governor Hannibal Hamlin. The clubs' name arose from an incident in which an alert young Republican punched an attacking Democrat, proving forcefully that he was "wide awake" to any danger. (A competing Democratic organization in Brooklyn dubbed itself, with typical Flatbush cheek, the Chloroformers, vowing "to put the Wide Awakes to sleep.") Within a few months' time, membership in the Wide Awakes numbered more than 400,000, with chapters in every northern state. "Ain't I glad I joined the Republicans," the men sang over and over, trooping along in their faintly military black oilcloth capes behind banners that hailed "Honest Old Abe, Our Western Star." One such parade in Springfield took several hours to wind past the candidate's house. "A Political Earthquake! The Prairies on Fire for Lincoln!" streamed the *Illinois State Journal*.[14]

Lincoln, for his part, found such displays more tiresome than grati-fying. Such "parades and shows and monster meetings," he groused, were just part of the "dry and irksome labor" of getting the people to the polls. At the only campaign rally he attended, in Springfield, a huge crowd surrounded his carriage and nearly smothered him in all the ex-citement before a quick-thinking friend pulled Lincoln out of the car-riage and slipped him onto the back of a horse to escape.[15]

Leaving nothing to chance, Lincoln met with Seward's former cam-paign manager, Thurlow Weed, to make peace and plot strategy. De-spite Weed's well-earned reputation as a political fixer, Lincoln found in him "no signs whatever of the intriguer." Reiterating his instructions to Davis on the eve of the convention—instructions that Davis had obeyed mainly in the breach—Lincoln assured the New Yorker that he had made no deals with anyone, and that the Empire State could expect "fair deal-ings" from a Lincoln administration. Weed went away happy. The candi-date also consented to be interviewed for various campaign biographies, although, as he told would-be chronicler John Locke Scripps, his early years were yawningly unexciting. "Why, Scripps, it is a great piece of folly to attempt to make anything out of my early life," Lincoln said. "It can be condensed into a single sentence you will find in Gray's Elegy: 'The short and simple annals of the poor.'"[16]

That did not stop Scripps, or a young journalist from Ohio, William Dean Howells, whose own campaign biography was his first national publication in what would become one of the great careers in American literature. In due time, Howells's book would get him out of the Civil War, when a grateful Lincoln appointed the twenty-three-year-old diplomatic neophyte the American consul in Venice. Scripps, in particular, was rather creative with the facts, describing the notably unreligious Lincoln as "a regular attendant upon religious worship, and . . . a pew-holder and liberal supporter of the Presbyterian church in Springfield." Despite the questionable accuracy of its claims, the thirty-two-page pamphlet sold over a million copies before Election Day.[17]

Predictably, the Democrats dragged up old charges, including Lincoln's near-duel with James Shields and earlier accusations that he was a practicing pagan. Once again, Lincoln was tarred with the dirty brush of Know-Nothingism. "Our adversaries think they can gain a point, if they could force me to openly deny this charge," he cautioned one Jewish supporter. "For this reason, it must not publicly appear that I am paying any attention to the charge." At one point, even Mary entered the fray, writing to a concerned Ohio minister, "Mr. Lincoln has never been a Mason or belonged to any secret order." More serious—and true—were the charges that Lincoln had opposed the Mexican War. Democratic speakers railed against Lincoln's "traitorous" stance and recalled his infamous demand on the floor of the House for President Polk to tell the nation on what spot the first drop of American blood had been spilled. Opponents chanted: "Mr. Speaker! Where's the spot?/Is it in Spain or is it not?/Mr. Speaker! Spot! Spot! Spot!" There was not much the Republicans could do to combat the charge, but when one Democrat scoffed that Lincoln would be "a nullity" in his own administration, Horace Greeley fired back dryly: "A man who by his own genius and force of character has raised himself from being a penniless and uneducated float boatman on the Wabash River to the position Mr. Lincoln now occupies is not likely to be a nullity anywhere."[18]

♦ ♦ ♦

While Douglas restlessly roamed the countryside and Lincoln stayed more or less serenely in the background, the other two candidates for president attempted to combine approaches. Breckinridge, in the hands of administration handlers, issued a formal letter of acceptance that was noticeably more moderate than the stance taken by his ultra supporters in Baltimore. There was no need for a special slave code, Breckinridge said, and Congress did not have the constitutional power to legislate over personal or property rights. "The Constitution and the equality of the states," he concluded. "These are the symbols of everlasting union. Let these be the rallying cries of the people." It was not exactly a stirring call to arms, and it simultaneously threw a wet blanket over his most ardent supporters, while failing to reassure those on the other side. "Mr. Breckinridge claims that he isn't a disunionist," fumed the *San Antonio Alamo Express.* "An animal not willing to pass for a pig shouldn't stay in the sty."[19]

After three weeks of organizing his campaign in Washington, Breckinridge headed home to Kentucky. He made a few impromptu speeches en route, confining his remarks to his acceptance letter, much to the dissatisfaction of the ultras. "If he has a fault as a statesman," Mississippi senator Albert Gallatin Brown observed, "it is in being too cautious. Prudence is a virtue, but too much is a fault." The widow of his longtime political opponent, Linn Boyd, scathingly pronounced Breckinridge "all ruffles and no shirt." Moving into the Phoenix Hotel in Lexington, the vice president maintained an uneasy silence that reflected the untenable position in which he found himself. "To those who take advantage of the position of a silent man, to heap upon him execrations, I say, pour on, I can endure," he said manfully. Unfortunately, Americans expected their presidential candidates to say something, occasionally, about the issues. After his personal choice for clerk of the Kentucky Court of Appeals was defeated in a landslide by a candidate supported by the combined forces of Douglas and Bell, Breckinridge was prevailed upon to make a public appearance. Henry Clay's son, James, helpfully offered the use of his grounds at Ashland for a giant campaign picnic. Thousands of Kentuckians turned out for the event—or nonevent, as it transpired. Breckinridge managed to speak for three hours, the longest speech of his life, without saying anything more riveting than "The truth will prevail." The general tenor of the speech, said one Virginia ultra, was "union-lauding." He did not mean it as a compliment.[20]

The fourth candidate in the field, Constitutional Unionist John Bell, was sixty-three years old and looked even older. The balding, grim-visaged Bell had entered public life as a Jacksonian Democrat, but broke ranks with his fellow Tennessean over the national bank and joined the Whigs. Bell served in the House of Representatives from 1827 to 1841, including a stint as Speaker. He was secretary of war in the Harrison and Tyler administrations and served two terms in the Senate before retiring in 1859. Bell owned slaves at his estate near Nashville, but opposed extending the practice into the territories, voting against both the Kansas-Nebraska Act and the Lecompton Constitution. Like Douglas, he became persona non grata at the White House, while winning few converts among the abolitionists. Horace Greeley "venture[d] to say that Bell's record is the most tangled and embarrassing to the party which shall run him for president of any man's in America." Despite Bell's long service in Congress, his running mate, Massachusetts-born Edward Everett, was actually the better known of the two, having won a national reputation as an orator of fulsome and ornate gifts. Three years later, the former Harvard president would find himself on the same speaker's platform as Abraham Lincoln, at a little southern Pennsylvania town called Gettysburg.[21]

The Constitutional Union ticket did not excite anyone. It was, said the Springfield, Massachusetts, *Republican*, "worthy to be printed on gilt-edged satin paper, laid away in a box of musk, and kept there. It is the party of no idea and no purpose." The cardboard-strength platform, calling merely for support of the Constitution and the enforcement of existing laws, had "no North, no South, no East, no West, no Anything," sniffed a New York newspaper. One Boston observer watched Bell-Everett supporters marching behind a horse-drawn wagon carrying an enormous bell. "It was too bad to laugh at," he said. "A more orderly and respectful funeral procession I have never seen, though the mourners were few." A generation after "Tippecanoe and Tyler, too," old-line Whigs had forgotten how to hurrah a candidate.[22]

✦ ✦ ✦

The indefatigable Douglas would do his own hurrahing. Following his notorious swing through New England, he headed south. His ostensible motive was to settle his former mother-in-law's estate in North Carolina, but he had also been invited to speak at the Democratic state convention in Raleigh. Given the demonstrable weakness of the Breckinridge and Bell candidacies, Douglas sensed an opportunity in the Upper South.

Stopping first at Norfolk, Virginia, he told a large crowd gathered at the courthouse: "I did not come here to purchase your votes. I came here to compare notes, and to see if there is not some common principle, some line of policy around which all Union-loving men, North and South, may rally to preserve the glorious Union against northern and southern agitators. I desire no man to vote for me unless he hopes and desires to see the Union maintained." If anyone attempted to break up the Union, Douglas said, the new president should treat the revolters as Andrew Jackson had treated South Carolina's nullifiers in 1832. "There is no evil, and can be none, for which disunion is a legitimate remedy," he warned. "You cannot sever this Union unless you cut the heartstrings that bind father to son, daughter to mother and brother to sister in all our new states and territories."[23]

From Norfolk, Douglas headed deeper into the South, which more than ever was enemy territory. Arriving in North Carolina to oversee the division of his former mother-in-law's property—she had left instructions to sell her slaves and give the proceeds to Douglas's sons—the candidate told a crowd in Raleigh that he loved his children and did not want them to live in a divided country. "The only mistake we Democrats made was in tolerating disunionist sentiments in our bosoms so long," he said, warning darkly that there was "a mature plan throughout the southern states to break up the Union" following the election. As Douglas explained privately to Massachusetts congressman Charles Francis Adams, a plot was in the works by southerners to overthrow Buchanan and replace him with Breckinridge. A new cotton kingdom would then be created among the states bordering the Gulf of Mexico, along with Cuba, Mexico, and certain Central American countries. The fact that Adams saw Douglas drinking heavily during the campaign might explain, in part, some of the senator's more lurid imaginings.[24]

Douglas's threats did not sit well with touchy southerners. As the torrid summer wore on—it was the hottest and driest in a generation—tempers rose accordingly. Jefferson Davis, who scoffed at Douglas as "an itinerant advocate of his own claims," reportedly told his fellow Mississippians to prepare a twin gallows for Douglas and Lincoln, taking into account the difference in their heights. In Montgomery, Alabama, the *Weekly Advertiser* said with glinting menace: "Douglas did well to turn his course northward—there are some portions of the South where the utterance of such sentiments might have led to the hoisting of that coat tail of his that hangs so near the ground to the limb of a tree, preceded by a short neck with grapevine attachment." That such warnings were not completely hollow was demonstrated in New Orleans, where future writer George Washington Cable, then a teenager, saw a crowd chase a man down Royal Street, crying, "Hang him! Hang him!" After the man was rescued, it transpired that he was a vendor of campaign buttons who somehow had failed to notice a Lincoln-Hamlin medal among his wares. Rumors sped through southern towns of slave uprisings, John Brown–type revolts, rapes, arsons, murders—even well poisonings. It was all enough, said South Carolina congressman Lawrence Keitt, "to risk disunion on."[25]

Except for Douglas, who had years of painful experience on which to base his views, few northerners took such talk seriously. The South, said the *New York Herald*, was at "the old game of scaring and bullying the North into submission to southern demands and southern tyranny." Massachusetts poet James Russell Lowell (who in a few years would lose a beloved nephew in the Civil War) called it the "old Mumbo-Jumbo." And William Seward, having for years fulminated about an "irrepressible conflict," now seemed to dare southerners to act. "They cry out that they will tear the Union to pieces," he sneered at one campaign stop for Lincoln. "Who's afraid? Nobody's afraid."[26]

Lincoln, safe in his protective cocoon in Springfield, affected a placid nonchalance. "The people of the South have too much good sense, and good temper, to attempt the ruin of the government," he told one supporter. Ohio journalist Donn Piatt, a close observer of his southern neighbors across the Ohio River from Cincinnati, tried unsuccessfully to warn the candidate. "He considered the movement South as a sort of political game of bluff, gotten up by politicians, and meant to solely frighten the North," wrote Piatt. "He believed that when the leaders saw their efforts in that direction unavailing, the tumult would subside. 'They won't give up the offices,' I remember he said, and added, 'Were it believed that vacant places could be had at the North Pole, the road there would be lined with dead Virginians.'"[27]

Douglas knew better, and his speeches took on a more desperate aspect as the long summer gave way to fall. He followed his southern tour with a swing through the crucial states of the Lower North—Ohio, Indiana, and Pennsylvania—where the election likely would be decided. With a total of 303 electoral votes at stake, the winning candidate would have to receive a majority of 152 votes. Lincoln and the Republicans could safely count on 114 electoral votes from the eleven free states that Frémont had carried in 1856. They could also add Minnesota, which had entered the Union since the last election. If they won Pennsylvania, with its 27 votes, they would only need to add one more state from among Illinois, Indiana, and New Jersey.[28]

It was eminently doable, particularly since Buchanan, with his typical combination of malice and ineptitude, had presented the Republicans with another ready-made issue when he vetoed the Homestead bill, which would have given 160 acres of public land to anyone living on the land for five years. Southerners opposed the act, fearing that it would populate the territories with hardworking, antislavery white farmers. "Better for us that these territories should remain a waste, a howling wilderness, trod only by red hunters than to be so settled," said one Mississippi lawmaker. Despite Douglas's long-standing support for such legislation, the issue became a powerful tool for Republican opinion makers during the campaign. "Does anybody suppose that Abraham Lincoln would ever veto such a bill?" Horace Greeley wondered.[29]

Douglas did what he could, speaking to large crowds in Syracuse, Rochester, and Buffalo before dropping down to campaign in Ohio and Indiana. In mid-September, he summoned his running mate, Herschel Johnson, to New York City for a quick strategy session. Republican candidates had already carried state elections in Maine and Vermont—Douglas's home state—by landslide margins, but the Little Giant surprised Johnson by still appearing upbeat about their chances. Johnson hastened to disagree. "I told him, he underestimated the power of Mr. Buchanan's army of office holders, in the northern states," recalled Johnson, "that although they could not carry a single one for Breckinridge, they would bring him enough votes to give them all to Lincoln, that he would not carry a single southern state & that I regarded Lincoln's election as certain." "If you be correct in your views," said a shaken Douglas, "then God help our poor country."[30]

◆ ◆ ◆

For once in his political life, Lincoln felt no need to campaign. Trusty stand-ins, including Massachusetts senator Henry Wilson, the old-time "Natick Cobbler," Tom Corwin, "the Wagon Boy," and Thomas Ewing, who grandly billed himself "the last of the Whigs," made Lincoln's case for him. While industrious townspeople turned the streets of Springfield into what one observer called "a Hindoo Bazaar," selling wooden souvenirs supposedly made from rails split by Lincoln like medieval pardoners hawking pieces of the True Cross, the candidate kept determinedly to his game plan. He would say or do nothing that might give offense to his enemies or frighten his friends. Sometimes it was hard to keep silent. After one worried supporter wrote to him about mounting southern belligerence, an exasperated Lincoln fired back: "What is it I could say which would quiet alarm? Is it that no interference by the government, with the slaves and slavery within the states, is intended? I have said this so often already, that a repetition of it is but mockery, bearing an appearance of weakness, and cowardice, which perhaps should be avoided. Why do not uneasy men *read* what I have already said and what our *platform* says?"[31]

As a way, perhaps, of escaping such letters, Lincoln gave serious thought to appearing at a Massachusetts horse show, a trip that would allow him to look in on Robert at Harvard. With some difficulty, he was dissuaded. Lincoln was glad of the diversion when William Seward's campaign train pulled into Springfield for a brief stopover en route to Chicago. Again, he was tempted to join the fun, but settled instead for an impromptu strategy session with Seward in which he urged him to stop Long John Wentworth from promising publicly that the Republicans, if successful, would end slavery altogether. It was the first face-to-face meeting of Lincoln and Seward in a dozen years. Lincoln reminded Seward of his words then. "Twelve years ago you told me that this cause would be successful," he said, "and ever since I have believed that it would be." Gratified by the attention, Seward returned to the campaign trail to vigorously make the case for Lincoln. In Toledo, Ohio, he shared an awkward moment with Stephen Douglas, after Seward's train arrived at the station while a Democratic rally was taking place. Douglas, carrying a whiskey bottle and "plainly drunk," in the view of Seward aide Charles Francis Adams, Jr., burst into the New Yorker's sleeping car, woke him up, and invited him to join the rally. Seward, startled, hastily declined.[32]

To sympathetic observers, Douglas had taken on the look of "a way-worn backwoods traveler," and his constant campaigning again aggravated his chronically enflamed throat. His booming baritone reduced to a "spasmodic bark," he frequently interrupted his speeches to squeeze lemon juice down his aching throat. In Cincinnati, he was so hoarse that he could not speak a word to the thousands who had gathered to hear him. Not even the presidency was worth such trouble, one follower observed. Watching from afar, Alexander Stephens lamented the cost to Douglas, both personally and politically. "I am pained and grieved at the folly which thus demanded the sacrifice of such a noble and gallant spirit as I believe Douglas to be," he wrote. Still, Douglas carried on. In Chicago, on October 5, he spoke to a massive crowd at the lakefront. Seward had preceded him into the city, and Douglas took the occasion to lambaste both him and Lincoln, warning that loose talk about irrepressible conflicts and houses divided "means revolution—undisguised revolution." "I am no alarmist," Douglas said, "but I believe that this country is in more danger now than at any other moment since I have known anything of public life." The only way to save the Union was to ensure that "northern abolitionism and southern disunion are buried in a common grave." That same day, South Carolina governor William H. Gist sent a round-robin letter to his fellow southern governors, advising them that his state was prepared to secede if Lincoln were elected.[33]

The October elections in Pennsylvania, Ohio, and Indiana made that event appear likely. In Pennsylvania, home of the sitting president, a nasty intraparty feud between Republican senator Simon Cameron and gubernatorial candidate Andrew Curtin gave momentary hope to the Democrats. But when the Buchanan forces rallied behind Breckinridge, Douglas supporter John W. Forney fired back: "No true friend of Douglas, in Pennsylvania or elsewhere, can touch an electoral ticket which contains upon it the single name of a Breckinridge Disunionist." "The Douglas and Breckinridge men," said Republican activist Carl Schurz happily, "would give [Pennsylvania] to us to spite each other." That was precisely what happened, with Curtin defeating Democratic nominee Henry D. Foster by 30,000 votes.[34]

The results were just as dire for the Democrats in Ohio and Indiana. The Buckeye State, under the leadership of Governor Salmon P. Chase, elected thirteen Republican congressmen, to eight for the opposition party, and added a state supreme court justice. Indiana went Republican as well, helped by a monster rally of 50,000 Wide Awakes and "Rail Maulers" in Indianapolis and a large infusion of money from the Republican National Committee. ("Men work better with money in hand," the ever-pragmatic David Davis observed.) Lincoln, keeping a gimlet eye on the results, exulted to Seward: "It now really looks as if the government is about to fall into our hands. Pennsylvania, Ohio, and Indiana have surpassed all expectation."[35]

◆ ◆ ◆

Douglas was campaigning in Iowa when he heard the news from Indiana. "Mr. Lincoln is the next president," he told his secretary, James B. Sheridan. "We must try to save the Union. I will go South." Accompanied by Sheridan, Adele, and brother-in-law James Madison Cutts, Jr., Douglas set out for St. Louis a few days later to begin his final descent into the simmering cauldron of southern politics. The emotional atmosphere in the South had grown even worse in the past two months. Continuing rumors of slave uprisings had led to the arrest of thirty-six black men in Dalton, Georgia, and the lynching of a white man in Talladega, Alabama. In Texas, the Methodist Church had split into northern and southern branches over the question of slavery. The northern branch was said to have organized a secret society, the Mystic Red, to "produce disaffection among our Negroes" and "to force their fair daughters into the embrace of buck Negroes for wives." On the floor of Congress, Texas representative John H. Reagan repeated the ridiculous claim that nearly a dozen towns in his state had been burned to the ground by black agitators, who allegedly had murdered an untold number of white citizens in the process. It was all "part of the legitimate fruits of Republicanism," Reagan charged.[36]

Against such a backdrop, Douglas's second southern tour took on a certain desperate grandeur. Having privately conceded the presidency to Lincoln, he was now concerned with preventing the breakup of the Union (and also preserving his viability as a presidential candidate four years hence). He began his tour in St. Louis, where he addressed a nighttime crowd from atop the levee beside the Mississippi River. "I am not here tonight to ask for your votes for the presidency," Douglas said. "I am here to make an appeal to you on behalf of the Union and the peace of the country." It was more a concession speech than a call to arms.[37]

Boarding a steamer, the Little Giant and his party headed downriver to Memphis, where two years earlier he had given a well-received, racist speech comparing blacks to crocodiles. Times had changed. The *Memphis Appeal* marked Douglas's arrival on southern soil with an editorial denouncing his visit as "the most impudent, the most disgraceful, the

191

most indefensible of his acts during the campaign." Another Memphis newspaper mocked his "bloated visage" and called him "an itinerant peddler of Yankee notions." Undeterred, Douglas spoke for three hours to an enormous crowd, insisting that Lincoln's election, in itself, would not constitute a mortal threat to southern interests, since the Democrats still controlled Congress and the Supreme Court. "I traveled yesterday through West Tennessee and looked out upon one of the loveliest countries the eye of man ever beheld," he said lyrically, "a country bearing the evidence of a kind providence that hath smiled upon and cherished its people, and I reflected what manner of man he must be who would precipitate this Union into revolution."[38]

One such man was the relentless William Yancey, whose path Douglas inadvertently crossed at Nashville, Chattanooga, and Kingston, Georgia. There were no run-ins with the violent Alabaman, although a few weeks earlier in Knoxville, Yancey had threatened to grab a bayonet "and plunge [it] to the hilt through and through [the] heart" of local abolitionist newspaperman William Brownlow. In Chattanooga, a little frontier town that within a few years would feel the full brunt of military occupation, siege, and starvation, residents greeted Douglas's arrival at the train depot with "an outburst of deafening salutations," augmented by a combination of what Tennessee journalist K. N. Pepper, Jr., termed "the spirit of politics and the rectified spirit of alcohol."[39]

From Chattanooga, Douglas crossed the border into Georgia, where he met up with Alexander Stephens. Little Aleck, loyal to the last, continued praising Douglas as the only man capable of preventing a civil war, "a lordly buffalo" being hounded to death by a lupine crowd of "malicious and envious pettifoggers." Moving west to Montgomery, Alabama, the seething heart of secessionist sentiment, Douglas and Adele were greeted by a large crowd and a torchlight procession to their hotel. En route, someone threw rotten eggs and spoiled tomatoes at the senator, knocking off his hat and spattering Adele. "I fear that we are in the midst of a revolution," *Mobile Register* editor John Forsyth told the seething Douglas. "The storm rages to such a madness that it is beyond the control of those who raised it. Our own people are becoming frantic."[40]

The next day, standing on the steps of the Alabama state capitol, Douglas gave his reply. Assuring his listeners that "your title to your slave property is expressly recognized by the Federal Constitution . . . where no power on earth but yourselves can interfere with it," he attempted to put the issue in climatological terms. "This question of slavery is one of political economy depending upon the class of climate, production and self-interest," he explained. "You cannot compel slavery to exist in a cold, northern latitude any more than by an act of Congress you can make cotton grow upon the tops of the Rocky Mountains. Whenever you make up your minds to maintain slavery in those cold northern regions, where the people do not want it and will not have it, you must first get an act of Congress compelling cotton, rice, sugar and tobacco to grow there, and then you can have Negroes."[41]

It was vintage Douglas, offering practical solutions to political problems, or political solutions to practical problems, but it failed to recognize that many northerners and southerners had moved beyond mere politics into a realm of theoretical certitude as exacting and precise as a hard-shell Baptist's understanding of sin. Lincoln realized this; so did those in the crowd. Slavery was not (or not strictly) what Douglas maintained that day in Montgomery, a mere accounting term—"horses, Negroes, merchandize, every kind of property"—but rather a tangible, physical act of control. If southerners could not feel secure in physically transporting their slaves, one man, woman, or child at a time, wherever they wished to take them, the entire multimillion-dollar system of slavery would soon be as dead as any sclerotic old master strangled in his bed by his houseboy.[42]

Douglas and Adele suffered another painful mishap while they were preparing to leave Montgomery for Selma. As the senator was making his farewell remarks on the top deck of their riverboat, the railing abruptly gave way under the weight of the surging crowd. The couple fell through the splintered wood to the deck below. Douglas wrenched his leg so badly that he needed a crutch to get around, and Adele was too shaken and bruised to continue the trip. (Five months later, literally adding insult to injury, Douglas received a bill for the crutch.) Hobbling like a pirate, Douglas made it to Mobile, where he gave the last speech of his presidential campaign the night before the election. It was, said the *Mobile Daily Advertiser*, with perhaps backhanded praise, "a triumphant vindication of his consistency since 1850." In a last flourish of defiance, Douglas vowed not to participate if the election were thrown into the House of Representatives. "I scorn to accept the presidency as a minority candidate," the Little Giant declared. Deep down, he knew it would not come to that.[43]

✦ ✦ ✦

Election Day, November 6, finally arrived. There was no reported violence, although the mood in the South was sepulchral. Not so in Springfield, where the Republican candidate spent the day relaxing in his office at the capitol. Lincoln, in fact, was so relaxed that Herndon had to urge him to leave the office to vote. Lincoln demurred, not wanting to be seen voting for himself. Only after Herndon convinced him that his vote was needed for the other Republican candidates did Lincoln go to the polling place. Greeted by shouts and cheers from his neighbors, he carefully cut off the top of the ballot sheet (which included the names of his own electors) before casting his vote. In the evening, Lincoln ate supper at home with his family, then headed back over to the capitol to await returns. The crowd grew so large that someone suggested he ask all but his closest friends to leave. Lincoln wouldn't hear of it—everyone who came was welcome to stay.[44]

Outwardly, Lincoln was calm and collected, but a *Missouri Democrat* reporter noted a slight nervous twitch whenever a messenger arrived from the telegraph office. All the news was good. Illinois fell to the Republicans, occasioning a great shout of joy from the listeners. Indiana fell. New England fell. The Old Northwest fell. Lincoln, increasingly excited, headed over to the telegraph office to eliminate the wait between returns. Sprawling across an old sofa in the superintendent's room, he received a dispatch from Simon Cameron in Pennsylvania: "Pennsylvania 70,000 for you. New York safe. Glory enough." Lincoln was not so sure. "The news would come quick enough if it was good," he fretted, "and if bad, I am not in any hurry to hear it."[45]

Around ten o'clock, Lincoln and his party headed over to Watson's Saloon, where a bevy of Republican women had taken over the premises and prepared a late-night snack for the candidate, Mrs. Lincoln, and their friends. When Lincoln entered the room, the women chorused: "How do you do, Mr. President!" He had scarcely taken his seat beside Mary at the long table when another telegram arrived. It was from New York politico Simeon Draper, an intimate of William Seward. "We have made steady gains everywhere throughout the state," Draper said, and although New York City had not yet reported, "we are quite sanguine a great victory has been won." The hall echoed with cheers; a spontaneous outburst of the campaign song "Ain't I Glad I Joined the Republicans" shook the rafters. "Not too fast, my friends," Lincoln cautioned. "Not too fast, it may not be over yet."[46]

But it was over, or soon would be. A belated effort by New York Democrats to fuse the backers of Douglas, Breckinridge, and Bell had come too late. (The brilliant New York City politician Samuel Tilden, who sixteen years later would lose—or have stolen from him—the closest presidential election in American history, estimated that a switch of 24,000 votes in selected districts would have kept New York out of the Republican column and thrown the election into the House of Representatives, where Lincoln would almost certainly have lost.) While Mary went home to check on the boys, Lincoln returned to the telegraph office, where word came in around midnight that he had indeed won New York, giving him a sure 180 electoral votes and putting him in line to become the sixteenth president of the United States. Crowds surged into the streets, climbed onto rooftops. The entire town of Springfield, reported Mary Lincoln's friend Mercy Conkling, was "perfectly wild: the republicans were singing, yelling, shouting! Old men, young, middle-aged, clergymen and all!" Church bells began clanging and cannons booming. Lincoln, putting the historical telegram in his pocket for safekeeping, hurried home to tell his most loyal, long-standing, and fiercest supporter the news. "Mary, Mary!" he called, bursting through the front door of their home. "We are elected!"[47]

◆ ◆ ◆

A thousand miles away, in a newspaper office in Mobile, Stephen Douglas was getting the same results. Resigned to defeat, he had spent the day quietly, reading his mail and accepting congratulations for a race which, if lost, had been gallantly run. To his companion, John Forsyth, the Little Giant seemed "less excited by the election than perhaps any other man in the city." The returns showed why. Douglas had carried only one state outright—Missouri—and split New Jersey (where fusion efforts finally had taken hold) with Lincoln, for a pitiful total of twelve electoral votes. Breckinridge, as expected, won all the Deep South states, along with Delaware and Maryland, giving him seventy-two electoral votes. Bell's Constitutional Union Party, somewhat surprisingly, carried the border states of Virginia and Kentucky, along with his home state of Tennessee, for thirty-nine electoral votes. All the rest went to Lincoln. The Old Railsplitter carried every northern and midwestern state—sixteen in all—and added California and Oregon on the West Coast. The extreme sectionalism of the results disguised the fact that Lincoln had won a decisive, if not overwhelming, victory. Except for Kentucky, New Jersey, and the two far western states, he had received a popular majority of the votes in every state where he was on the ballot. Only in California, Oregon, and Illinois was his margin of victory less than 7 percent, and he still beat Douglas by 12,000 votes in their own backyard. The only solace Douglas could take was in besting Breckinridge by more than 500,000 votes. He remained the clear leader of the Democratic Party, the only one of the four presidential candidates who had won electoral votes in both free and slave states. Already, there was talk of another run for the White House in 1864.[48]

Eighteen sixty-four would take care of itself. For the time being, Douglas was "more hopeless than I had ever before seen him," in the words of aide James Sheridan. The day after the election, he was rejoined by Adele, and the couple traveled to New Orleans, where a driving rain allowed him to indulge in another of his favorite meteorological metaphors. "This is no time to despair or despond," he told the crowd from the steps of the St. Charles Hotel. "The bright sun will soon chase away these clouds and the patriots of the country will rally as one man and throttle the enemies of our country." In an open letter to residents of the city, Douglas lamented Lincoln's victory, but pointed out again that the Democrats still held both houses of Congress, along with a voting majority on the Supreme Court. "Four years will soon pass away," he said, "when the ballot-box will furnish a peaceful, legal and constitutional remedy for all the evils and grievances with which the country may be affected."[49]

Perhaps. But with the states of the Deep South already planning to hold constitutional conventions on the issue of secession, it was questionable, at best, whether the nation would have the luxury of waiting that long. "I think the Union is gone," Herschel Johnson wrote to Douglas a few days after the election. Forsyth said much the same thing, lamenting, "With your defeat, the cause of the Union was lost." The editor of the provocatively named *Atlanta Confederacy* framed the issue more vividly, if less succinctly: "Let the consequences be what they may—whether the Potomac is crimsoned in human gore, and Pennsylvania Avenue is paved ten fathoms in depth with mangled bodies, or whether the last vestige of liberty is swept from the face of the American continent, the South will never submit to such humiliation and degradation as the inauguration of Abraham Lincoln." Having lost, and lost badly, the third presidential bid of his career, Douglas headed back to Washington to attend the traditional swearing-in ceremony formalizing that defeat, however humiliating and degrading it might be.[50]

9

༺༒༻

We Must Not Be Enemies

In Springfield, the president-elect awoke early on November 7, having spent a sleepless night prickled by worries about his new responsibilities and punctuated by window-rattling blasts from the incessant cannon fire in the courthouse square. Even in the first blush of victory, Lincoln had no illusions about the difficulties facing him and the nation in the days to come. He did not question the legitimacy of his election. Still, his 39.9 percent share of the popular vote was the lowest since John Quincy Adams had won his tarnished victory in 1824, and only Stephen Douglas had managed—however meagerly—to win votes both above and below the Mason-Dixon Line. If Lincoln was not exactly a minority president, he was a sectional one, and no one before him had ever been elected without at least some support in all sections of the country. Electorally speaking, the Deep South had walled itself off from the rest of the country. It remained to be seen how strong that wall would be.

Unable to sleep, Lincoln took out a blank note card and jotted down the last names of seven potential cabinet members: Seward, Bates, Dayton, Judd, Chase, Blair, and Welles. Counting Lincoln himself, the preliminary cabinet was equally composed of old-line Whigs and free-soil Democrats—the strength-bearing walls of the new Republican Party.

Seward would be asked to be secretary of state; Lincoln would divide the other cabinet chairs as he saw fit. By inviting his principal rivals for the nomination to join him in the government, he was exhibiting either deep-seated self-confidence or uneasy self-doubt in his ability to govern—perhaps a little of both. He would run the list by his running mate, Hannibal Hamlin, when they met in Chicago in a couple weeks. For the time being, the list seemed nicely "balanced and ballasted" to Lincoln. The next morning, as he entered his office in the state capitol, he greeted the assembled newsmen with a jaunty but revealing quip. "Well, boys," he said, "your troubles are over now, mine have just begun."[1]

To handle the expected crush of office seekers, Lincoln decided to hold two receptions each day, one in the morning, the other in the late afternoon. His personal secretary, John Nicolay, signed up an old prep school friend, John Hay, to assist him with the bushels of correspondence piling up in the office. Visitors were treated to the novel sight of Lincoln sporting facial whiskers. During the campaign, he had received a letter from eleven-year-old Grace Bedell of Westfield, New York, who promised to get her brothers to vote for Lincoln if he would grow a beard. Miss Bedell, an unusually self-possessed preteen, assured the candidate: "You would look a great deal better for your face is so thin. All the ladies like whiskers and they would tease their husbands to vote for you and then you would be president." By the end of November, Lincoln was sporting a closely cropped beard—actually, more a chin-topping goatee—and regaling visitors with an almost manic cascade of jokes, puns, and tall tales. When former Kentucky governor Charles S. Morehead called on the president-elect to urge him to make concessions to southern moderates, Lincoln favored him with a retelling of Aesop's fable about the lion who agrees to trim his fangs and claws before marrying a beautiful young woman, only to be knocked on the head by his prospective in-laws once he is defenseless. "That was an exceedingly interesting anecdote, and very *apropos*," said the unimpressed Morehead, "but not altogether a satisfactory answer."[2]

Another close observer of the South, Cincinnati journalist Donn Piatt, endured a similarly unsatisfactory session with the incoming president. After vividly warning Lincoln that the countryside would be "white with army tents" within three months' time if events continued in the direction they were headed, Piatt said Lincoln brushed him off with an airy "Well, we won't jump that ditch until we come to it." An indication that he was not always so unconcerned might be inferred from an eerie experience Lincoln had one afternoon while taking a break from office seekers. According to Ward Hill Lamon, who got the account straight from Lincoln, the president-elect was lying on his sofa in his study when he saw his reflection in a bureau mirror. His body was intact, but there were two faces in the mirror—one normal and ruddy, the other deathly pale. Inconsiderately, perhaps, Lincoln told Mary of the vision. It scared her to death. She interpreted the strange encounter as a sign that her husband would die during his second term in the White House. Lincoln was unusually sensitive to dreams and portents, and although he tried to put it out of his mind, "the thing would come up once in a while and give me a little pang, as though something uncomfortable had happened." Adding to his discomfort, he was regularly receiving hate mail from disgruntled southerners, some of it decorated with ghoulish drawings of guns, daggers, and hangmen's nooses. One showed Lincoln being tossed into hell by the devil's three-pronged pitchfork.[3]

Despite all warnings, portents, and threats, Lincoln refused to be pressured into making untimely, if not indeed unseemly, concessions to the South, particularly since he had not yet taken office. The hot breath of secession, he told Nicolay, was "just the trick by which the South breaks down every Northern man." He did go as far as inserting a couple of conciliatory paragraphs into a speech Lyman Trumbull gave in Springfield on November 20. In the appended passage, Lincoln pledged that "each and all of the States will be left in . . . complete control of their own affairs respectively." At the same time, a reporter for the *New York Tribune* observed Lincoln reading an account of Andrew Jackson's heavy-handed treatment of the nullification crisis in South Carolina three decades earlier, when Jackson had threatened to hang John C. Calhoun and send in the army to enforce federal laws. Lincoln's assurance that the states would be treated "as they have been under any administration," was received, perhaps understandably, with less-than-complete magnanimity by the "political fiends" he now saw at work in the South.[4]

✦ ✦ ✦

Fresh from his own encounters with the clamorous fiends, Stephen Douglas returned to the nation's capital on the morning of December 1, a beaten but by no means broken man. Mainly, he was a worried one. The election had justified his eleventh-hour campaigning in the South, even if it had proven a crushing failure at the ballot box. Now all his efforts would be directed at holding the Union together, at least until the new administration was in place and the next Congress took its seats in loyal opposition, with Douglas at its head. Time, however, was running out. In Charleston, at the same Institute Hall where the fire-eaters had blocked his nomination eight months earlier, delegates were meeting to debate an ordinance of secession. Other cotton states were making similar noises. Douglas called for southern legislators to "sink their bickerings" and return to Washington for the short winter session. "Let all asperities drop, all ill feelings be buried, and all real patriots strive to save the Union," he urged. With the exceptions of South Carolina senators James Chesnut and James H. Hammond, all southern lawmakers did return to their seats when Congress reopened for business on December 3. How long they would remain there was an open question.[5]

Buchanan, as usual, was no help. In his annual message to Congress, the lame-duck president went out of his way to blame Republicans for "the incessant and violent agitation of the slavery question," which he said had "produced its malign influence on the slaves and inspired them with vague notions of freedom," causing "many a matron throughout the South [to] retire at night in dread of what may befall herself and her children before morning." He called on northerners to stop criticizing slavery, obey the Fugitive Slave Law, and adopt a constitutional amendment protecting slavery in the territories. The South, he said, was responsible for its own domestic institutions, and "the people of the North are not more responsible and have no more right to interfere than with similar institutions in Russia or in Brazil." If abolitionist agitation did not cease, Buchanan warned, the South would "be justified in revolutionary resistance to the government." Such resistance was illegal, the president maintained, but there was nothing he could do about it. "The fact is," said Buchanan, "that our Union rests upon public opinion, and can never be cemented by the blood of its citizens shed in civil war. If it cannot live in the affections of the people, it must one day perish."[6]

William Seward, who had no such scruples, sneered openly at the president, scoffing that what Buchanan really was saying was that "no state has the right to secede unless it wishes to, and that it is the President's duty to enforce the laws, unless somebody opposes him." The message, added Massachusetts abolitionist Charles Francis Adams, was "in all respects like the author, timid and vacillating in the face of slaveholding rebellion, bold and insulting towards his countrymen whom he does not hear." Buchanan, said one northern newspaper, was a "Pharasaical old hypocrite."[7]

Two days later, the appropriately named Senator Lazarus Powell of Kentucky sought to revive the Senate's waning influence by calling for the appointment of a special committee to consider ways to preserve the Union. Douglas was one of thirteen senators named to the committee—his bête noire, Jefferson Davis, was another—and the panel immediately began debating how best to meet the newest southern threat. Kentucky senator John J. Crittenden, in the spirit of his late home-state hero, Henry Clay, proposed a series of constitutional amendments designed to preserve and protect slavery by restoring the Missouri Compromise and extending the dividing line all the way to the Pacific. Douglas, who had sponsored similar legislation six years earlier, did what he could to help, supporting the Crittenden amendments in the committee and offering his own suggestion—which Lincoln had favored for years—that freed blacks be colonized to Africa or South America.

Douglas was hopeful the Crittenden plan would win widespread Republican support, since it "would not add a foot of slave territory to the Union, except where climate and soil render it more profitable than free labor." Once again, he failed to take into account the moral objections to what he persisted in seeing as a purely economic matter. Lincoln, back in Illinois, was unyielding on the issue. He signaled Republicans in Washington to oppose any compromise measure, writing to Trumbull: "Entertain no proposition for a compromise in regard to the extension of slavery. The tug has to come & better now than later. Republicans have only to stand firm acting firmly, but in a kind spirit & all will yet be well. Concession on our part . . . would be fatal." To a *New York Herald* reporter, the president-elect insisted, "I will suffer death before I consent or will advise my friends to consent to any concession or compromise which looks like buying the privilege to take possession of this government to which we have a constitutional right." Ultimately, the compromise was defeated in committee, seven to six, with Jefferson Davis and fellow southerner Robert Toombs joining the five Republicans in voting no.[8]

Douglas was disappointed by Lincoln's resistance to the compromise, but he was not surprised. He still considered his old rival a hopeless provincial in the game of national politics, telling an acquaintance that Lincoln was "eminently a man of the atmosphere which surrounds him.

He has not yet got out of Springfield. He does not know that he is president-elect of the United States. He does not see that the shadow he casts is any bigger than it was last year. It will not take him long when he has got established in the White House. But he has not found it out yet."[9]

Meanwhile, as Douglas understood better than Lincoln, time was not on their side. After ever-troublesome South Carolina—"too small to be a republic, too large to be a lunatic asylum," went the joke—voted on December 20 to secede, he tried unsuccessfully to get Congress to stay in session over the holidays. "I know we do not feel like going abroad and enjoying a holiday," Douglas said. "I trust there may be something done to restore peace to the country. This is a good time to do it, and I hope we shall remain in session." Congress dutifully continued to meet, but nothing was done. Meanwhile, on December 26, Major Robert Anderson moved his small garrison of soldiers from Fort Moultrie, on the South Carolina mainland, to Fort Sumter, in Charleston harbor. By the second week in January, five other southern states had "gone out" of the Union: Florida, Georgia, Alabama, Mississippi, and Louisiana. Texas was teetering on the brink. Douglas considered secession "wrong, unlawful, unconstitutional, criminal," but he opposed armed resistance to the act. "Surely you do not expect to exterminate or subjugate ten million people, the entire population of one section, as means of preserving amiable relations between the two sections?" he wondered aloud.[10]

There were signs, subtle but unmistakable, that Lincoln was considering doing just that. The *Illinois State Journal*, his longtime mouthpiece, editorialized: "Disunion by armed force is treason, and treason must and will be put down at all hazards. . . . The laws of the United States must be executed—the President has no discretionary power on the subject—his duty is emphatically pronounced in the Constitution. Mr. Lincoln will perform that duty." To young Nicolay, Lincoln maintained, "The right of a state to secede is not an open or debatable question." And to Thurlow Weed, Lincoln reiterated: "No state can, in any way lawfully, get out of the Union, without the consent of the others." Lincoln did not intend to give such consent, and nothing was likely to sway him. As his wife observed, Lincoln "was a terribly firm man when he set his foot down. No man or woman could rule him after he had made up his mind." When Nicolay reported rumors that Buchanan was preparing to surrender Fort Sumter, Lincoln snapped uncharacteristically, "If that is true, they ought to hang him." He would simply retake the fort once he entered office.[11]

✦ ✦ ✦

By late January, Lincoln was making the final preparations for a twelve-day train trip to Washington. He resisted Seward's pleas to come to Washington early, but he agreed to his suggestion to make a highly publicized journey east to rally support for the Union. Faced with leaving the town where he had made his home for the past twenty-four years, Lincoln was in a somber mood. He paid an emotional visit to his beloved stepmother, Sarah, who was still living with her daughter in rural isolation in Farmington, Illinois. Sarah, who had loved Abe like her own son after his mother died and had encouraged his reading in the face of his father's resistance, worried tearfully that something would happen to the president-elect. "No, no, Mama," Lincoln assured her. "Trust in the Lord and all will be well. We will see each other again." He also visited his father's grave, promising to have a better gravestone erected on the site, but as with most dealings between Lincoln and his father, alive or dead, it was a promise he did not keep.[12]

A few days later, Lincoln and Mary held a huge reception for their friends, standing side by side for five hours in the parlor to personally greet the 700 well-wishers who turned out for the festivities. The day before he was scheduled to leave, Lincoln climbed the stairs to his law office on the town square and bade his old partner Billy Herndon a wistful farewell. Taking a last look at the sign hanging outside their office, he assured the damp-eyed younger man, "If I live, I'm coming back some time, and then we'll go right on practicing law as if nothing had ever happened." For the time being, Lincoln added fatalistically, "I am decided; my course is fixed."[13]

More than 1,000 people turned out at the Springfield railroad depot on the morning of February 11 to see him off. Mary and the two younger boys were traveling separately and would meet him in Indianapolis. In the waiting room at the station, a visibly moved Lincoln shook hands ceremonially with each of his friends. "His face was pale, and quivered with emotion so deep as to render him almost unable to utter a single word," reported the correspondent for the *New York Herald*. Stepping onto the platform at the rear of the train, Lincoln removed his hat and asked for silence. He had not intended to make a formal farewell, but the solemnity of the moment seemed to call for a few heartfelt words. "My friends," he began, "no one, not in my situation, can appreciate my feeling of sadness at this parting. To this place, and the kindness of these people, I owe every thing. Here I have lived a quarter of a century, and have passed from a young to an old man. Here my children have been born, and one is buried. I now leave, not knowing when, or whether ever, I may return, with a task before me greater than that which rested upon Washington. Without the assistance of that Divine Being, who ever attended him, I cannot succeed. With that assistance I cannot fail. Let us confidently hope that all will yet be well. To his care commending you, as I hope in your prayers you will commend me, I bid you an affectionate farewell."[14]

A special four-car train carried Lincoln on the roundabout journey to Washington. Accompanying him were his oldest son, Robert, immediately dubbed by the press "the Prince of Rails"; private secretaries John Nicolay and John Hay; personal physician William S. Wallace; political backers David Davis and Norman Judd; and burly, pistol-packing Ward Hill Lamon, who had appointed himself Lincoln's bodyguard. Somewhat surprisingly, the government had not supplied a military escort for the president-elect, but three army officers, their eyes clearly on their own careers, volunteered to protect him. (As proof of their self-interested acuity, all three—Colonel Edwin Sumner, Major David Hunter, and Captain John Pope—would be promoted to major general by Lincoln within a year.) A chesty young militia captain, Elmer Ellsworth, was also along for the ride, having traded his law books for the manual of arms. Local politicians jumped on and off the train every few miles, seeking to share the luster of the moment. At Indianapolis, Lincoln was reunited with his family at the Bates House, where he delivered a preplanned speech from the hotel balcony. "By what principle of original right is it that one-fiftieth or one-ninetieth of a great nation, by calling themselves a state, have the right to break up and ruin that nation as a matter of original principle?" he wondered aloud. "Now, I ask the question—I am not deciding anything. Where is the mysterious right for a certain district of country with inhabitants to play tyrant over all its own citizens, and deny the authority of everything greater than itself?"[15]

The trip quickly took on the trappings of a vacation jaunt for Lincoln and his family. Robert lost his usual Todd-like reserve, flirting with girls along the way, throttling the locomotive beside the engineer, and, on one occasion at least, drinking too much Catawba wine. His abstemious father was not amused, particularly when Robert nearly lost the satchel containing the only copies of the inaugural address that Lincoln had entrusted to his care. Willie and Tad tickled themselves by asking other train passengers if they wanted to see "Old Abe," then pointing out someone other than their father. Even tightly wound Mary allowed herself to join her husband on the rear platform of the train when it pulled away from the various whistle stops. As for Lincoln, he relaxed more into the role of president-elect with each passing mile. He was determined not to say anything concrete on the national crisis, for fear of committing himself to a specific course of action, but he perfected the rhetorical trick of saying very little, satisfyingly. He devised a joke at his own expense—a proven crowd-pleaser—telling the people who turned out to see him that he wanted to see them as well, and "in that arrangement I have the best of the bargain." In Westfield, New York, he stopped the train long enough to single out little Grace Bedell and give her a newly bewhiskered kiss.[16]

Not everyone was pleased with Lincoln's performance. Charles Francis Adams, Jr., son of the Massachusetts congressman, complained that Lincoln was "perambulating the country, kissing little girls and growing whiskers." And his patrician father worried in his diary that Lincoln's folksy appearances "are rapidly reducing the estimate put upon him. I am much afraid that in this lottery we may have drawn a blank." The northern public seemed not to agree, turning out in massive numbers in Cincinnati, Columbus, Pittsburgh, Cleveland, Buffalo, Albany, New York City, Trenton, Camden, and Philadelphia. At tiny Dunkirk, in upstate New York, some 12,000 people gathered for a glimpse of the president-elect. Saying that he had no time to speak, Lincoln placed his hand on the flagstaff and intoned portentously: "I stand by the flag of the Union, and all I ask of you is that you stand by me as long as I stand by it."[17]

It was well enough to make such promises in the North—enforcing them in the South would be a different matter. While Lincoln was still en route to Washington for his inauguration, the Confederate States of America held its own inauguration ceremony in Montgomery, Alabama. Jefferson Davis, at last gaining the ascendancy he had been seeking for the past decade over his turbulent fellow southerners, assumed the presidency. More surprisingly, Lincoln's and Douglas's old friend, Alexander Stephens, agreed to serve as Davis's vice president. Still, Lincoln maintained a stubborn serenity in the face of the news. "There is nothing going wrong," he assured a crowd at Pittsburgh. "We entertain different views on political questions, but nobody is suffering anything." He continued to assert his belief that the current crisis was an artificial one, gotten up by "designing politicians" in the South. "Why are southerners so incensed?" he asked in Cleveland. "Have they not all their rights now as they ever had? What then is the matter with them? Why all this excitement? Why all these complaints?"[18]

When Lincoln's train arrived in Philadelphia on February 21, a hitherto unknown railroad detective named Allan Pinkerton, who was working for the Philadelphia, Wilmington & Baltimore line, warned the president-elect that a plot was in the works to assassinate him as he changed trains in Baltimore. Pinkerton even had the name of the plot's leader—local barber Cypriano Ferrandini. The detective advised Lincoln to alter his schedule and leave for Washington immediately, passing through Baltimore under cover of darkness. Lincoln refused—he had symbolically important speaking engagements at Independence Hall and the Pennsylvania state capital in Harrisburg. He kept his appointments, alluding cryptically to the threats in the building where the Declaration of Independence was signed. "If [the government] can't be saved upon that principle, it will be truly awful," Lincoln warned. "I would rather be assassinated on this spot than to surrender it." Pinkerton continued to urge Lincoln to take a night train from Philadelphia, and after additional warnings arrived from William Seward and General Winfield Scott, Lincoln reluctantly agreed.[19]

Leaving the official party, Lincoln boarded a different train to Baltimore, accompanied only by Pinkerton and Lamon—"a brainless egotistical fool," in the detective's professional judgment—and wearing a faintly ridiculous "Kossuth" hat that drooped over his ears and a long overcoat thrown, invalid-like, across his shoulders. The sleeping berth Pinkerton had reserved for Lincoln was too short for him to stretch out, and the president-elect rode, knees up, all the way to Baltimore, where he secretly changed trains for the final leg of his unheralded entry into the nation's capital. Alighting at dawn, Lincoln and his bodyguards were startled by a loud voice echoing down the platform: "Abe, you can't play that on me!" Guns drawn, Pinkerton and Lamon whirled around and were about to fire on the approaching stranger when Lincoln recognized him at the last moment as Illinois congressman Elihu Washburne, who had appointed himself a one-man welcoming committee. Badly rattled, Lincoln was driven to Willard's Hotel at the corner of Fourteenth Street and Pennsylvania Avenue. Waiting for him at the desk was an unsigned letter warning, somewhat baroquely, "If you do not resign we are going to put a spider in your dumpling and play the Devil with you," and closing with the less subtle salutation "You are nothing but a goddamn black nigger."[20]

The press had a field day at Lincoln's expense. *New York Times* reporter Joseph Howard wrote inaccurately that Lincoln had made his getaway from Harrisburg wearing a Scottish plaid cap and a long military coat. Cartoonists immediately elaborated on the disguise, changing it into a tam-o'-shanter and kilts and depicting a scarecrowlike Lincoln doing "the Mac Lincoln Harrisburg Highland Fling." The final leg of the trip was termed "the flight of Abraham," and even the pro-Lincoln *New York Tribune* demanded some proof of the "imminent and great danger" that had caused the president-elect to make such a seriocomic arrival. Diarist George Templeton Strong worried that "this surreptitious nocturnal dodging or sneaking of the President-elect into the capital city will be used to damage his moral position and throw ridicule on his Administration." Mainly, it damaged Lincoln's self-respect. Days later, he was still explaining, a little huffily, that he had never believed he would be assassinated, "but I thought it wise to run no risk where no risk was necessary." Whatever the case, it was an inauspicious beginning to his presidency.[21]

Stephen Douglas was among to first to meet with Lincoln after his arrival in the capital. Hurrying over to Willard's that afternoon, the Little Giant reunited with the man who had bested him for the presidency. It was their first face-to-face meeting since the senatorial debates in Illinois two and a half years earlier. By all accounts, the reunion went surprisingly well—Douglas pronounced it "peculiarly pleasant." He took the opportunity to urge Lincoln to support an eleventh-hour national peace conference chaired by former president John Tyler and attended by a number of Lincoln's old Whig associates, including David Wilmot, Stephen Logan, Thomas Ewing, and Caleb Smith. "In God's name," said Douglas, "act the patriot and save our children a country to live in." Lincoln listened "respectfully and kindly," Douglas reported, but would not throw his support behind a conference that was being boycotted by thirteen of the thirty-four states, including all the southern states and the free states of Michigan, Minnesota, Wisconsin, California, and Oregon. In the end, the peace conference got no further than a Senate committee, where it was tabled without comment. Douglas took his leave after assuring Lincoln of his personal support. Later, Lincoln told another visitor, a little wistfully, "What a noble man Douglas is."[22]

The next ten days were spent in a dizzying whirl of courtesy calls—on the president, Congress, the Supreme Court, even the mayor of Washington, D.C. At night, Lincoln and Mary entertained visitors in the hotel parlor. President Buchanan's supercilious niece, Harriet Lane, the reigning doyenne of Washington society, compared Lincoln to her "tall, awkward" Irish doorman, and sniffed disapprovingly that Mary was "awfully *western*, loud & unrestrained." The Dutch ambassador complained that Lincoln's "conversation consists of vulgar anecdotes at which he himself laughs uproariously," and a Virginia aristocrat compared the president-elect to "a cross between a sandhill crane and an Andalusian jackass." Understandably weary of his official duties, and smarting a little from his cool reception, Lincoln's temper grew short. When New York financier William E. Dodge, whose suite the Lincolns were using before the inauguration, fretted that the nation was headed for bankruptcy, with "grass growing in the streets of our commercial cities," Lincoln snapped: "Let the grass grow where it may."[23]

◆ ◆ ◆

Inauguration Day dawned cloudy and cool, more late winter than early spring, and a sharp northwesterly wind blew through the bare-branched elm trees on Capitol Hill. Beneath the temporary wooden speaker's stand on the east portico of the Capitol, a sleepy group of volunteer soldiers shivered and stretched in the lightening air. They were part of the rapidly expanding federal militia now taking shape in Washington. Their commanding officer, Colonel Charles P. Stone, had been dragooned back into the army by his old Mexican War commander, General-in-Chief Winfield Scott, a few weeks earlier. The men had been there all night, dispatched by Stone to guard the platform after an anonymous warning that someone was planning to blow it up. Posted in the shadows beneath the stand, the soldiers had watched and waited for something to happen, fingering their muskets and jingling their canteens, but they had seen nothing more menacing in the blue-black night than the spectral waving of the elms in the wind or the disembodied statue of Armed Freedom standing watch on the Capitol lawn, clutching her bronze sword and wreath of flowers and staring up forlornly at the unfinished dome.

A few blocks away, at Willard's Hotel, the president-elect was dressing himself with unaccustomed care: new black suit, polished boots, stovepipe hat, and gold-headed cane. Abraham Lincoln was no one's idea of a clotheshorse—least of all his own—but he had a politician's innate respect for public ceremony and a historian's awareness of the timeless moment. Both were coming. Lincoln had just enough time to finish dressing and read his much-worked-over inaugural address to his family and friends. Unlike most of his speeches, this one had been vetted by a number of hands, most especially those of his newly designated secretary of state, William Seward. The conclusion, in particular, had been Seward's idea, although Lincoln had improved upon it with his surprisingly delicate gift for language. "Guardian angel of the nation" had been changed to "the better angels of our nature," and "ancient music" had been transformed into the infinitely more evocative "mystic chords of memory." It was the difference between a statesman and a poet, Today, of all days, Lincoln would need to be both.

Outside, the crowd was beginning to gather on Pennsylvania Avenue, the main Washington thoroughfare down which Lincoln and outgoing President Buchanan were scheduled to lead a rather truncated parade to the Capitol. Above the crowd, on the sloping rooftops of finely appointed mansions, army sharpshooters were moving into position, while below in the dusty street, squads of cavalrymen cantered into place to seal off intersections along the parade route. General Scott himself commanded a section of flying artillery on the far slope of Capitol Hill. The whole city was on edge, and with good reason. With seven southern states now out of the Union, no one was really sure who, exactly, Lincoln would be addressing, beyond the crowds now jockeying for position below the speaker's stand. Were there still thirty-four states in the Union, or only twenty-seven? Was Lincoln the president-elect of a transcontinental nation, or merely a transnorthern one? Lincoln intended to address these questions.

Precisely at noon, the carriage bearing Buchanan, Maryland senator James A. Pearce, and Lincoln's closest friend, Oregon senator Edward Baker, pulled up to the front door of Willard's Hotel. Buchanan went inside alone and emerged a few minutes later, arm in arm with Lincoln. The two presented a dramatic contrast. Buchanan was "pale, sad, preoccupied," while Lincoln was "grave and impassive as an Indian martyr." The sky had cleared to a bleached-out blue, but it was still unpleasantly cool. The weather inside the carriage was scarcely warmer. Buchanan and Lincoln said little as the procession moved down Pennsylvania Avenue. The two senators took their cues from the president and president-elect and said nothing. Along the avenue, people strained to catch a glimpse inside the carriage, but the cavalry escort blocked their view. There was a smattering of cheers, and an equal amount of boos. One onlooker called out, "Three cheers for the southern Confederacy!" Lincoln typically kept his feelings to himself.[24]

In contrast to Buchanan's gala inaugural four years earlier, the festivities surrounding Lincoln's advent were decidedly low-key. Five hundred Republican stalwarts, including representatives from the Wide Awakes, led the way, followed by a company of West Point cadets and a float carrying thirty-four pretty girls, one for each state in (or out of) the Union. Alongside the presidential carriage, Stone and his horsemen purposely reared and swerved, the better to block an assassin's aim. Bringing up the rear was a contingent of Washington-based militia, their rifles topped with bayonets. It looked, one observer said, less like a parade than a military march.

Entering the Capitol through a door guarded by marines and shielded from the public by a high board fence, Lincoln and his escort walked directly to the Senate, where they witnessed the unadorned swearing-in of Vice President Hannibal Hamlin. Then, as marksmen crouched in every window overlooking the Capitol, the official party walked out onto the speaker's platform in the wan sunlight. Overhead, an American flag dangled limply from a broken halyard on the derrick atop the sheared-off dome—a bad omen, some thought. Silver-haired Senator Baker, more handsome and mellifluous than either the outgoing or incoming president, strode to the front of the podium and said, with little fanfare, "Fellow citizens, I introduce to you Abraham Lincoln, president-elect of the United States of America." There was the slightest ripple of applause.[25]

Standing behind a small table placed at the front of the podium, Lincoln fumbled momentarily with his top hat and cane. Stephen Douglas, seated nearby, stepped forward graciously and took the hat, saying, "Permit me, sir." Those were the only words they exchanged all morning. As Douglas returned to his seat, Lincoln laid the cane underneath the table, then fiddled with a pair of reading glasses. The crowd waited silently, surprised by both the glasses and the new beard the president-elect had sprouted in the sixteen weeks since the election. He looked both unfamiliar and uncomfortable, like a man who had wandered into the wrong wedding party. In the background, leaning against a column in the Capitol doorway, Texas senator Louis Wigfall, a leading spokesman for southern secession, folded his arms and glared contemptuously at Lincoln's back.[26]

With long experience acquired from outdoor meetings in Illinois, Lincoln's naturally high-pitched voice carried easily to the back row of the crowd. "Fellow citizens of the United States," he began, and was greeted with his first big cheer. "Good, good," his old opponent Douglas murmured, holding Lincoln's top hat in his lap. "Apprehension seems to exist among the people of the southern states, that by the accession of a Republican administration, their property, and their peace, and personal security, are to be endangered," Lincoln continued, downplaying intentionally the current state of affairs. "There has never been any reasonable cause for such apprehension." At this, Wigfall smirked in the background. Lincoln quoted from an earlier speech in which he had declared, "I have no purpose, directly or indirectly, to interfere with the institution of slavery in the states where it exists. I believe I have no lawful right to do so, and I have no inclination to do so." Unmentioned was his less-ambiguous statement of intent to "place slavery in the course of its ultimate extinction," or his personal opinion that it was "a moral, social, and political evil."[27]

It was not Lincoln's intention to reopen that particular can of worms. Most people knew his views on the matter, and nothing he could say would be likely to change anyone's mind. Instead, he devoted the majority of his speech to the legal question of secession, which he argued was both unconstitutional and illegal. "I therefore consider that, in view of the Constitution and the laws, the Union is unbroken," Lincoln said, "and, to the extent of my ability, I shall take care that the laws of the Union be faithfully executed in all the states." Such execution of laws need not be accompanied by force, he argued, "and there shall be none, unless it be forced upon the national authority." Federal officers would be protected and the mails would be delivered, he promised, but "my best discretion will be exercised with a view and a hope of a peaceful solution of the national troubles, and the restoration of fraternal sympathies and affections."[28]

The crowd listened quietly and respectfully, although at one point in Lincoln's speech he was badly startled by a sudden commotion directly down front. A little man with a red beard who had been sitting in the crook of a tree and regaling those close to him with a sort of counter inaugural address, somehow contrived to fall out of the tree. Soldiers immediately rushed over and hustled him away, but *Louisville Journal* correspondent Henry Watterson thought that "Mr. Lincoln was thrown completely off his balance for a moment."[29]

With order restored in the crowd below, Lincoln turned to the question of restoring order in the nation as a whole. Secession, "the essence of anarchy," would not be tolerated. "The rule of a minority, as a permanent arrangement, is wholly inadmissible," he said. "Anarchy, or despotism in some form, is all that is left." With a backhanded slap at the much-derided *Dred Scott* decision and the author of that decision, Supreme Court chief justice Roger Taney, who was sitting on the platform behind him, Lincoln noted punctiliously that the court's rulings were binding, even when "it is obviously possible that such a decision may be erroneous," but there was always "the chance that it may be overruled." It was also possible, Lincoln continued, that the Constitution itself could be amended. For his part, Lincoln pledged that he would "make no recommendation of amendments," but he left the door open for the individual states to recommend their own future changes to the Constitution. Few listeners were in doubt as to what part of the document Lincoln wanted to see changed. He had made it obvious a few paragraphs earlier: "One section of our country believes slavery is *right*, and ought to be extended, while the other believes it is *wrong*, and ought not to be extended. This is the only substantial dispute."[30]

In the speech's original form, Lincoln had planned to tell rebellious southerners, "With you, and not with me, is the solemn question of 'Shall it be peace, or a sword?'" But Seward, who had contributed as much as any single person to the present difficulties between the regions with his talk of an "irrepressible conflict" and "a higher law," had advised Lincoln to end on a more conciliatory note. "Some words of affection, of calm and cheerful confidence" were needed, Seward urged. These Lincoln provided. "I am loth to close," he told the crowd. "We are not enemies, but friends. We must not be enemies. Though passion may have strained, it must not break our bonds of affection. The mystic chords of memory, stretching from every battlefield, and patriot grave, to every living heart and hearthstone, all over this broad land, will yet swell the chorus of the Union, when again touched, as surely they will be, by the better angels of our nature."[31]

That was all. The crowd applauded politely, if not enthusiastically. Senator Wigfall melted back into the shadows. Chief Justice Taney, looking, someone said, "like a galvanized corpse," tottered forward on his eighty-three-year-old legs to formally administer the oath of office. Placing his hand on a gilt-edged, cinnamon-colored, velvet-trimmed Bible, Lincoln swore the time-honored pledge to "preserve, protect, and defend the Constitution of the United States." Cannons boomed a twenty-one-gun salute. Standing alongside the guns on Capitol Hill, Winfield Scott threw up his hands and cried: "God be praised! We have a government!" But of whom, and for how long, no one could say.[32]

◆ ◆ ◆

Douglas's first reaction to Lincoln's address was positive. During the speech, he had audibly murmured, "Good," "That's so," and "Good again." Afterward, he praised Lincoln to a *New York Times* reporter, observing: "He does not mean coercion; he says nothing about retaking the forts or federal property—he's all right." That night, Douglas personally escorted his old Springfield dance partner, Mary Lincoln, into the inaugural ball. Mary, resplendent in a blue silk gown, pearls, diamonds, and gold bracelets, shared a reminiscent quadrille with the Little Giant. Two days after the inauguration, Douglas gave a gloss of the president's speech in the Senate. Lincoln, he repeated, did not intend to use forcible coercion on the South. His inaugural address had been "a peace offering rather than a war message," and "on this one question, that of preserving the Union by peaceful solution of our present difficulties . . . I am with him." The *New York Times*, among others, was a little skeptical of Douglas's apparent change of heart. "What means this evident weakness of Mr. Douglas for Mr. Lincoln?" it wondered.[33]

Douglas's newfound amiability did not extend to his abolitionist colleagues in the Senate. During a sharp exchange with Daniel Clark of New Hampshire and Timothy Howe of Wisconsin over his demand to know the War Department's plans for protecting federal property in the South, Douglas lost his temper. Referring to his recent defeat for the presidency—the only direct reference he ever made to the election—he observed: "Seven states are out of the Union, civil war is impending . . .

213

commerce is interrupted, confidence destroyed, the country going to pieces, just because I was unable to defeat you. You can boast that you have defeated me, but you have defeated your country with me. You . . . have triumphed over the unity of these States. Your triumph has brought disunion; and God only knows what consequences may grow out of it."[34]

The answer to that question was not long in coming. On the night of April 12–13, Confederate cannons fired on Fort Sumter. The war of words was over; the shooting war had begun. The next afternoon, Douglas met privately with Lincoln for two hours at the White House. Lincoln showed him the draft of a presidential order asking for 75,000 three-month volunteers to put down the insurrection; Douglas recommended raising the total to 200,0000 and strengthening other federal installations at Fortress Monroe, Washington, Harpers Ferry, and Cairo, Illinois. "You do not know the dishonest purposes of those men as well as I do," he warned. The meeting, Douglas told the press afterward, was marked by "a cordial feeling of a united, friendly, and patriotic purpose." While he remained "unalterably opposed" to the administration on political issues, he was prepared to sustain the president in all his attempts to preserve the Union. "I've known Mr. Lincoln a longer time than you have, or than the country has," Douglas assured a doubtful friend. "He'll come out all right, and we will all stand by him."[35]

Lincoln's call for volunteers had the unwelcome consequence of driving the border states into the southern camp. At the urging of Illinois Democrats, Douglas set out for Springfield with Adele on April 21 to pump up support for the Union cause. What he saw back home was not encouraging. "I found the state of feeling here and in some parts of our State much less satisfactory than I could have desired or expected when I arrived," he reported to Lincoln. But, he assured his old Prairie State rival, "There will be no outbreak however and in a few days I hope for entire unanimity in the support of the government and the Union." Some whispered that Lincoln had sent Douglas on a secret mission to raise an army in the Northwest, with him serving at its head. Given the fact that Douglas had even less active military experience than Lincoln, the image of the Little Giant galloping boldly at the forefront of an army was comical. Asked about the rumor by the *Chicago Tribune*, Lincoln said diplomatically that he had not considered appointing Douglas to a military position, but that if he did, "there were many who would be inferior" to the senator. Considering the quality of Lincoln's initial appointments as commander in chief, it would prove in retrospect to be faint praise indeed.[36]

Riding through Confederate Virginia, Douglas's train was stopped and searched by southern militia, some of whom wanted to throw the apostate Democrat into jail. Douglas was defiant. If he were arrested, he warned, a huge northern army would invade Virginia immediately and release him. Allowed to proceed, Douglas rode into the border town of Bellaire, Ohio, where he delivered a saber-rattling speech to listeners on both sides of the Ohio River. Denouncing "the new system of resistance by the sword and bayonet to the results of the ballot box," Douglas called on "the people in this great valley" to stand by the Union. "I have almost exhausted strength, and voice, and life, in the last two years, in my efforts to point out the dangers upon which we were rushing," he said. "Unite as a band of brothers and rescue your government and your country from the enemy who have been the authors of your calamity." Continuing to Springfield, he spoke for two hours before a full house at a special session of the legislature on April 25. In the same hall where he had fought so many battles with Lincoln in the past, Douglas now openly acknowledged that he had made a mistake "by leaning too far to the southern section of the Union against my own." He urged his listeners to stand with him against "the piratical flag" of the secessionists and "protect this government from every assailant."[37]

Douglas followed that defiant speech with another combative appearance in Chicago six days later. Speaking inside the Wigwam, where Lincoln had won the Republican presidential nomination almost exactly twelve months earlier, Douglas pointed out that he had struggled for years to find a peaceful solution to the sectional controversies. "I have gone to the very extreme of magnanimity," he said, only to be thwarted by "an enormous conspiracy" on the part of southern militants to overthrow the government. "The slavery question is a mere excuse," Douglas charged. "The election of Lincoln is a mere pretext." After conjuring up the horrors of the French Revolution, he ended with another ringing call to arms: "There are only two sides to the question. Every man must be for the United States or against it. There can be no neutrals in this war, only patriots—or traitors."[38]

Douglas was treated like a hero by Chicagoans, who greeted his arrival with resounding cheers and an informal parade. The chairman of the Illinois Democratic state committee, Virgil Hickox, was less impressed. Citing Douglas's public conversion to Unionism, if not Lincolnism, Hickox urged the senator "to make a full explanation" of his views, adding that party members were beginning to "distrust him on account of the great love that the Republicans profess now to have for him." In an answering letter, Douglas protested, "I am neither the supporter of the partisan policy nor the apologist for the errors of the administration." But, he added, "If we hope to regain and perpetuate the ascendancy of our party we should never forget that a man cannot be a true Democrat unless he is a loyal patriot." Hickox, a personal friend of Douglas's father-in-law, was not entirely persuaded by the Little Giant's logic. Still, he released the letter to the public—against Douglas's wishes—in an attempt to reassure restive Democrats.[39]

Douglas was forced to dictate the letter to Hickox; he had temporarily lost the use of his arms due to "a severe attack of rheumatism." As had often been the case during his life, personal and political disappointments had been followed closely by a sudden onslaught of illness. Douglas was confined to his bed at the Tremont House, where a steady procession of friends and family trooped in to see him. At first, they expected him to recover quickly, as he had always done in the past. As early as May 17, however, biographer James Sheahan was warning privately that "Douglas is very ill, and I am afraid is past all surgery." Afflictions mounted. To the persistent rheumatism, apparently brought on by emotional distress, were added typhoid fever, an ulcerated throat, constipation, and "torpor of the liver"—polite language, perhaps, for alcohol-induced cirrhosis. Lapsing in and out of consciousness, Douglas at one point shouted: "Telegraph to the president and let the column move!" Thoroughly alarmed, Adele called in Catholic bishop James Duggan, who asked the feverish senator if he had ever been baptized. "Never," Douglas replied. When Duggan offered to perform that service for him, the dying man held firm. "No sir," he said. "When I do I will communicate with you freely." Shortly after sunrise on June 3, he suddenly raised up from his pillow and cried: "Death! Death! Death!" When Adele leaned closer and asked if he had any last words for his sons, Robbie and Stevie, Douglas replied—so the story went, at any rate—"Tell them to obey the laws and uphold the Constitution." He died four hours later, at 9:00 a.m.[40]

Notified immediately of Douglas's death, Lincoln ordered the White House and other government buildings wrapped in black crepe as a show of mourning. The next day, Secretary of War Simon Cameron sent out a circular to the Union armies in the field announcing "the death of a great statesman . . . a man who nobly discarded party for his country. A Senator who forgot all prejudices in an earnest desire to serve the republic. A patriot, who defended with equal zeal and ability the constitution as it came to us from our fathers, and whose last mission upon earth was that of rallying the people of his own State of Illinois, as one man, around the glorious flag of our Union." Cameron, as strong a Republican partisan as there was in the country, directed the various colonels to read the message aloud to their regiments and likewise crape their colors in mourning out of respect for the fallen Democrat.[41]

As the crowd began gathering in Chicago for Douglas's funeral—Adele initially had wanted her husband buried in Washington, alongside their daughter, but the state of Illinois claimed pride of place—his old Sangamon County rival remained in seclusion in the White House. Abraham Lincoln had much on his mind. On the same day that Douglas died, Union and Confederate forces had fought the first real battle of the Civil War at Philippi, Virginia. The dispute was no longer an abstract political quarrel—families were beginning to bury their sons and brothers and fathers. No one, least of all Lincoln, knew what direction the war would take, only that it would be a long, hard slog. "The bottom," he would say, "is out of the tub." Now, for the first time in nearly three decades, he would have to make the journey alone, without the familiar, short-legged shadow of Stephen Douglas huffing alongside him every step of the way. The long pursuit was over; Lincoln had won the race. But for the time being at least, the victory seemed hollow, the platform of fame a little less crowded, now that the Little Giant had left the stage and passed irrevocably out of the limelight.[42]

Acknowledgments

With the possible exceptions of Jesus Christ and William Shakespeare, more books have been written about Abraham Lincoln than about any other figure in human—certainly American—history. No one, even with the best of intentions, could read them all, or should wish to. Most are pure hagiography, as is to be expected when dealing with one of the nation's most revered secular saints. Nevertheless, there are some authors whose scholastic rigor allowed them to portray the mythical Lincoln in a more recognizably human light. Some of the works that I found particularly useful included David Herbert Donald's *Lincoln*; Stephen Oates's *With Malice Toward None*; Kenneth J. Winkle's *The Young Eagle*; Paul Simon's *Lincoln's Preparation for Greatness*; Jean H. Baker's *Mary Todd Lincoln*; and Harold Holzer's *Lincoln at Cooper Union* and *The Lincoln-Douglas Debates*.

Far fewer books have been written about Lincoln's greatest—or, at any rate, most frequent—rival, Stephen Douglas. Anyone assaying a study of Douglas's multifarious career must acknowledge a large debt of gratitude to Robert W. Johannsen, who almost single-handedly has labored to preserve Douglas's life and letters for future generations. Without Johannsen's Herculean efforts, the onetime Little Giant of American politics would be even less remembered than he is today. Johannsen's

1973 biography, *Stephen A. Douglas*, remains unequaled. George Fort Milton's *The Eve of Conflict: Stephen A. Douglas and the Needless War*, although somewhat dated, is still a valuable study of the political climate that gave rise to Douglas and Lincoln, and Damon Wells's *Stephen Douglas: The Last Years, 1857–1861*, is also insightful.

Among the general histories of the time, Allan Nevins's multivolume *Ordeal of the Union* remains authoritative, and Sean Wilentz's *The Rise of American Democracy: Jefferson to Lincoln* is a beautifully written modern account of that tumultuous era. Reinhard Luthin's *The First Lincoln Campaign*, the only modern study of that epochal election, provides a useful road map to the 1860 race, if skewed rather heavily toward the Republican side of affairs. On matters of purely political partisanship, Michael Holt's *The Rise and Fall of the American Whig Party*, William E. Gienapp's *The Origins of the Republican Party, 1852–1856*, and Eric H. Walther's *The Fire-Eaters* and *The Shattering of the Union* are solid and enlightening works.

To all these authors, and to dozens of others on whom I relied, I offer my sincere professional gratitude.

I would like to thank my editor at Smithsonian Books, Elisabeth Kallick Dyssegaard, for her consistent kindness and support—not least of which lay in contributing a far better title for this book than the one I came up with originally. Thanks also to my agent, Georges Borchardt, for his always cogent and courtly advice. Finally, to my immediate family—Leslie, Lucy, and Phil—thanks beyond thanks for giving me the benefit of your wisdom, patience, and love, all of which I needed in copious amounts to complete this book. The dedication at the beginning is slight recompense, indeed, for your unfailingly good-natured and long-suffering support.

Notes

Introduction

1. Roy P. Basler, ed., *The Collected Works of Abraham Lincoln*, 9 vols. (New Brunswick, N.J.: Rutgers University Press, 1953–55), 2:382. Hereafter cited as *CW*. Stephen B. Oates, *With Malice Toward None: The Life of Abraham Lincoln* (New York: Harper & Row, 1977), 106; Paul Simon, *Lincoln's Preparation for Greatness: The Illinois Legislative Years* (Urbana: University of Illinois Press, 1971), 110.
2. Robert W. Johannsen, *Stephen A. Douglas* (Urbana: University of Illinois Press, 1997), xi; *CW*, 2:266.

Chapter 1: The Paradise of the World

1. CW, 2:382–83.
2. David Herbert Donald, *Lincoln* (New York: Touchstone, 1996), 21–26; *CW*, 4:61; Kenneth J. Winkle, *The Young Eagle: The Rise of Abraham Lincoln* (Dallas: Taylor Trade Publishing, 2001, 7.
3. Donald, *Lincoln*, 33–34; Winkle, *Young Eagle*, 20.
4. Donald, *Lincoln*, 38–39; Douglas L. Wilson and Rodney O. Davis, eds., *Herndon's Informants: Letters, Interviews and Statements About Abraham Lincoln* (Urbana: University of Illinois Press, 1998), 429.
5. Winkle, *Young Eagle*, 42; Donald, *Lincoln*, 40, 44; William H. Herndon and Jesse W. Weik, *Herndon's Lincoln: The True Story of a Great Life*, 3 vols. (Chicago: Belford-Clarke, 1890), 1:79–80.

6. Donald, *Lincoln*, 40; Oates, *With Malice Toward None*, 20.

7. Donald, *Lincoln*, 41–42; Oates, *With Malice Toward None*, 19–23; Winkle, *Young Eagle*, 84.

8. Donald, *Lincoln*, 42–43; *Sangamo Journal*, Mar. 15, 1832; *CW*, 1:5–9.

9. Winkle, *Young Eagle*, 86–90, 104.

10. Donald, *Lincoln*, 44–45; Winkle, *Young Eagle*, 91; Alvin M. Josephy, Jr., *The Patriot Chiefs: A Chronicle of American Indian Leadership* (New York: Viking, 1961), 252.

11. Donald, *Lincoln*, 46; Herndon and Weik, *Herndon's Lincoln*, 1:103; *CW*: 4:64.

12. Donald, *Lincoln*, 47–50; *CW*, 4:65.

13. Johannsen, *Stephen A. Douglas*, 6–7.

14. Stephen A. Douglas, Autobiographical Sketch, Sept. 1, 1838, in Robert W. Johannsen, ed., *The Letters of Stephen A. Douglas* (Urbana: University of Illinois Press, 1961), 57. Hereafter cited as *Letters*. George Fort Milton, *The Eve of Conflict: Stephen A. Douglas and the Needless War* (Boston: Houghton Mifflin, 1934), 15.

15. Douglas, Autobiographical Sketch, Sept. 1, 1838, *Letters*, 57; Johannsen, *Stephen A. Douglas*, 9. For the Jackson-Adams feud, see Paul F. Boller, Jr., *Presidential Campaigns* (New York: Oxford University Press, 1984), 33–52.

16. Boller, *Presidential Campaigns*, 42, 44–45.

17. Johannsen, *Stephen A. Douglas*, 9; Douglas, Autobiographical Sketch, Sept. 1, 1838, *Letters*, 58.

18. Johannsen, *Stephen A. Douglas*, 10–11.

19. Ibid., 11–12; Sean Wilentz, *The Rise of American Democracy: Jefferson to Lincoln* (New York: W. W. Norton, 2005), 272–79, 349–52.

20. Johannsen, *Stephen A. Douglas*, 13–15; Douglas, Autobiographical Sketch, Sept. 1, 1838, *Letters*, 59; Milton, *Eve of Conflict*, 16.

21. Johannsen, *Stephen A. Douglas*, 16–21; Douglas to Julius N. Granger, July 13, 1834, *Letters*, 7; Douglas to Julius N. Granger, Nov. 14, 1834, *Letters*, 10; Douglas to Julius N. Granger, Dec. 15, 1833, *Letters*, 3.

22. Donald, *Lincoln*, 51, 54–55; Oates, *With Malice Toward None*, 27; *CW*, 4:62.

23. Donald, *Lincoln*, 51.

24. Ibid., 52–53; Winkle, *Young Eagle*, 115–16; Benjamin P. Thomas, *Lincoln's New Salem* (New York: Alfred A. Knopf, 1954), 85.

25. Michael Burlingame, ed., *An Oral History of Abraham Lincoln: John G. Nicolay's Interviews and Essays* (Carbondale: Southern Illinois University Press, 1996), 10.

26. Donald, *Lincoln*, 53; Simon, *Lincoln's Preparation for Greatness*, 21; *CW*, 2:382.

27. Johannsen, *Stephen A. Douglas*, 29–30; Milton, *Eve of Conflict*, 19.

28. Milton, *Eve of Conflict*, 19–20; Douglas to Julius N. Granger, May 9, 1835, *Letters*, 17; Douglas to Julius N. Granger, Feb. 22, 1835, *Letters*, 12; Douglas to Julius N. Granger, Apr. 25, 1835, *Letters*, 13.

29. Douglas, Autobiographical Sketch, Sept. 1, 1838, *Letters*, 65–67.

30. Douglas to Julius N. Granger, May 9, 1835, *Letters*, 15; Johannsen, *Stephen A. Douglas*, 39.

31. Johannsen, *Stephen A. Douglas*, 38–44; Simon, *Lincoln's Preparation for Greatness*, 34; *Chicago Democrat*, Jan. 6, 1836.

32. Johannsen, *Stephen A. Douglas*, 43–45; Douglas to Julius N. Granger, Apr. 8, 1836, *Letters*, 36; Milton, *Eve of Conflict*, 21; Simon, *Lincoln's Preparation for Greatness*, 47.

33. *Sangamo Journal*, Jan. 6, 1837; Simon, *Lincoln's Preparation for Greatness*, 49–51; Johannsen, *Stephen A. Douglas*, 47.

34. Donald, *Lincoln*, 53, 55, 64; Winkle, *Young Eagle*, 120.

35. *Sangamo Journal*, Apr. 1, 1837; Johannsen, *Stephen A. Douglas*, 56–57.

36. Johannsen, *Stephen A. Douglas*, 61–62; *Sangamo Journal*, Nov. 4, 1837; Douglas to Levi Woodbury, Oct. 6, 1837, *Letters*, 41.

37. Johannsen, *Stephen A. Douglas*, 63–64; Oates, *With Malice Toward None*, 53; *CW*, 1:107.

38. Milton, *Eve of Conflict*, 22; *Quincy Whig*, Sept. 22, 1838; Johannsen, *Stephen A. Douglas*, 66–69.

39. Johannsen, *Stephen A. Douglas*, 66, 90–91; Winkle, *Young Eagle*, 211.

40. Winkle, *Young Eagle*, 211; Johannsen, *Stephen A. Douglas*, 66–68.

41. Johannsen, *Stephen A. Douglas*, 70; Milton, *Eve of Conflict*, 22; *CW*, 1:154.

42. Oates, *With Malice Toward None*, 55–56.

43. *Illinois State Register*, Nov. 23, 1839; Donald, *Lincoln*, 79.

44. For a lively account of the 1840 election, see Robert Gray Gunderson, *The Log-Cabin Campaign* (Lexington: University Press of Kentucky, 1957).

45. Roy Morris, Jr., "Tippecanoe and Cider Too: The Improbable, Irrepressible Election of 1840," *Timeline* 22, no. 4 (Oct.–Dec. 2005), 13.

46. Simon, *Lincoln's Preparation for Greatness*, 211–13; *CW*, 1:205; *Alton Telegraph*, Apr. 11, 1840; *Sangamo Journal*, May 8, 1840.

47. Simon, *Lincoln's Preparation for Greatness*, 219; *Illinois State Register*, Nov. 23, 1839; Johannsen, *Stephen A. Douglas*, 73; Jean H. Baker, *Mary Todd Lincoln* (New York: W. W. Norton, 1997), 84–85.

48. Johannsen, *Stephen A. Douglas*, 79–80; *CW*, 1:206.

49. Johannsen, *Stephen A. Douglas*, 82, 84–87, 96.

50. Ibid., 97, 104–5.

51. Milton, *Eve of Conflict*, 24–25; *Illinois State Register*, May 14, 1841.

52. Douglas to Julius N. Granger, Apr. 3, 1841, *Letters*, 99; Johannsen, *Stephen A. Douglas*, 113–14, 116–22.

Chapter 2: Whigs and Polkats

1. *CW*, 1:305; Donald, *Lincoln*, 90, 95; Oates, *With Malice Toward None*, 60.

2. Donald, *Lincoln*, 87, 90; Baker, *Mary Todd Lincoln*, 94.

3. *Sangamo Journal*, Sept. 2, 8, 1842; Baker, *Mary Todd Lincoln*, 95–97.

4. Donald, *Lincoln*, 91–92; Baker, *Mary Todd Lincoln*, 97.

5. Donald, *Lincoln*, 93; Oates, *With Malice Toward None*, 68; Baker, *Mary Todd Lincoln*, 97–98; Winkle, *Young Eagle*, 212.

6. Donald, *Lincoln*, 94–97; Oates, *With Malice Toward None*, 64.

7. Donald, *Lincoln*, 97, 104–5; John P. Frank, *Lincoln as a Lawyer* (Chicago: Americana House, 1991), 18–20.

8. Donald, *Lincoln*, 105–6; Frank, *Lincoln as a Lawyer*, 22–24.

9. Donald, *Lincoln*, 106.

10. Ibid., 111; *CW*, 1:320.

11. Donald, *Lincoln*, 112; Oates, *With Malice Toward None*, 74.
12. Johannsen, *Stephen A. Douglas*, 125–26.
13. Ibid., 129–30.
14. Ibid., 144–47. For the annexation of Texas, see Wilentz, *Rise of American Democracy*, 559–66.
15. Johannsen, *Stephen A. Douglas*, 148–49; Milton, *Eve of Conflict*, 28.
16. Johannsen, *Stephen A. Douglas*, 149; William A. DeGregorio, *The Complete Book of U.S. Presidents* (New York: Dembner Books, 1984), 167.
17. Wilentz, *Rise of American Democracy*, 572–73; Boller, *Presidential Campaigns*, 80–81.
18. *CW*, 1:334; *Illinois State Register*, Mar. 15, 1844; Donald, *Lincoln*, 110.
19. Milton, *Eve of Conflict*, 28; *Nashville Union*, Sept. 2, 1844; *Illinois State Register*, Sept. 20, 1844; Johannsen, *Stephen A. Douglas*, 150–51.
20. Richard Carwardine, *Lincoln: A Life of Purpose and Power* (New York: Alfred A. Knopf, 2006), 18; Donald, *Lincoln*, 118; Oates, *With Malice Toward None*, 75; *CW*, 1:313, 378–79, 385–86.
21. Wilentz, *Rise of American Democracy*, 574; Winkle, *Young Eagle*, 202–3.
22. Boller, *Presidential Campaigns*, 82; *New York Tribune*, Nov. 11, 1844; *CW*, 1:315, 347–48.
23. Donald, *Lincoln*, 101–2; David Herbert Donald, *Lincoln's Herndon* (New York: Alfred A. Knopf, 1948), 18–21.
24. Donald, *Lincoln*, 102–3.
25. *CW*, 1:353, 356; Donald W. Riddle, *Lincoln Runs for Congress* (New Brunswick, N.J.: Rutgers University Press, 1948), 102.
26. *CW*, 1:382–84; Oates, *With Malice Toward None*, 83.
27. *Sangamo Journal*, June 4, 1846; Johannsen, *Stephen A. Douglas*, 156.
28. Milton, *Eve of Conflict*, 29–30; Johannsen, *Stephen A. Douglas*, 192–93.
29. Johannsen, *Stephen A. Douglas*, 189, 196.
30. Milo Milton Quaife, ed., *The Diary of James Knox Polk During His Presidency, 1845–1849*, 4 vols. (Chicago: A. C. McClurg, 1910), 2:75.
31. Johannsen, *Stephen A. Douglas*, 202, 204–5; *Chicago Western Citizen*, Mar. 4, 1846.
32. Johannsen, *Stephen A. Douglas*, 207–9, 251, 334; Milton, *Eve of Conflict*, 32–35.
33. Oates, *With Malice Toward None*, 85; Donald, *Lincoln's Herndon*, 26.
34. *CW*, 1:439–442.
35. Oates, *With Malice Toward None*, 85; Donald, *Lincoln*, 120; Baker, *Mary Todd Lincoln*, 139; *CW*, 1:465.
36. Baker, *Mary Todd Lincoln*, 138–41; *CW*, 1:465, 477.
37. *CW*, 1:431, 446–47; Donald, *Lincoln*, 124–25. For more adverse reaction to Lincoln's stand, see Donald W. Riddle, *Congressman Abraham Lincoln* (Westport, Conn.: Greenwood Press, 1979), 35–39, 56.
38. Wilentz, *Rise of American Democracy*, 628. For Taylor's background, see DeGregorio, *Complete Book of U.S. Presidents*, 175–81.
39. *CW*, 1:452.
40. Ibid., 2:63, 75–76.
41. Johannsen, *Stephen A. Douglas*, 228, 231–32; *Raleigh Register*, Apr. 2, 1848.

42. Douglas to Robert Smith, Sept. 20, 1848, *Letters*, 163–64; Donald, *Lincoln*, 131–32; *CW*, 2:3–4.

43. Donald, *Lincoln*, 132; Doris Kearns Goodwin, *Team of Rivals: The Political Genius of Abraham Lincoln* (New York: Simon & Schuster, 2005), 127; Oates, *With Malice Toward None*, 91.

44. *CW*, 1:491; Donald, *Lincoln*, 133; Winkle, *Young Eagle*, 244.

45. Donald, *Lincoln*, 133–34.

46. Riddle, *Congressman Abraham Lincoln*, 170; Oates, *With Malice Toward None*, 94; Donald, *Lincoln*, 135.

47. *CW*, 2:41, 46, 49, 58, 60, 79; Donald, *Lincoln*, 140–41.

48. Johannsen, *Stephen A. Douglas*, 252–54.

49. Baker, *Mary Todd Lincoln*, 153; Donald, *Lincoln*, 108.

Chapter 3: A Hell of a Storm

1. *CW*, 2:77; *CW*, 3:512; Donald, *Lincoln*, 142.

2. Oates, *With Malice Toward None*, 109; Donald, *Lincoln*, 150–51.

3. Donald, *Lincoln*, 146; Oates, *With Malice Toward None*, 111.

4. *CW*, 4:67; DeGregorio, *Complete Book of U.S. Presidents*, 183.

5. *CW*, 2:82–90; Oates, *With Malice Toward None*, 102.

6. Donald, *Lincoln*, 153; *CW*, 2:96–97, 111–13.

7. Goodwin, *Team of Rivals*, 141–43.

8. Johannsen, *Stephen A. Douglas*, 276.

9. Ibid., 277.

10. Milton, *Eve of Conflict*, 66; Allan Nevins, *Ordeal of the Union*, 4 vols (New York: Charles Scribner's Sons, 1947–1971), 1:300–301; Wilentz, *Rise of American Democracy*, 641.

11. Johannsen, *Stephen A. Douglas*, 278–79.

12. Ibid., 295–98.

13. Ibid., 280, 298–99; *New York Herald*, Jan. 29, 1851; *Washington National Intelligencer*, Mar. 27, 1851.

14. Milton, *Eve of Conflict*, 79–80; *New York Herald*, Mar. 22, 1851.

15. Milton, *Eve of Conflict*, 83; Johannsen, *Stephen A. Douglas*, 360–63.

16. Johannsen, *Stephen A. Douglas*, 335, 358; Nevins, *Ordeal of the Union*, 1:11.

17. DeGregorio, *Complete Book of U.S. Presidents*, 197, 200; Boller, *Presidential Campaigns*, 89–90.

18. Johannsen, *Stephen A. Douglas*, 371.

19. *CW*, 2:121–124.

20. Ibid., 2:132; Donald, *Lincoln*, 165.

21. *CW*, 2:140–41; Donald, *Lincoln*, 163.

22. *CW*, 2:205; Donald, *Lincoln*, 155.

23. Donald, *Lincoln*, 155–56.

24. Ibid., 163; Boller, *Presidential Campaigns*, 89–90; Milton, *Eve of Conflict*, 94; Johannsen, *Stephen A. Douglas*, 373.

25. Johannsen, *Stephen A. Douglas*, 375–77; Douglas to Charles H. Lanphier, Dec. 3, 1852, *Letters*, 258; Milton, *Eve of Conflict*, 97.

26. Johannsen, *Stephen A. Douglas*, 381–83.

27. Ibid., 384–85; *Providence Journal*, Sept. 1, 1853; *Washington National Intelligencer*, Nov. 10, 1853.

28. Johannsen, *Stephen A. Douglas*, 389; Milton, *Eve of Conflict*, 98; Nevins, *Ordeal of the Union*, 1:75.

29. Douglas to Charles H. Lanphier, Nov. 11, 1853, *Letters*, 267–68; Milton, *Eve of Conflict*, 98.

30. Johannsen, *Stephen A. Douglas*, 394, 435; Milton, *Eve of Conflict*, 105–6.

31. Johannsen, *Stephen A. Douglas*, 391; Nevins, *Ordeal of the Union*, 1:90, 93.

32. Milton, *Eve of Conflict*, 112–116; Nevins, *Ordeal of the Union*, 1:98–99.

33. Nevins, *Ordeal of the Union*, 1:111–112; *Washington National Era*, Jan. 24, 1854.

34. Milton, *Eve of Conflict*, 122–24.

35. Johannsen, *Stephen A. Douglas*, 420–421; Nevins, *Ordeal of the Union*, 1:114.

36. Eric H. Walther, *The Shattering of the Union: America in the 1850s* (Wilmington, Del.: Scholarly Resources, 2004), 46–48.

37. Johannsen, *Stephen A. Douglas*, 425; Milton, *Eve of Conflict*, 131.

38. Johannsen, *Stephen A. Douglas*, 428–430; *New York Tribune*, Mar. 7, 1854; Goodwin, *Team of Rivals*, 162–63.

39. *New York Times*, May 12, 1854; Johannsen, *Stephen A. Douglas*, 432–34.

40. *CW*, 2:282; Donald, *Lincoln*, 170.

41. Walther, *Shattering of the Union*, 59–60; James M. McPherson, *Battle Cry of Freedom: The Civil War Era* (New York: Oxford University Press, 1988), 145, 146.

42. Walther, *Shattering of the Union*, 49–50.

43. Johannsen, *Stephen A. Douglas*, 446; *Detroit Democrat*, Feb. 4, 1854.

44. Milton, *Eve of Conflict*, 175–76; Nevins, *Ordeal of the Union*, 1:149.

45. Donald, *Lincoln*, 172–73.

46. Ibid., 174, 178.

47. *CW*, 2:282.

48. Ibid., 2:262–65.

49. *Illinois Journal*, Oct. 10, 1854; Donald, *Lincoln*, 178.

50. Johannsen, *Stephen A. Douglas*, 460–61.

51. Donald, *Lincoln*, 186.

52. *CW*, 2:9; Oates, *With Malice Toward None*, 130–31; Donald, *Lincoln*, 184.

53. Donald, *Lincoln*, 184–85; Johannsen, *Stephen A. Douglas*, 464.

Chapter 4: Defiant Recreancy

1. *CW*, 2:308; Donald, *Lincoln*, 185–86.

2. Donald, *Lincoln*, 186; Goodwin, *Team of Rivals*, 174–75.

3. Donald, *Lincoln*, 186; Herndon and Weik, *Herndon's Lincoln*, 2:356.

4. Johannsen, *Stephen A. Douglas*, 478–79; *St. Louis Missouri Democrat*, Sept. 22, 1855.

5. Johannsen, *Stephen A. Douglas*, 484–85; Milton, *Eve of Conflict*, 209.

6. David M. Potter, *The Impending Crisis, 1848–1861* (New York: Harper & Row, 1976), 199–201; McPherson, *Battle Cry of Freedom*, 145–47; Walther, *Shattering of the Union*, 63–64; Nevins, *Ordeal of the Union*, 1:384–85.

7. Walther, *Shattering of the Union*, 66; Nevins, *Ordeal of the Union*, 1:386–87; Potter, *Impending Crisis*, 206.

8. Potter, *Impending Crisis*, 205; Wilentz, *Rise of American Democracy*, 692.
9. Nevins, *Ordeal of the Union*, 1:420, 424; *New York Tribune*, Apr. 11, 1856.
10. Nevins, *Ordeal of the Union*, 1:439–40.
11. Johannsen, *Stephen A. Douglas*, 502–3.
12. Walther, *Shattering of the Union*, 99; Johannsen, *Stephen A. Douglas*, 504.
13. Walther, *Shattering of the Union*, 99–100; *Richmond Enquirer*, June 2, 1856; Wilentz, *Rise of American Democracy*, 691.
14. Walther, *Shattering of the Union*, 90–91; Potter, *Impending Crisis*, 208–9.
15. Potter, *Impending Crisis*, 212–13.
16. For the beginnings of the Republican Party, see William E. Gienapp, *The Origins of the Republican Party, 1852–1856* (New York: Oxford University Press, 1987); *CW*, 2:322–23.
17. Donald, *Lincoln*, 191–92.
18. Ibid., 192.
19. Don E. Fehrenbacher, *Prelude to Greatness: Lincoln in the 1850's* (New York: McGraw-Hill, 1964), 44; *CW*, 2:342–43; Boller, *Presidential Campaigns*, 92; Donald, *Lincoln*, 193.
20. Boller, *Presidential Campaigns*, 92; Johannsen, *Stephen A. Douglas*, 515–21.
21. *CW*, 2:374–75; Baker, *Mary Todd Lincoln*, 107; Johannsen, *Stephen A. Douglas*, 527.
22. Walther, *Shattering of the Union*, 108; Jean H. Baker, *James Buchanan* (New York: Times Books, 2004), 20–22, 25–26, 71; Boller, *Presidential Campaigns*, 97.
23. Arthur M. Schlesinger, Jr., and Fred L. Israel, eds., *History of American Presidential Elections, 1789–1968*, 4 vols. (New York: Chelsea House, 1971), 1:1029; Andrew Rolle, *John Charles Frémont: Character as Destiny* (Norman: University of Oklahoma Press, 1991), 1–3, 169.
24. *Richmond Enquirer*, Oct. 11, 1856; McPherson, *Battle Cry of Freedom*, 159; Schlesinger and Israel, *History of American Presidential Elections*, 1:1028.
25. Nevins, *Ordeal of the Union*, 1:514; Johannsen, *Stephen A. Douglas*, 537–38.
26. Johannsen, *Stephen A. Douglas*, 540–44; *Washington States Union*, Jan. 20, 1858.
27. Donald, *Lincoln*, 197–98.
28. Ibid., 157.
29. Oates, *With Malice Toward None*, 148–50.
30. Ibid., 142–43; Donald, *Lincoln*, 198–99, 202–3; *CW*, 2:412–13.
31. For the *Dred Scott* decision, see McPherson, *Battle Cry of Freedom*, 170–76.
32. Ibid., 180; Johannsen, *Stephen A. Douglas*, 569.
33. Johannsen, *Stephen A. Douglas*, 569–71.
34. *CW*, 2:401–5.
35. Johannsen, *Stephen A. Douglas*, 533, 537.
36. Ibid., 551, 557; *New York Tribune*, Oct. 13, 1857.
37. McPherson, *Battle Cry of Freedom*, 164; Milton, *Eve of Conflict*, 270–71.
38. Baker, *James Buchanan*, 102–3; Nevins, *Ordeal of the Union*, 2:239; Johannsen, *Stephen A. Douglas*, 581.
39. Johannsen, *Stephen A. Douglas*, 590–91; *New York Times*, Dec. 11, 1857.
40. Walther, *Shattering of the Union*, 135; Johannsen, *Stephen A. Douglas*, 585–86, 593.

41. McPherson, *Battle Cry of Freedom*, 168; Johannsen, *Stephen A. Douglas*, 608, 626.
42. Potter, *Impending Crisis*, 321; Donald, *Lincoln*, 204; *CW*, 2:430, 448.
43. Oates, *With Malice Toward None*, 112; Donald, *Lincoln*, 204; Johannsen, *Stephen A. Douglas*, 633; *New York Tribune*, Feb. 12, 1858.
44. Oates, *With Malice Toward None*, 151–52; *CW*, S:29–30; Johannsen, *Stephen A. Douglas*, 638; Simon, *Lincoln's Preparation for Greatness*, 117; *Dixon Republican and Telegraph*, May 20, 27, 1858.
45. Donald, *Lincoln*, 205.
46. *CW*, 2:461–65.
47. Ibid., 2:466–69.
48. Johannsen, *Stephen A. Douglas*, 640–43.
49. Oates, *With Malice Toward None*, 158; Donald, *Lincoln*, 210; *CW*, 2:484–501.
50. Oates, *With Malice Toward None*, 163; Johannsen, *Stephen A. Douglas*, 655; Donald, *Lincoln*, 210–11.
51. *CW*, 2:529; Douglas to Abraham Lincoln, July 24, 1858, *Letters*, 423–24.

Chapter 5: Thunder Tones

1. Harold Holzer, ed., *The Lincoln-Douglas Debates: The First Complete, Unexpurgated Text* (New York: HarperCollins, 1994), 40–41.
2. *Chicago Press and Tribune*, Aug. 26, 1858; Paul M. Angle, ed., *Created Equal? The Complete Lincoln-Douglas Debates of 1858* (Chicago: University of Chicago Press, 1958), 102.
3. Angle, *Created Equal*, 102–3; Holzer, *Lincoln-Douglas Debates*, 41–42.
4. Holzer, *Lincoln-Douglas Debates*, 54–55.
5. Ibid., 42, 63, 66, 69.
6. Ibid., 60, 79, 2; Baker, *Mary Todd Lincoln*, 155.
7. *Chicago Times*, Aug. 22, 1858; Holzer, *Lincoln-Douglas Debates*, 43.
8. *CW*, 3:37; Donald, *Lincoln*, 217; Fehrenbacher, *Prelude to Greatness*, 124–25.
9. Holzer, *Lincoln-Douglas Debates*, 86–89.
10. Ibid., 91, 92, 93, 96, 105; Angle, *Created Equal*, 152.
11. Potter, *Impending Crisis*, 336; Holzer, *Lincoln-Douglas Debates*, 90, 110–11.
12. Holzer, *Lincoln-Douglas Debates*, 136–37; *Chicago Press and Tribune*, Sept. 17, 1858.
13. Holzer, *Lincoln-Douglas Debates*, 143, 148, 149, 151.
14. Ibid., 156, 157; *Chicago Times*, Sept. 17, 1858.
15. Holzer, *Lincoln-Douglas Debates*, 185–86.
16. Ibid., 189–90.
17. Ibid., 190.
18. Ibid., 204, 209, 223.
19. Ibid., 234–35.
20. Ibid., 236, 242, 243, 247.
21. Ibid., 254, 258.
22. Ibid., 277–79.
23. Ibid., 279, 318, 320.
24. Ibid., 321, 322, 329.
25. Ibid., 354, 359.
26. Ibid., 373; Douglas to Charles H. Lanphier, Jan. 6, 1859, *Letters*, 433.

27. Johannsen, *Stephen A. Douglas*, 680.
28. Damon Wells, *Stephen Douglas: The Last Years, 1857–1861* (Austin: University of Texas Press, 1971), 149; *New York Tribune*, Dec. 6, 1858; Milton, *Eve of Conflict*, 360.
29. Milton, *Eve of Conflict*, 360–62; *Memphis Daily Appeal*, Nov. 30, 1858; *Port Gibson, Daily Southern Reveille*, Dec. 4, 1858.
30. Milton, *Eve of Conflict*, 362; Johannsen, *Stephen A. Douglas*, 683–84; *New York Tribune*, Dec. 14, 1858.
31. Oates, *With Malice Toward None*, 174; CW, 3:39, 336–37, 342.
32. CW, 3:396; Donald, *Lincoln*, 150, 230.
33. Donald, *Lincoln*, 231; Carwardine, *Lincoln*, 100; Oates, *With Malice Toward None*, 184.
34. Oates, With *Malice Toward None*, 174–75; CW, 3:511–12.
35. Donald, *Lincoln*, 237; Douglas to Follett and Foster Company, June 9, 1860, *Letters*, 489–90.
36. Donald, *Lincoln*, 232; CW, 3:367, 379.
37. Johannsen, *Stephen A. Douglas*, 686–87; Wells, *Stephen Douglas*, 157.
38. Wells, *Stephen Douglas*, 167; *New York Tribune*, Dec. 31, 1858; Milton, *Eve of Conflict*, 364.
39. Johannsen, *Stephen A. Douglas*, 689; Milton, *Eve of Conflict*, 357.
40. Milton, *Eve of Conflict*, 364; Johannsen, *Stephen A. Douglas*, 690.
41. Milton, *Eve of Conflict*, 366n; Johannsen, *Stephen A. Douglas*, 694–95; *New York Tribune*, Feb. 25, 1859.
42. *Washington States and Union*, Jan. 31, 1859; Douglas to , Jan. 1859, *Letters*, 432; Johannsen, *Stephen A. Douglas*, 695–96.
43. CW, 2:530–31; Oates, *With Malice Toward None*, 177; Johannsen, *Stephen A. Douglas*, 704–5; *Washington Daily National Intelligencer*, June 24, 1859.
44. *Jackson Weekly Mississippian*, Aug. 3, 1859; Milton, *Eve of Conflict*, 384; Johannsen, *Stephen A. Douglas*, 705.
45. Wells, *Stephen Douglas*, 183–85; *Richmond Enquirer*, Sept. 9, 1859.
46. CW, 3: 365–70, 394; *Chicago Press and Tribune*, Sept. 14, 1859; Donald, *Lincoln*, 233; *Columbus Ohio Statesman*, Sept. 20, 1859.
47. Johannsen, *Stephen A. Douglas*, 713; Milton, *Eve of Conflict*, 390–91.
48. Roy F. Nichols, *The Disruption of American Democracy* (New York: Macmillan, 1948), 263–64; Nevins, *Ordeal of the Union*, 2:69.
49. Walther, *Shattering of the Union*, 168–70; McPherson, *Battle Cry of Freedom*, 206–7.
50. Walther, *Shattering of the Union*, 170, 176; Wells, *Stephen Douglas*, 195; Johannsen, *Stephen A. Douglas*, 724; McPherson, *Battle Cry of Freedom*, 212.
51. Harold Holzer, *Lincoln at Cooper Union: The Speech That Made Abraham Lincoln President* (New York: Simon & Schuster, 2004), 270; CW, 3:496.
52. Goodwin, *Team of Rivals*, 226; Walther, *Shattering of the Union*, 174–79; McPherson, *Battle Cry of Freedom*, 209–10.

Chapter 6: Gentlemen of the South, You Mistake Us

1. CW, 3:496–503.
2. Holzer, *Lincoln at Cooper Union*, 10, 73, 80.

3. Donald, *Lincoln*, 237; Holzer, *Lincoln at Cooper Union*, 84, 88–89; Mary Panzer, *Mathew Brady and the Image of History* (Washington: Smithsonian Institution Press, 1997), 28.

4. Holzer, *Lincoln at Cooper Union*, 92–94.

5. Ibid., 105–7, 265–66. Lincoln's speech is reprinted as an appendix to Holzer's book.

6. Ibid., 267–74, 283–84.

7. *New York Times*, Feb. 28, 1860; *New York Tribune*, Feb. 28, 1860; *New York Post*, Feb. 28, 1860.

8. *Providence Journal*, Mar. 1, 1860; *CW*, 4:18.

9. Holzer, *Lincoln at Cooper Union*, 183, 189, 246. For Lincoln's full New England itinerary, see ibid., 177; Douglas to James Walker, n.d., *Letters*, 481.

10. *CW*, S:49–50; Herndon and Weik, *Herndon's Lincoln*, 3:457; *CW*, 4:33, 44–45.

11. Johannsen, *Stephen A. Douglas*, 725, 727–728; *Richmond Enquirer*, Aug. 31, 1860.

12. Johannsen, *Stephen A. Douglas*, 730–732; Milton, *Eve of Conflict*, 391.

13. *New York Herald*, Feb. 28, 1860; Johannsen, *Stephen A. Douglas*, 740.

14. William B. Hesseltine, ed., *Three Against Lincoln: Murat Halstead Reports the Caucus of 1860* (Baton Rouge: Louisiana State University Press, 1976), 18–20; Nevins, *Ordeal of the Union*, 2:212.

15. Johannsen, *Stephen A. Douglas*, 748–49; Norman A. Graebner, ed., *Politics and the Crisis of 1860* (Urbana: University of Illinois Press, 1961), 74; Douglas to Peter Cagger, Feb. 19, 1860, *Letters*, 485.

16. *Opelika Weekly Southern Era*, Apr. 18, 1860; Avery O. Craven, *The Growth of Southern Nationalism, 1848–1861* (Baton Rouge: Louisiana State University Press, 1953), 316.

17. Douglas to James W. Singleton, Mar. 21, 1859, *Letters*, 439; Johannsen, *Stephen A. Douglas*, 699, 747.

18. Hesseltine, *Three Against Lincoln*, 3, 7–8; Nichols, *Disruption of American Democracy*, 294.

19. Hesseltine, *Three Against Lincoln*, 13; *Charleston Mercury*, Apr. 16, 1860.

20. Eric H. Walther, *The Fire-Eaters* (Baton Rouge: Louisiana State University Press, 1992), 52, 55, 58, 71.

21. *St. Paul Pioneer and Democrat*, Jan. 27, 1860; Johannsen, *Stephen A. Douglas*, 751.

22. Hesseltine, *Three Against Lincoln*, 11, 13, 18.

23. Ibid., 20–24.

24. Ibid., 25–28; Milton, *Eve of Conflict*, 432.

25. Gerald M. Capers, *Stephen A. Douglas: Defender of the Union* (Boston: Little Brown, 1959), 194; Hesseltine, *Three Against Lincoln*, 34–35, 39.

26. Nichols, *Disruption of American Democracy*, 293.

27. Ibid., 292–93; Graebner, *Politics and the Crisis of 1860*, 75.

28. Hesseltine, *Three Against Lincoln*, 45–46, 51; Milton, *Eve of Conflict*, 433–34.

29. Hesseltine, *Three Against Lincoln*, 49; Nevins, *Ordeal of the Union*, 2:215; Dwight Lowell Dumond, *The Secession Movement, 1860–1861* (New York: Macmillan, 1931), 46.

30. Hesseltine, *Three Against Lincoln*, 24, 50; Nevins, *Ordeal of the Union*, 2:215.

31. Nevins, *Ordeal of the Union*, 2:216–17; Hesseltine, *Three Against Lincoln*,

52–53; Dumond, *Secession Movement*, 47; Walther, *Fire-Eaters*, 74; Walther, *Shattering of the Union*, 186.

32. Nevins, *Ordeal of the Union*, 2:217; Johannsen, *Stephen A. Douglas*, 754.

33. Nevins, *Ordeal of the Union*, 2:217; *Charleston Courier*, Apr. 30, 1860; Hesseltine, *Three Against Lincoln*, 48, 55–56.

34. Nevins, *Ordeal of the Union*, 2:217; Milton, *Eve of Conflict*, 436–37; Johannsen, *Stephen A. Douglas*, 755.

35. Nichols, *Disruption of American Democracy*, 301, 303; Hesseltine, *Three Against Lincoln*, 60–61.

36. Nevins, *Ordeal of the Union*, 2:219; *Cleveland Plain Dealer*, May 4, 1860; Hesseltine, *Three Against Lincoln*, 65–66.

37. Hesseltine, *Three Against Lincoln*, 67; Nevins, *Ordeal of the Union*, 2:219.

38. Hesseltine, *Three Against Lincoln*, 69–70.

39. Ibid., 79–84.

40. Ibid., 86.

41. Ibid., 88–100.

42. Ibid., 102–4; Johannsen, *Stephen A. Douglas*, 758.

43. Hesseltine, *Three Against Lincoln*, 113–15; Johannsen, *Stephen A. Douglas*, 758.

Chapter 7: The Rush of a Great Wind

1. Donald, *Lincoln*, 241–44; Oates, *With Malice Toward None*, 189–90; *CW*, 4:43–47.

2. Oates, *With Malice Toward None*, 184; Donald, *Lincoln*, 244–45; *CW*, 4:48.

3. Nevins, *Ordeal of the Union*, 2:245–46 ; Boller, *Presidential Campaigns*, 106–7; Carwardine, *Lincoln*, 103.

4. *CW*, 4:34, 50; Donald, *Lincoln*, 246.

5. Johannsen, *Stephen A. Douglas*, 759–60; Hesseltine, *Three Against Lincoln*, 119; Milton, *Eve of Conflict*, 453.

6. Milton, *Eve of Conflict*, 452–54.

7. Wells, *Stephen Douglas*, 232; Milton, *Eve of Conflict*, 454; Johannsen, *Stephen A. Douglas*, 765–66.

8. Johannsen, *Stephen A. Douglas*, 764; Boller, *Presidential Campaigns*, 101, 113; Nevins, *Ordeal of the Union*, 2:240.

9. Nevins, *Ordeal of the Union*, 2:248; Goodwin, *Team of Rivals*, 237–39.

10. Donald, *Lincoln*, 248; *CW*, 3:517; Goodwin, *Team of Rivals*, 214–16.

11. Donald, *Lincoln*, 248; Carwardine, *Lincoln*, 109.

12. DeGregorio, *Complete Book of U.S. Presidents*, 237; Donald, *Lincoln*, 248–49; *CW*, 4:50; Goodwin, *Team of Rivals*, 246; Nevins, *Ordeal of the Union*, 2:257.

13. Goodwin, *Team of Rivals*, 241; Hesseltine, *Three Against Lincoln*, 146.

14. Goodwin, *Team of Rivals*, 247; Hesseltine, *Three Against Lincoln*, 165.

15. Nevins, *Ordeal of the Union*, 2:260; Hesseltine, *Three Against Lincoln*, 165, 171.

16. Carwardine, *Lincoln*, 110; Donald, *Lincoln*, 250; Oates, *With Malice Toward None*, 194.

17. Oates, *With Malice Toward None*, 194; Goodwin, *Team of Rivals*, 253, 259; Donald, *Lincoln*, 251.

18. Johannsen, *Stephen A. Douglas*, 761; Milton, *Eve of Conflict*, 458–62.
19. Milton, *Eve of Conflict*, 464–66; Johannsen, *Stephen A. Douglas*, 762.
20. Nevins, *Ordeal of the Union*, 2:265–66; Hesseltine, *Three Against Lincoln*, 185–86; John T. Hubbell, "The Douglas Democrats and the Election of 1860," *Mid-America* 55 (1973), 118–19.
21. Johannsen, *Stephen A. Douglas*, 767; Nevins, *Ordeal of the Union*, 2:268; Hesseltine, *Three Against Lincoln*, 221.
22. Dumond, *Secession Movement*, 81–82.
23. Ibid., 82–85; Hesseltine, *Three Against Lincoln*, 220–21.
24. Hesseltine, *Three Against Lincoln*, 227–28, 238–39, 246; *New York Tribune*, June 23, 1860; Nevins, *Ordeal of the Union*, 2:270.
25. Hesseltine, *Three Against Lincoln*, 233–35; Nevins, *Ordeal of the Union*, 2:270.
26. Johannsen, *Stephen A. Douglas*, 769–70; Douglas to William A. Richardson, June 20, 1860, *Letters*, 492; Hesseltine, *Three Against Lincoln*, 262.
27. Hesseltine, *Three Against Lincoln*, 244–45.
28. Ibid., 251–53.
29. Ibid., 267–69, 276–77.
30. Ibid., 263; Johannsen, *Stephen A. Douglas*, 772; *Washington States and Union*, June 25, 1860.
31. William C. Davis, *Breckinridge: Statesman, Soldier, Symbol* (Baton Rouge: Louisiana State University Press, 1974), 226.
32. Ibid., 223, 227, 230.
33. Ibid., 224–27; Nevins, *Ordeal of the Union*, 2:285; Johannsen, *Stephen A. Douglas*, 775.
34. Johannsen, *Stephen A. Douglas*, 776–77; Douglas to Nathaniel Paschall, July 4, 1860, *Letters*, 497; Nevins, *Ordeal of the Union*, 2:284.
35. Donald, *Lincoln*, 252; Nevins, *Ordeal of the Union*, 2:262, 278; *CW*, 4:90.

Chapter 8: The Prairies Are on Fire

1. Douglas to Charles H. Lanphier, July 4, 1860, *Letters*, 498; Johannsen, *Stephen A. Douglas*, 777.
2. *New York Times*, July 3, 1860; Boller, *Presidential Campaigns*, 110.
3. Nevins, *Ordeal of the Union*, 2:291; *Springfield Republican*, July 28, 1860.
4. Boller, *Presidential Campaigns*, 110; Johannsen, *Stephen A. Douglas*, 780.
5. *New York Times*, Aug. 6, 1860; *Brandon Northern Visitor*, Aug. 2, 1860; Johannsen, *Stephen A. Douglas*, 3–4.
6. *New York Times*, Aug. 10, 1860; Boller, *Presidential Campaigns*, 109–10.
7. Johannsen, *Stephen A. Douglas*, 782; Milton, *Eve of Conflict*, 490.
8. Nevins, *Ordeal of the Union*, 2:291–92.
9. *New York Times*, Aug. 4, 1860; *Brandon Northern Visitor*, Aug. 2, 1860; Johannsen, *Stephen A. Douglas*, 783–84.
10. Reinhard H. Luthin, *The First Lincoln Campaign* (Cambridge, Mass.: Harvard University Press, 1944), 170; *Chicago Press and Tribune*, May 23, 1860.
11. *Missouri Democrat*, Sept. 29, 1860; Baker, *Mary Todd Lincoln*, 159–60; *New York Evening Post*, May 24, 1860; *Springfield Daily Republican*, May 23, 1860.
12. Donald, *Lincoln*, 252–54; *CW*, 4:68, 83.
13. Boller, *Presidential Campaigns*, 107, 111; *Southern Advocate*, Dec. 12, 1860.

14. Boller, *Presidential Campaigns*, 111–12; Luthin, *First Lincoln Campaign*, 174; Oates, *With Malice Toward None*, 201.
15. *CW*, 4:109; Donald, *Lincoln*, 254.
16. Oates, *With Malice Toward None*, 199; Donald, *Lincoln*, 19.
17. Carwardine, *Lincoln*, 123; Oates, *With Malice Toward None*, 197.
18. *CW*, 4:86; Baker, *Mary Todd Lincoln*, 161; Oates, *With Malice Toward None*, 202; *New York Tribune*, May 26, 1860.
19. Davis, *Breckinridge*, 231–32; *New York Times*, July 26, 1860.
20. Davis, *Breckinridge*, 234–41; *Lexington Kentucky Statesman*, July 20, 1860.
21. Potter, *Impending Crisis*, 417–18; DeGregorio, *Complete Book of U.S. Presidents*, 234; *New York Tribune*, May 11, 1860.
22. McPherson, *Battle Cry of Freedom*, 221–22; Boller, *Presidential Campaigns*, 101, 113; Luthin, *First Lincoln Campaign*, 190.
23. *Washington States and Union*, Aug. 25, Sept. 1, 1860; Johannsen, *Stephen A. Douglas*, 788–89.
24. *New York Herald*, Aug. 30, 1860; Johannsen, *Stephen A. Douglas*, 789–90; Nevins, *Ordeal of the Union*, 2:293.
25. Wells, *Stephen Douglas*, 241; Johannsen, *Stephen A. Douglas*, 791; *Montgomery Weekly Advertiser*, Sept. 19, 1860; Nevins, *Ordeal of the Union*, 2:287; Ollinger Crenshaw, *The Slave States in the Presidential Election of 1860* (Baltimore: Johns Hopkins University Press, 1945), 108.
26. *New York Herald*, Aug. 1, Oct. 18, 1860; Potter, *Impending Crisis*, 431.
27. Oates, *With Malice Toward None*, 204–5; Potter, *Impending Crisis*, 432.
28. Luthin, *First Lincoln Campaign*, 194.
29. McPherson, *Battle Cry of Freedom*, 193; *New York Daily Tribune*, June 25, 1860.
30. Johannsen, *Stephen A. Douglas*, 792–93.
31. Oates, *With Malice Toward None*, 201; Luthin, *First Lincoln Campaign*, 170, 171, 182.
32. Donald, *Lincoln*, 254; Goodwin, *Team of Rivals*, 270; Wells, *Stephen Douglas*, 247–48.
33. Schlesinger and Israel, *History of American Presidential Elections*, 1:1116; Johannsen, *Stephen A. Douglas*, 795–96; Wells, *Stephen Douglas*, 247; *Illinois State Register*, Oct. 8, 1860.
34. Luthin, *First Lincoln Campaign*, 204, 208.
35. Ibid., 197–99; *CW*, 4:126–27.
36. Johannsen, *Stephen A. Douglas*, 797–98; Nevins, *Ordeal of the Union*, 2:306–8.
37. Milton, *Eve of Conflict*, 497–98.
38. Ibid., 498; *Memphis Appeal*, Oct. 20, 1860; Johannsen, *Stephen A. Douglas*, 798; *Memphis Avalanche*, Oct. 25, 1860; Wells, *Stephen Douglas*, 253–54.
39. Milton, *Eve of Conflict*, 498–99; Walther, *Fire-Eaters*, 76; *Knoxville Chronicle*, Oct. 31, 1860.
40. Nevins, *Ordeal of the Union*, 2:296; *Augusta Constitutionalist*, Sept. 6, 1860; Johannsen, *Stephen A. Douglas*, 800; Milton, *Eve of Conflict*, 499.
41. David R. Barbee and Milledge L. Bonham, Jr., eds., "The Montgomery Address of Stephen A. Douglas," *Journal of Southern History* 5 (Feb. 1939), 531, 543.
42. Ibid., 546–47.
43. Johannsen, *Stephen A. Douglas*, 801–2; *Mobile Daily Advertiser*, Nov. 6, 1860.

44. Nevins, *Ordeal of the Union*, 2:314; Goodwin, *Team of Rivals*, 276.
45. *Missouri Democrat*, Nov. 9, 1860; Goodwin, *Team of Rivals*, 277.
46. Donald, *Lincoln*, 255; Oates, *With Malice Toward None*, 206; Goodwin, *Team of Rivals*, 277.
47. Luthin, *First Lincoln Campaign*, 218; Oates, With *Malice Toward None*, 206; Baker, *Mary Todd Lincoln*, 162.
48. Johannsen, *Stephen A. Douglas*, 802–5; Wells, *Stephen Douglas*, 255–56; *Illinois State Register*, Nov. 16, 1860.
49. Johannsen, *Stephen A. Douglas*, 803, 806; Douglas to Ninety-six New Orleans Citizens, Nov. 13, 1860, *Letters*, 500–2.
50. Johannsen, *Stephen A. Douglas*, 805, 809; Nevins, *Ordeal of the Union*, 2:316.

Chapter 9: We Must Not Be Enemies

1. Goodwin, *Team of Rivals*, 279–80; Oates, *With Malice Toward None*, 211.
2. Goodwin, *Team of Rivals*, 280–81; *CW*, 4:129–30; Donald, *Lincoln*, 259.
3. Donald, *Lincoln*, 260; Oates, *With Malice Toward None*, 212.
4. Donald, *Lincoln*, 260–61; *CW*, 4:146; Oates, *With Malice Toward None*, 213.
5. Johannsen, *Stephen A. Douglas*, 809–10; Wells, *Stephen Douglas*, 262–63; *Washington Daily National Intelligencer*, Dec. 4, 1860.
6. Potter, *Impending Crisis*, 518–20; McPherson, *Battle Cry of Freedom*, 250–51; Nevins, *Ordeal of the Union*, 2:352–53.
7. McPherson, *Battle Cry of Freedom*, 248, 251; Potter, *Impending Crisis*, 520n.
8. Johannsen, *Stephen A. Douglas*, 817, 825; McPherson, *Battle Cry of Freedom*, 252–53; *New York Herald*, Jan. 28, 1861.
9. Wells, *Stephen Douglas*, 278.
10. Carwardine, *Lincoln*, 140; Wells, *Stephen Douglas*, 261, 263–64.
11. *Illinois State Journal*, Nov. 14, 20, 1861; Donald, *Lincoln*, 269–70; *CW*, 4:154; Oates, *With Malice Toward None*, 217.
12. Donald, *Lincoln*, 271.
13. Ibid., 272.
14. Goodwin, *Team of Rivals*, 307; *CW*, 4:190.
15. Donald, *Lincoln*, 273–75; *CW*, 4:196.
16. Donald, *Lincoln*, 275; *CW*, 4:218.
17. Donald, *Lincoln* , 276; Goodwin, *Team of Rivals*, 310; *CW*, 4:137.
18. Oates, *With Malice Toward None*, 226–27.
19. Ibid., 228–29; Donald, *Lincoln*, 277.
20. Donald, *Lincoln*, 278; Oates, *With Malice Toward None*, 230.
21. Donald, *Lincoln*, 278–79; Oates, *With Malice Toward None*, 231.
22. Johannsen, *Stephen A. Douglas*, 842; Milton, *Eve of Conflict*, 545.
23. Goodwin, *Team of Rivals*, 313; Donald, *Lincoln*, 280; *New York Evening Post*, Mar. 3, 1861.
24. Paul F. Boller, Jr., *Presidential Inaugurations* (New York: Harcourt, 2001), 92; Margaret Leech, *Reveille in Washington, 1860–1865* (New York: Harper & Brothers, 1941), 44.
25. Carl Sandburg, *Abraham Lincoln: The War Years*, 4 vols. (New York: Harcourt, Brace, 1939), 1:122.
26. Leech, *Reveille in Washington*, 44; Donald, *Lincoln*, 283.

27. *CW*, 4:262–63; Holzer, *Lincoln-Douglas Debates*, 157.
28. *CW*, 4:265–66.
29. Leech, *Reveille in Washington*, 44; Sandburg, *Abraham Lincoln*, 1:123.
30. *CW*, 4:268–69.
31. Donald, *Lincoln*, 283–84; *CW*, 4:261, 271.
32. Sandburg, *Abraham Lincoln*, 1:122–23.
33. Johannsen, *Stephen A. Douglas*, 844–46; *New York Times*, Mar. 5, 11, 1861; Baker, *Mary Todd Lincoln*, 178–79.
34. Johannsen, *Stephen A. Douglas*, 851; Wells, *Stephen Douglas*, 280.
35. Johannasen, *Stephen A. Douglas*, 859; Wells, *Stephen Douglas*, 281.
36. Johannsen, *Stephen A. Douglas*, 862–63, 868; Douglas to Abraham Lincoln, Apr. 29, 1861, *Letters*, 511; Wells, *Stephen Douglas*, 282–85.
37. Johannsen, *Stephen A. Douglas*, 863–67.
38. Ibid., 867–68; *Chicago Tribune*, May 2, 1861.
39. Johannsen, *Stephen A. Douglas*, 869–70; Douglas to Virgil Hickox, May 10, 1861, *Letters*, 512–13.
40. Douglas to Virgil Hickox, May 10, 1861, *Letters*, 511; Johannsen, *Stephen A. Douglas*, 871–72.
41. Oates, *With Malice Toward None*, 259; General Orders, No. 29, June 4, 1861, reprinted in Wells, *Stephen Douglas*, 290.
42. Johannsen, *Stephen A. Douglas*, 873; Donald, *Lincoln*, 330.

Bibliography

Angle, Paul M., ed. *Created Equal? The Complete Lincoln-Douglas Debates of 1858.* Chicago: University of Chicago Press, 1958.

———. *"Here I Have Lived": A History of Lincoln's Springfield, 1821–1865.* New Brunswick, N.J.: Rutgers University Press, 1950.

Baker, Jean H. *James Buchanan.* New York: Times Books, 2004.

———. *Mary Todd Lincoln: A Biography.* New York: W. W. Norton, 1987.

Barbee, David R., and Milledge L. Bonham, Jr., eds. "The Montgomery Address of Stephen A. Douglas." *Journal of Southern History* 5 (February 1939), 527–52.

Baringer, William E. *Lincoln's Rise to Power.* Boston: Little, Brown, 1937.

Basler, Roy P., ed. *The Collected Works of Abraham Lincoln.* 9 vols. New Brunswick, N.J.: Rutgers University Press, 1953–55.

Blight, David W. *Race and Reunion: The Civil War in American Memory.* Cambridge, Mass.: Harvard University Press, 2001.

Boller, Paul F., Jr. *Presidential Campaigns.* New York: Oxford University Press, 1984.

———. *Presidential Inaugurations.* New York: Harcourt, 2001.

Boritt, G. S. "Was Lincoln a Vulnerable Candidate in 1860?" *Civil War History* 27 (Mar. 1981), 32–48.

Burlingame, Michael, ed. *An Oral History of Abraham Lincoln: John G. Nicolay's Interviews and Essays.* Carbondale: Southern Illinois University Press, 1996.

Caldwell, J.W. "John Bell of Tennessee." *American Historical Review* 4 (July 1899), 652–64.

Capers, Gerald M. *Stephen A. Douglas: Defender of the Union.* Boston: Little, Brown, 1959.

Carwardine, Richard. *Lincoln: A Life of Purpose and Power.* New York: Alfred A. Knopf, 2006.

Channing, Steven A. *Crisis of Fear: Secession in South Carolina*. New York: Simon & Schuster, 1970.

Collins, Bruce. "The Lincoln-Douglas Contest of 1858 and Illinois' Electorate." *Journal of American Studies* 20 (1986), 391–420.

Craven, Avery O. *The Growth of Southern Nationalism, 1848–1861*. Baton Rouge: Louisiana State University Press, 1953.

Crenshaw, Ollinger. *The Slave States in the Presidential Election of 1860*. Baltimore: Johns Hopkins University Press, 1945.

Davis, William C. *Breckinridge: Statesman, Soldier, Symbol*. Baton Rouge: Louisiana State University Press, 1974.

———. *Lincoln's Men: How President Lincoln Became Father to an Army and a Nation*. New York: Touchstone, 2000.

DeGregorio, William A. *The Complete Book of U.S. Presidents*. New York: Dembner Books, 1984.

Dodd, William E. "The Fight for the Northwest, 1860." *American Historical Review* 16 (July 1911), 774–86.

Donald, David Herbert. "1860: The Road Not Taken." *Smithsonian* (Oct. 2004), 54–56.

———. *Lincoln*. New York: Touchstone, 1996.

———. *Lincoln's Herndon*. New York: Alfred A. Knopf, 1948.

Douglas, Stephen A. Autobiographical Sketch. In *The Letters of Stephen A. Douglas*, ed. Robert W. Johannsen. Urbana: University of Illinois Press, 1961.

Dumond, Dwight Lowell. *The Secession Movement, 1860–1861*. New York: Macmillan, 1931.

Fehrenbacher, Don E. *Prelude to Greatness: Lincoln in the 1850's*. New York: McGraw-Hill, 1964.

Frank, John P. *Lincoln as a Lawyer*. Chicago: Americana House, 1991.

Freehling, William W. *The Road to Disunion: Secessionists at Bay 1776–1854*. New York: Oxford University Press, 1990.

Gienapp, William E. *Abraham Lincoln and Civil War America*. New York: Oxford University Press, 2002.

———. *The Origins of the Republican Party, 1852–1856*. New York: Oxford University Press, 1987.

Goodwin, Doris Kearns. *Team of Rivals: The Political Genius of Abraham Lincoln*. New York: Simon & Schuster, 2005.

Graebner, Norman A., ed. *Politics and the Crisis of 1860*. Urbana: University of Illinois Press, 1961.

Gunderson, Robert Gray. *The Log-Cabin Campaign*. Lexington: University Press of Kentucky, 1957.

Herndon, William H., and Jesse W. Weik. *Herndon's Lincoln: The True Story of a Great Life*. 3 vols. Chicago: Belford-Clarke, 1890.

Hesseltine, William B., ed. *Three Against Lincoln: Murat Halstead Reports the Caucus of 1860*. Baton Rouge: Louisiana State University Press, 1960.

Hodder, F. H. "Stephen A. Douglas." *Kansas Historical Quarterly* 8 (Aug. 1939), 227–37.

Holt, Michael F. *The Fate of Their Country: Politicians, Slavery Extension, and the Coming of the Civil War*. New York: Hill & Wang, 2004.

———. *The Political Crisis of the 1850s*. New York: W. W. Norton, 1983.

————. *The Rise and Fall of the American Whig Party: Jacksonian Politics and the Onset of the Civil War*. New York: Oxford University Press, 1999.

Holzer, Harold. *Lincoln at Cooper Union: The Speech That Made Abraham Lincoln President*. New York: Simon & Schuster, 2004.

————, ed. *The Lincoln-Douglas Debates: The First Complete, Unexpurgated Text*. New York: HarperCollins, 1994.

Hubbell, John T. "The Douglas Democrats and the Election of 1860." *Mid-America* 55 (1973), 108–11, 133.

Huston, James L. "Democracy by Scripture versus Democracy by Process: A Reflection on Stephen A. Douglas and Popular Sovereignty." *Civil War History* 63 (Sept. 1997), 189–200.

Jaffa, Harry V. *Crisis of the House Divided: An Interpretation of the Issues in the Lincoln-Douglas Debates*. Chicago: University of Chicago Press, 1982.

————. *A New Birth of Freedom: Abraham Lincoln and the Coming of the Civil War*. Oxford: Rowman & Littlefield, 2000.

Johannsen, Robert W. "America's Little Giant: Stephen A. Douglas." *Civil War Times Illustrated* (Apr. 1974), 18–29.

————. *The Frontier, the Union, and Stephen A. Douglas*. Urbana: University of Illinois Press, 1989.

————, ed. *The Letters of Stephen A. Douglas*. Urbana: University of Illinois Press, 1961.

————. *Stephen A. Douglas*. Urbana: University of Illinois Press, 1997.

————. "Stephen A. Douglas and the South." *Journal of Southern History* 33 (1967), 26–50.

Johnson, Paul. *A History of the American People*. New York: HarperCollins, 1998.

Josephy, Alvin M., Jr. *The Patriot Chiefs: A Chronicle of American Indian Leadership*. New York: Viking, 1961.

Knoles, George Harmon, ed. *The Crisis of the Union, 1860–1861*. Baton Rouge: Louisiana State University Press, 1965.

Leech, Margaret. *Reveille in Washington 1860–1865*. New York: Harper & Brothers, 1941.

Luthin, Reinhard H. "Abraham Lincoln Becomes a Republican." *Political Science Quarterly* 69 (Sept. 1944), 420–38.

————. *The First Lincoln Campaign*. Cambridge, Mass.: Harvard University Press, 1944.

McPherson, James M. *Battle Cry of Freedom: The Civil War Era*. New York: Oxford University Press, 1988.

Mering, John V. "Allies or Opponents? The Douglas Democrats and the Constitutional Unionists." *Southern Studies* (Winter 1984), 376–85.

————. "The Slave-State Constitutional Unionists and the Politics of Consensus." *Journal of Southern History* 43 (Aug. 1977), 395–410.

Milton, George Fort. *The Eve of Conflict: Stephen A. Douglas and the Needless War*. Boston: Houghton Mifflin, 1934.

————. "Stephen A. Douglas' Efforts for Peace." *Journal of Southern History* 1 (1935), 261–75.

Morris, Roy, Jr. *Fraud of the Century: Rutherford B. Hayes, Samuel Tilden, and the Stolen Election of 1876*. New York: Simon & Schuster, 2003.

————. "Tippecanoe and Cider Too: The Improbable, Irrepressible Election of 1840." *Timeline* 22, no. 4 (Oct.–Dec. 2005), 2–17.

Morrison, Michael A. *Slavery and the American West: The Eclipse of Manifest Destiny and the Coming of the Civil War.* Chapel Hill: University of North Carolina Press, 1997.

Nevins, Allan. *Ordeal of the Union.* 4 vols. New York: Charles Scribner's Sons, 1947–1971.

Nichols, Roy F. *The Disruption of American Democracy.* New York: Macmillan, 1948.

Niderost, Eric. "The Great Debate." *America's Civil War* (May 1993), 47–53.

Oates, Stephen B. *With Malice Toward None: The Life of Abraham Lincoln.* New York: Harper & Row, 1977.

Panzer, Mary. *Mathew Brady and the Image of History.* Washington: Smithsonian Institution Press, 1997.

Parks, Joseph. *John Bell of Tennessee.* Baton Rouge: Louisiana State University Press, 1950.

Peterson, Merrill D. *Lincoln in American Memory.* New York: Oxford University Press, 1994.

Pinsker, Matthew. "Senator Abraham Lincoln." *Journal of the Abraham Lincoln Association* 14 (Summer 1993), 1–21.

Potter, David. M. *The Impending Crisis, 1848–1861.* New York: Harper & Row, 1976.

———. *Lincoln and His Party in the Secession Crisis.* New Haven, Conn.: Yale University Press, 1942.

Quaife, Milo Milton, ed. *The Diary of James Knox Polk During His Presidency, 1845–1849.* 4 vols. Chicago: A. C. McClurg, 1910.

Rawley, James A. *Race and Politics: "Bleeding Kansas" and the Coming of the Civil War.* Philadelphia: J. B. Lippincott, 1969.

Riddle, Donald W. *Congressman Abraham Lincoln.* Westport, Conn.: Greenwood Press, 1979.

———. *Lincoln Runs for Congress.* New Brunswick, N.J.: Rutgers University Press, 1948.

Rolle, Andrew. *John Charles Frémont: Character as Destiny.* Norman: University of Oklahoma Press, 1991.

Sandburg, Carl. *Abraham Lincoln: The War Years.* 4 vols. New York: Harcourt, Brace, 1939.

Schlesinger, Arthur M., Jr., and Fred L. Israel, eds. *History of American Presidential Elections, 1789–1968.* 4 vols. New York: Chelsea House, 1971.

Sewell, Richard H. *A House Divided: Sectionalism and Civil War, 1848–1865.* Baltimore: Johns Hopkins University Press, 1988.

Simon, Paul. *Lincoln's Preparation for Greatness: The Illinois Legislative Years.* Urbana: University of Illinois Press, 1971.

Stampp, Kenneth M. *America in 1857: A Nation on the Brink.* New York: Oxford University Press, 1990.

———. *And the War Came: The North and the Secession Crisis.* Baton Rouge: Louisiana State University Press, 1950.

———. *The Imperiled Union: Essays on the Background of the Civil War.* New York: Oxford University Press, 1980.

Stevens, Frank E. "Life of Stephen Arnold Douglas." *Journal of the Illinois State Historical Society* 16 (Oct. 1923–Jan. 1924), 655–56, 668.

Thomas, Benjamin P. *Lincoln's New Salem.* New York: Alfred A. Knopf, 1954.

Venable, Austin. L "The Conflict Between the Douglas and Yancey Forces in the Charleston Convention." *Journal of Southern History* 8 (1942), 226–41.

Walther, Eric H. *The Fire-Eaters*. Baton Rouge: Louisiana State University Press, 1992.

———. *The Shattering of the Union: America in the 1850s.* Wilmington, Del.: Scholarly Resources, 2004.

Wells, Damon. *Stephen Douglas: The Last Years, 1857–1861*. Austin: University of Texas Press, 1971.

Wilentz, Sean. *The Rise of American Democracy: Jefferson to Lincoln*. New York: W. W. Norton, 2005.

Wilson, Douglas L. *Honor's Voice: The Transformation of Abraham Lincoln*. New York: Alfred A. Knopf, 1998.

Wilson, Douglas L., and Rodney O. Davis, eds. *Herndon's Informants: Letters, Interviews and Statements About Abraham Lincoln*. Urbana: University of Illinois Press, 1998.

Winkle, Kenneth J. *The Young Eagle: The Rise of Abraham Lincoln*. Dallas: Taylor Trade Publishing, 2001.

Zarefsky, David. "The Lincoln-Douglas Debates Revisited: The Evolution of Public Argument." *Quarterly Journal of Speech* 72 (1986), 162–84.

Index

Breinigsville, PA USA
24 September 2010
245991BV00001B/1/P